T0330301

Japan's Great Stagnation

To

Holly and Finn

with love

Japan's Great Stagnation

Forging Ahead, Falling Behind

W. R. Garside

Waseda University, Japan

Edward Elgar

Cheltenham, UK • Northampton, MA, USA

Published by
Edward Elgar Publishing Limited
The Lypiatts
15 Lansdown Road
Cheltenham
Glos GL50 2JA
UK

Edward Elgar Publishing, Inc.
William Pratt House
9 Dewey Court
Northampton
Massachusetts 01060
USA

A catalogue record for this book
is available from the British Library

Library of Congress Control Number: 2012935303

ISBN 978 0 85793 821 3

Typeset by Columns Design XML Ltd, Reading
Printed and bound by MPG Books Group, UK

Contents

List of figures   vi
List of tables   vii
Preface   viii

 1 Before stagnation: legacies of the high-growth period   1

 2 Catch-up growth and maturity: developmentalism in retrospect   25

 3 Developmentalism as ideology   43

 4 Economic and financial policy in a changing international
    environment: the origins and course of the bubble economy   60

 5 'Losing a decade': economic and financial hubris in recessionary
    Japan, 1990–97   80

 6 Funding a recovery: the impact and fate of fiscal policy, 1990–97   106

 7 Banking crises, monetary policy and deflation, 1997–2000   120

 8 Reform without salvation: Japan 1997–2000   133

 9 Recession, stagnation and the labour market: continuity and
    change in the 1990s   154

10 'Lost decades?' Japan's political economy in the new millennium   168

Bibliography   188
Index   215

Figures

4.1	Breakdown of corporate borrowers by size	69
4.2	Illustration of the bubble economy in Japan	78
5.1	Japanese stock and land price index, 1980–2001	81
6.1	Real nonresidential investment growth and real GDP growth, Japan 1975/I–1998/IV	107
6.2	Trends of private investment and government investment	112
8.1	Intra-group shareholding ratio, 1977–99	138
9.1a	Changes in the number of regular and nonregular workers (male)	162
9.1b	Changes in the number of regular and nonregular workers (female)	162

Tables

2.1	Real gross domestic product (GDP), 1960–89	31
2.2	Growth rates of labour productivity and total factor productivity in newly industrializing economies (NIEs) and developed industrial economies	32
2.3	Keiretsu loans, 1965–85	34
3.1	Characteristics of Japan's economic systems	55
5.1	Average annual growth rates of real GDP by decade	84
5.2	Selected banking crises and their effects	85
6.1	Contribution of demand components (per cent)	118
7.1	Measures of inflation in Japan, 1991–99 (per cent change)	128
9.1	Strategies for personnel adjustment by industry (January–February 2002)	164
10.1	The Japanese economy emerging from the lost decade	175

Preface

I am delighted to acknowledge the support and encouragement that I received from a considerable number of colleagues over the course of this study. They include Barry Eichengreen, Peter Mathias, Barry Supple, Mark Metzler and many in Japan, including Mariko Hatase, Kikuo Iwata, Michiya Kato, Takao Matsumura, Tamotsu Nishizawa, Osamu Saito, Kaoru Sugihara, Juro Teranishi, Ken'ichi Tomobe, Masazumi Wakatabe and Takeshi Yuzawa. I am especially grateful to Michal Marcik for transforming my draft bibliography into a form ready for publication. As a staff member of the School of Political Science and Economics, I have also derived considerable benefit from the intellectual and supportive environment of Waseda University in Tokyo.

Over the years my wife and family have become accustomed to my academic preoccupations, yet they have constantly made allowances beyond what I should have expected. I thank them again. This book is dedicated to my grandchildren. They bring so much joy.

W. R. Garside

1.   Before stagnation: legacies of the high-growth period

The contrast between Japan's 'bubble' years of the mid-to-late 1980s and the recession and stagnation experienced during the 1990s is fast becoming as legendary as its 'miracle' growth in the early 1960s. Japan had stunned both itself and the outside world by its capacity to mount a serious challenge to American hegemony, within just a few decades of wartime defeat. However, once the impulses of catch-up growth and the good fortune of an accommodating international environment faded, Japan appeared incapable of fully adjusting to shifting economic circumstance, with doleful consequences. To outside observers, Japan seemed almost mesmerized by its earlier success. It appeared to be wedded to a form of political economy better fitted to the exceptional needs of post-war reconstruction and economic convergence than to the demands of a rapidly globalizing world. However, success with pragmatic adjustment in the past (such as followed in the wake of the oil crisis in the early 1970s), the cementing of relational ties that had sustained economic, political and social order during the high-growth period, and a fear of alternative, essentially Western, forms of political economy helped to underwrite a continuing belief amongst the Japanese authorities during the troubled 1990s that the country possessed a distinct and superior form of economic management that only needed the return of benign growth to give it renewed legitimacy.

A recurring theme in this book is that the institutional and ideational matrix constructed to deliver catch-up growth down to the early 1970s affected the content, direction and fate of economic policy during the bubble, bust and reform years from the 1980s to the turn of the century. We distance ourselves, however, from the 'de-historicized economic rationality'[1] that pervades much of the literature on Japan's declining fortunes from the early 1990s. This often dismisses the range of contemporary policy choices and priorities as but a stubborn and woeful resistance to the self-evident truths

---

[1]   Ravi A. Palat, '"Eyes Wide Shut": Reconceptualizing the Asian Crisis', *Review of International Political Economy* 10, no. 2 (2003): 169–95.

of neoclassical economics, inviting 'one-sided analyses of the pre- and post-crisis periods – either exaggerating the success of the former and the failures of the latter or interpreting the past as pathological and the future as a new start provided the 'right' policies are made'.[2]

The reality, of course, was more nuanced. As Ozawa has noted, although the characteristics of the developmental agenda have been extensively explored, 'their interactions and evolutionary developments in the context of Japan's catch-up growth and [subsequent] economic malaise remain largely unexamined.'[3] It is our purpose to develop such an holistic approach. Given the vast literature available on Japan's high-growth experience, it would be counterproductive to repeat the detail of that narrative. If, however, as we contend, there is a continuum in Japan's experience of growth and decline from the 1960s to the turn of the century, we need to trace how a lingering attachment to the bureaucratic, financial and political underpinnings of high-growth success affected Japan's response to critical shifts in national and international economic circumstance after catch-up had been achieved. We also need to determine how it is possible, within the tensions that emerged between shifting circumstance and established practice, to trace both the origins and nature of the 'boom and bust' years, and the lacklustre reform programme that ensued.[4]

It might seem perverse to focus on the continuing legacy of Japan's high-growth experience when the developmental policies that initiated and

---

[2]   Bob Jessop, 'A Regulationist and State-Theoretical Analysis', in Richard Boyd and Tak-Wing Ngo (eds.), *Asian States: Beyond the Developmental Perspective* (London: RoutledgeCurzon, 2005), 19–42.

[3]   Terutomo Ozawa, 'Institutionally Driven Growth and Stagnation – and Struggle for Reform', in David Bailey, Dan Coffey and Phil Tomlinson (eds.), *Crisis or Recovery in Japan: State and Industrial Economy* (Cheltenham, UK and Northampton, MA: Edward Elgar, 2007), 106–11. A notable exception is Thomas F. Cargill and Takayuki Sakamoto, *Japan Since 1980* (Cambridge: Cambridge University Press, 2008), which provides a detailed treatment of economic and political policy during the 1980s and 1990s. In recent years there has been renewed interest in the links between growth, stagnation and reform from 1997. The published results are often in edited volumes that offer eclectic appraisals of only particular episodes or characteristics of Japan's economic experience. See, for example, Koichi Hamada, Keijiro Otsuka, Gustav Ranis, and Ken Togo (eds.), *Miraculous Growth and Stagnation in Post-War Japan* (London: Routledge, 2011); Koichi Hamada, Anil K. Kayshap and David E. Weinstein (eds.), *Japan's Bubble, Deflation and Long-Term Stagnation* (Cambridge, MA: MIT Press, 2011).

[4]   In 'Institutionally Driven Growth' Ozawa makes the point but develops it only in part. Metzler writes that the 'deadlock of the mid-century "Japan Inc." system was ... at the root of the problems of the 1990s, and the thrust of structural reform

sustained it have attracted substantial criticism over the years. However, if we are to make sense of those criticisms and understand why, despite the shortcomings of the policies to which they draw attention, the core objectives and practices of the developmentalist agenda remained dominant for so long, we need first to identify and contextualize those elements of Japan's distinctive post-war political economy which are commonly regarded as underpinning its stellar economic success. Only then can we assess the extent to which the country subsequently fell into 'a trap of institutional obsolescence'[5] and with what consequences.

THE STYLIZED 'DEVELOPMENTAL STATE'

State Activity and Export-led Growth

It is a commonplace of the post-1945 period that Japan, wrought by wartime defeat, transformed itself into a dominant player on the world's economic stage in a relatively short period of time. In his seminal work, Johnson argued that Japan's post-war economic success could be attributed in large part to a strong 'developmental state' that adopted and promoted, through its economic and financial bureaucracies, state-prioritized development goals that built upon existing institutions and cultural legacies within the framework of a capitalist market economy.[6] The central role of government in strategic planning, 'picking winners' in sectors or firms, orchestrating cartels, and subsidizing industry stood in stark contrast to the practice of more mature industrialized nations. Export promotion lay at the heart of the Japanese post-war endeavour. It was critical to promote rapid growth in output and employment in industrial sectors of the economy in order to absorb underemployed workers in low-productivity sectors, such as agriculture and small business. Such expansion depended in turn upon enhanced investment and the ability to direct increased output beyond the limited domestic sector and to expanding overseas markets in order to provide the exchange earnings needed to pay for necessary imports. These priorities were clearly enunciated in the 1955 Five-Year Plan for Economic

---

was to deconstruct that system', Mark Metzler, 'Japan: Toward a Financial History of Japan's Long Stagnation, 1990–2003', *Journal of Asian Studies* 67, no. 2 (2008), 666.

   [5]   Ozawa, 'Institutionally Driven Growth', 106.

   [6]   Chalmers A. Johnson, *MITI and the Japanese Miracle: The Growth of Industrial Policy, 1925–1975* (Stanford: Stanford University Press, 1982), 3–34.

Independence and won popular support among politicians, business people and the press.[7]

The essential function of government in Japan was to supply incentives to the market to foster long-term growth, principally, though not exclusively, through industrial policy. It used quotas and high tariffs to protect sunrise industries in their infancy. The industries chosen for promotion did not conform to a single model of development. They spanned light industries and heavy industries; the selection driven essentially by considerations of economic rather than political criteria, not least the potential for high value-added and spillover effects.[8] Firms were encouraged to adapt foreign technology in order to spur increased production and returns to scale, thereby lowering production costs. Economic regulation was directed at fostering industrial activity and promoting business; this was unlike its American counterpart, which was often motivated by fear of the consequences of unbridled capitalism.[9] So far as corporate strategy was concerned, the aim was growth through diversification to gain increased sales and market share rather than maximum short-term profit. The government's objective was to 'raise the sights of private business'[10] and to lessen the risks involved in developing new enterprises on a large scale. The result was a form of Japanese capitalism 'with few national political guarantees for organized labor, little emphasis towards the social welfare state, high degrees of mercantilism, limited penetration by foreign investment, and ... exceptionally dependent on access to the U.S. market.'[11]

---

[7]   Hiromitsu Ishi, 'Macroeconomic Fundamentals of Postwar Economic Growth in Japan – A Great Success and Recent Frustration Lessons in Asian Economies', *Journal of Asian Economics* 10, no. 2 (1999): 252.

[8]   Saadia M. Pekkanen, *Picking Winners? From Technology Catch-Up to the Space Race in Japan* (Stanford, CA: Stanford University Press, 2003).

[9]   Tetsuji Okazaki, 'From Wartime Controls to Postwar Recovery', in Frank Gibney (ed.), *Unlocking the Bureaucrat's Kingdom: Deregulation and the Japanese Economy* (Washington, DC: Brookings Institution Press, 1998), 19–30.

[10]   Moses Abramovitz, 'Catch Up and Convergence in the Post-War Boom and After', in William J. Baumol, Richard R. Nelson and Edward N. Wolff (eds.), *Convergence of Productivity: Cross-National Studies and Historical Evidence* (New York: Oxford University Press, 1994), 104. See also Moses Abramovitz, 'Catching Up, Forging Ahead, and Falling Behind', *Journal of Economic History* 46, no. 2 (1986): 385–406.

[11]   T. J. Pempel, 'The Developmental Regime in a Changing World Economy', in Meredith Woo-Cumings (ed.), *The Developmental State* (Ithaca: Cornell University Press, 1999), 179.

The Japanese state, embedded within the political economy of the nation,[12] provided distinctive coordinating mechanisms that produced 'constellations of power and interest'[13] that for many years were regarded as fundamental to the country's economic success. An elite bureaucracy, unified by a common purpose, engaged with private economic agents through an array of incentives and administrative guidance to encourage and influence entrepreneurial behaviour to the benefit of themselves and the nation as a whole.[14] Control over finance enabled key economic agencies – notably the Ministry of International Trade and Industry (MITI) and the Ministry of Finance (MOF) – to formulate long-term plans and to set targets for growth, thus counterbalancing the benefits of tariffs, subsidies, cartels, credit and tax support for export promotion and access to foreign exchange for imported technology; punitive measures were taken against inefficient performers.[15]

Commercial activity was enhanced by encouraging a steady flow of information within government agencies and between these agencies and the private sector. Other sources of support came from reciprocally held cross-shareholdings among corporations and banks within horizontal business groupings (keiretsu), which cultivated a dense and stable network of long-term relationships. Vertically structured keiretsu buyer-supplier relationships (notably in the automobile industry) encouraged the supply of intermediate goods through sub-contracting arrangements and the sharing

---

[12] Peter B. Evans, *Embedded Autonomy: States and Industrial Transformation* (Princeton, NJ: Princeton University Press, 1995).

[13] Mark Beeson (ed.), *Reconfiguring East Asia: Regional Institutions and Organizations After the Crisis* (London: RoutledgeCurzon, 2002), 19.

[14] The literature developing this theme is voluminous, and the following are representative of the genre. Johnson, *MITI and the Japanese Miracle;* Chalmers A. Johnson (ed.), *The Industrial Policy Debate* (San Francisco, CA: ICS Press, 1984); Michael L. Gerlach, *Alliance Capitalism: The Social Organization of Japanese Businesses* (Berkeley: University of California Press, 1992); Michio Morishima, *Why Has Japan Succeeded? Western Technology and the Japanese Ethos* (Cambridge: Cambridge University Press, 1982); Mark W. Fruin, *The Japanese Enterprise System: Competitive Strategies and Cooperative Structures* (New York: Oxford University Press, 1992); Ronald P. Dore, *Flexible Rigidities: Industrial Policy and Structural Adjustment in the Japanese Economy, 1970–1980* (Stanford: Stanford University Press, 1986); Tetsuji Okazaki and Masahiro Okuno-Fujiwara (eds.), *The Japanese Economic System and Its Historical Origins* (Oxford: Oxford University Press, 1999); William Lazonick and William Mass (eds.), *Organizational Capability and Competitive Advantage: Debates, Dynamics and Policy* (Aldershot, UK and Brookfield, VT: Edward Elgar, 1995).

[15] Palat, 'Eyes Wide Shut', 172.

of technology and skilled personnel in order to spur innovation. The Japanese firm became 'a nexus of treaties with keiretsu relationships, employee relations and the financial structure all interrelated', thereby representing a much wider set of interests than is found in supposedly profit-maximizing Western corporations.[16] Some successful Japanese firms remained independent of such traditional corporate groups (such as Sony and Suntory) but the majority of firms from the 1960s to the 1990s reflected a fairly homogeneous national model that helped them to reduce uncertainty and gain legitimacy.[17]

Businesses competed in final markets but within a system where the rules and the limits of competition were directly influenced by the 'visible hand' of a state bureaucracy that was determined to nurture international export competitiveness, almost as a matter of national honour and security. Competition among firms was encouraged as a way of identifying which firms were worthy of support. The institutionalized government-business-banking interface and the deployment of subsidies, tax breaks, low-cost credit and support for industrial sectors that might otherwise have fallen victim to the brutal reality of market forces were not uniquely Japanese practices but they were pursued with such vigour and determination as to set 'Japan Inc.' aside from the industrialized West.[18]

This was a developmental strategy that seemingly promoted an authoritarian but paternalistic government, in which the bureaucracy, autonomous from societal forces, was able to devise long-term policies without undue influence from private interests. Its operational potency lay in its alleged capacity to anticipate change and to reorient developmental policies accordingly. Decision making was centralized and dominated by the power elite of an 'iron triangle': the bureaucracy, the Liberal Democratic Party (LDP)

---

[16] Keith Cowling and Philip R. Tomlinson, 'Revisiting the Roots of Japan's Economic Stagnation: The Role of the Japanese Corporation', *International Review of Applied Economics* 16, no. 4 (2002): 378; Gregory Jackson and Hideaki Miyajima, 'Introduction: The Diversity and Change of Corporate Governance in Japan', in Masahiko Aoki, Gregory Jackson and Hideaki Miyajima (eds.), *Corporate Governance in Japan: Institutional Change and Organizational Diversity* (New York: Oxford University Press, 2007), 3–4.

[17] Jackson and Miyajima, 'Diversity and Change', 6.

[18] Corrado Molteni, 'Structural Reforms in Japan: The Attempt to Transform the Country's Economic System', in Maria Weber (ed.), *Reforming Economic Systems in Asia: A Comparative Analysis of China, Japan, South Korea, Malaysia, and Thailand* (Cheltenham, UK and Northampton, MA: Edward Elgar, 2001), 43–4.

from 1955 and big business, with the bureaucracy taking the initiative.[19] In a country which lacked the means to judicially enforce administrative orders and where social and cultural mores inhibited resort to criminal sanctions, key government ministries made extensive use of 'administrative guidance' to effect voluntary compliance with those bureaucratic recommendations deemed beneficial to the business world. Given the discretionary power that MITI held during the 1950s and 1960s to grant or deny access to raw materials, foreign technology and foreign markets, compliance proved the more likely outcome. As Pempel puts it: 'For the Japanese bureaucracy to lead in the economic arena, it had to forge a consensus, not issue a command.'[20]

Bureaucracy was only one networked actor in the political economy. Lockwood neatly described the system as 'a typical Japanese web of influences and pressures interweaving through government and business, rather than a streamlined pyramid of authoritarian control ... a web with no spider.'[21] Businesses usually made decisions after consulting the appropriate government authority, the reverse also being true. In that way, the web of connections enabled the government to be both a minimalist state in day-to-day operations and an interventionist state when market processes conflicted with designated policy.[22]

Administrative guidance, defined by Johnson as 'the authority of the government ... to issue directives ... requests ... warnings ... suggestions ... and encouragements ... to the enterprises or clients within a particular ministry's jurisdiction',[23] involved detailed and regular exchanges of information between bureaucrats, industry officials and private firms. Such disclosures enabled key agencies, such as the MOF, to influence or impede particular developments. At the same time they enabled ministries to obtain

---

[19] Johnson, *MITI and the Japanese Miracle*, 1982, 198–241; T. J. Pempel, 'The Bureaucratization of Policymaking in Postwar Japan', *American Journal of Political Science* 18, no. 4 (1974): 647–64.

[20] T. J. Pempel, *Regime Shift: Comparative Dynamics of the Japanese Political Economy* (Ithaca: Cornell University Press, 1998), 76.

[21] William W. Lockwood, *The Economic Development of Japan: Growth and Structural Change* (Princeton, NJ: Princeton University Press, 1968), 503.

[22] Daniel I. Okimoto, *Between MITI and the Market: Japanese Industrial Policy for High Technology* (Stanford: Stanford University Press, 1989), 151; James R. Lincoln and Michael L. Gerlach, *Japan's Network Economy: Structure, Persistence, and Change* (Cambridge: Cambridge University Press, 2004), 14.

[23] Robert J. Brown, *The Ministry of Finance: Bureaucratic Practices and the Transformation of the Japanese Economy* (Westport, CN: Quorum Books, 1999), 32–3, 40.

feedback on the efficacy of regulations or policy changes. As university graduates, the majority of bureaucrats had little hands-on experience in the industries they regulated. By using the consultative process to learn from industry, bureaucrats could prepare policy responses for public consumption, thus strengthening the impression that they were the guiding hand behind change.[24] The 'descent from heaven' (amakudari) of well-informed retired bureaucrats into corporate boardrooms posed an awkward dialectic between being loyal to one's former government agency and being paid by a corporation. However, it was credited with providing the corporate sector with important perspectives on the function and objectives of the bureaucratic system and with smoothing the flow of information between government and the private sector, in what Schaede calls a process of 'consultative capitalism'.[25]

Japanese Post-war Political Economy

The Japanese state had long been regarded as having a legitimate role in shaping economic development. Ever since the Meiji restoration, Japan had had to cope with, and resist, foreign imperialist encroachment. In consequence, the Japanese nation-state had emerged as an intentional and self-conscious means of effecting a domestic response to this challenge.[26] The post-war developmental state can be seen as an expression of this long-held concept.

Before the late 1920s, Japan reflected many of the characteristics of a classic market economy. Companies sought funds predominately from the

---

[24]   Johnson, *MITI and the Japanese Miracle*, 265.

[25]   Ulrike Schaede, 'The "Old Boy" Network and Government-Business Relationships in Japan', *Journal of Japanese Studies* 21, no. 2 (1995): 293–317.

[26]   That is not to say that developmentalism, as defined in the post-1945 period, was an abiding characteristic. Early Meiji Japan was not a developmental plan-rational state. During the last quarter of the nineteenth century, the tension in the political economy within Japan was between warfare and developmental objectives, rather than between the pro-market camp and industry promotion. Over the long run (at least until the 1930s) the pro-market camp triumphed over the industry promotion camp, which did not have a clearly defined economic strategy. Thereafter, the fiscal-military state dominated until it was disestablished after 1945. See Osamu Saito, 'The Economic History of the Restoration Period, 1853–1885', Institute of Economic Research, Global COE Hi-Stat Discussion Paper Series, no. 163, Institute of Economic Research, Hitotsubashi University, Tokyo, 2011, available at http://gcoe.ier.hit-u.ac.jp/research/discussion/2008/pdf/gd10–163.pdf.

stock market, shareholders had a dominant presence in corporate govern-ance, labour was mobile (though at risk of rapid firing by firms) and trade unions were organized by trade rather than by company.[27] Deflation and unemployment in the 1930s cast a shadow on the workings of this free-market capitalist system. The subsequent push for a strong autarkic economy to stave off threats of recession strengthened the drive for government-led industrialization, especially in the heavy industry sector, though the critical spur was military aggression.

It was, however, the dramatic transformation of the market economy into a planned wartime economic system from 1940 that many see as the elemental influence upon Japan's post-war political economy. Wartime demands strengthened the central bureaucracy and intensified the pressure on firms to carry out production plans rather than enhance short-term profits. Banks became managing banks under the overall supervision of the Bank of Japan (BOJ). They established loan syndicates to monitor firms seeking to borrow funds.[28] Important supplier networks were established in the automobile and aircraft industries. Control associations within each principal industry gathered information from their enterprises to help inform planning. Management practices such as seniority wages and life-time employment co-existed with active government involvement in indus-trial policy.[29]

These and many other wartime developments were so recognizably part of economic activity from the 1950s that Japan's development is often regarded as an essentially transwar experience rather than one driven by any galvanising or rallying agenda dating from 1945. Distinctive features of the post-war Japanese economic system, such as the 'main bank system',[30] active industrial policy, corporate structures and managerial practice, gov-ernment administrative guidance and intervention, are regarded as the

---

[27] Okazaki, 'From wartime controls', 19–25.
[28] See below pp. 18, 56.
[29] Takafusa Nakamura, *The Postwar Japanese Economy: Its Development and Structure, 1937–1994* (Tokyo: University of Tokyo Press, 1995); Michio Morishima, *Why Has Japan Succeeded?;* Okazaki and Okuno-Fujiwara, *Japanese Economic System*; Tetsuji Okazaki, 'The Supply Network and Aircraft Production in Wartime Japan', *The Economic History Review*, 64, no. 3 (August 2011): 973–94; Yukio Noguchi, 'The 1940 System: Japan under the Wartime Economy', *American Economic Review* 88, no. 2 (1998): 404–7; Jerome B. Cohen, *Japan's Economy in War and Reconstruction* (Minneapolis, MN: University of Minnesota Press, 1949).
[30] See below pp. 22–4.

natural outcome of practices established during the early 1940s, when Japan sought to impose control over its wartime economy. From this perspective, the significant structural break for Japan occurred at the time the country was developing a command economy rather than during the post-war reform period.[31] As Okazaki puts it, though post-war Japan was a market economy, 'key elements of its systemic foundation were introduced under a planned and controlled economic system'.[32]

Whatever their relative significance,[33] the American Occupation of Japan, from 1945 to 1952, dramatically affected such transwar influences. A strong Japan was crucial to America's post-war fight against communism. As a consequence, the USA ultimately agreed not only to offer military security to Japan but also to underwrite its economic growth and stability by legitimising a fixed exchange rate and permitting Japanese export manufacturers access to the American market without demanding reciprocal access.

Significantly, the Occupying authorities, who lacked the essential knowledge needed to institute political and economic leadership in Japan, implemented reconstruction policies via indirect government, utilizing existing bureaucratic agencies which had themselves been reformed and strengthened during the wartime years. Since Japan had never developed a strong central government to undertake such tasks and with politicians weakened by the Occupation's purges, such responsibilities fell to the existing bureaucrats. By the time the Allied Occupation ended (in April 1952), the key institutions of the Japanese bureaucracy – the Economic Planning Agency, MITI (created in 1949) and the BOJ – had amassed considerable power and prestige.

Japan, aided by its strengthened bureaucracy and free of the burden of financing its own military/industrial complex, was thereafter able to flout the neoliberal emphasis upon the free movement of goods and capital. It could focus on economic self-development, promoting domestic industry while keeping foreign capital at bay. Buttressed by the foreign currency

---

[31]   Okazaki and Okuno-Fujiwara, *The Japanese Economic System*. Noguchi in particular has stressed that it was the continuation into the post-war period of 'the 1940 system' that saddled the economy with dominant bureaucratic institutional control and an over-emphasis upon production. This subsequently hindered pragmatic adjustment to changing economic circumstances. Noguchi, 'The 1940 system', 404–7.

[32]   Okazaki, 'Wartime controls', 29.

[33]   Conceding that wartime mobilization led to a system-wide shock during the 1940s does not necessarily explain the causes of or direction of post-war changes, or how and why continuities prevailed. We return to this issue below pp. 56–9.

earnings gained in supplying America's procurement needs during the Korean War and by the upgrading of workers' skills and organizational and technical knowledge during the execution of the war,[34] Japan from the early 1950s set firm upon an export-oriented strategy to nurture national rejuvenation. Economic development was to be financed by export revenues and domestic savings, not by foreign direct investment; this enabled outcomes to be determined by internal power holders, not by impersonal market forces.[35]

With funds allocated to domestic manufacturing rather than to domestic consumption or international lending, the mercantilist state was able to provide 'the protection and subsidies required to enhance the capacity of domestic business to conquer world export markets'.[36] The paramount goal was the expansion of productive capacity for the sake of national strength. Restricting the domestic market's access to foreign capital, marginalizing the link between growth and domestic consumption, and pursuing a macroeconomic policy of controlled inflation, low interest rates and balanced budgets down to the mid-1960s assisted this focus on export-driven and investment-driven development.

Herein lay another pivotal aspect of the developmental agenda. Firms focused on steady long-term growth. Input and output quantities were not always set to minimize cost or to produce maximum short-term profit; they could just as easily reflect a determination to expand in certain markets or to sustain a firm's social status by providing a product line akin to that of its competitors. With growth and market share rather than short-term profit taking being seen as the goals, and with industrial concentration needed to reap the benefits of economies of scale, it was imperative to keep industrial

---

[34] For further discussion see Richard Stubbs, *Rethinking Asia's Economic Miracle: The Political Economy of War, Prosperity and Crisis* (New York: Palgrave Macmillan, 2005). The USA was estimated to have spent some US$3 billion on war-related supplies. Ibid., 68.

[35] Taggart R. Murphy, 'A Loyal Retainer? Japan, Capitalism, and the Perpetuation of American Hegemony', *The Asia-Pacific Journal: Japan Focus* 41, no. 3 (2010); Mark Beeson, *Regionalism and Globalization in East Asia: Politics, Security and Economic Development* (Basingstoke: Palgrave Macmillan, 2007); Michael Schaller, *The American Occupation of Japan. The Origins of the Cold War in Asia* (New York: Oxford University Press, 1985); Aaron Forsberg, *America and the Japanese Miracle: The Cold War Context of Japan's Postwar Economic Revival, 1950–1960* (Chapel Hill: University of North Carolina Press, 2000).

[36] Robert Brenner, 'The Capitalist Economy, 1945–2000', in David Coates (ed.), *Varieties of Capitalism, Varieties of Approaches* (New York: Palgrave Macmillan, 2005), 220.

competition alive. Companies were encouraged to compete in the battle for market share, a reflection of their standing in the industrial pecking order. In order to prevent destructive, excessive competition, cartels were organized to contain competition amongst the controlled number of oligopolistic firms in selected value-added industries. Once a firm's ranking was established, industrial associations worked to ensure that it competed only to the point of keeping its ranking intact but not beyond. This was a distinctive Japanese view of competition, which rested on the belief that markets should be regulated and managed.

Labour, Welfare and Enterprise Unionism

This post-war developmental agenda relied upon firms in the private sector delivering a welfare function so that the government could concentrate on sustaining competitive export industries rather than on having to deflect resources to social support systems. Although Japan's 'employment system', which emphasized loyalty, consensus, cooperation, harmony and productive efficiency, is commonly regarded as one of the institutional bedrocks of post-war economic success down to the 1990s, it was not socially or culturally endemic. It emerged in the post-war period as a functional requirement built around the need to train and retain skilled labour in a market-conforming environment.

During 1945–47 the Supreme Commander for the Allied Powers (SCAP) gave Japanese workers the rights to organize, to bargain collectively and to strike. By the end of 1948 around 56 per cent of the industrial labour force were in their own labour unions. However, following democratization, labour went on the offensive to seek a voice in shopfloor conditions, explicit agreements with management, and regulation and control of the workplace. Between 1949 and 1954 violent labour disputes occurred within major corporations, such as Toshiba, Hitachi, Toyota and Nissan. In the steel and coal industries, in particular, battles over wage setting and working conditions continued down to 1960.

Corporate managers and the state authorities regarded such developments as a direct threat to the country's latent economic transformation. Both the government and the Occupying forces were determined to ensure that Japan would remain a fortress against communism and so they worked from 1948 to isolate militancy within labour ranks and to curtail newly won rights to strike and bargain collectively. In the 'contest for the workplace' during the first two decades after the war, the consensual cooperative industrial order of later repute was conspicuously absent.

By the 1960s managers had asserted their control, replacing democratic worker ideals with 'the hegemony of a corporate-centred society'.[37] The bitter defeat of the Miike coalmining union in 1960 came to represent the ascendancy of the managerial prerogative within the private sector. Managers thereafter generally forged new personnel policies with compliant segments of the trade union movement ('second unions' comprising many white-collar and supervisory workers). Core workers in large and medium-sized manufacturing firms enjoyed the benefits of such 'enterprise' unionism – 'lifetime employment',[38] housing, health and accident benefits, seniority-linked wages, and the fostering of firm-specific skills – rather than the embrace of strong, independent trade unions that neither the Japanese state nor the corporate sector wished to foster. Workers were offered a mixture of affluence and security, so long as they accepted corporate goals as their own and a much narrower concept of democracy in the workplace.

---

[37] Andrew Gordon, *The Wages of Affluence: Labor and Management in Post-war Japan* (Cambridge, MA: Harvard University Press, 1998), 197.

[38] It is important to recognise that these celebrated features of the post-war Japanese employment system trace their origins to the corporate welfarism that emerged during the inter-war period. The rapid growth of heavy industries and the shortage of skilled labour after World War One encouraged a small group of leading employers to introduce human resource management practices, including company training, incentive pay and employment security, to help retain skilled workers. Labour gradually began to expect such benefits to be part of their 'just reward' and protested against reductions in employment and the elimination of such benefits during economic downturns. Although labour remained essentially mobile in the pre-1939 period, managers began to develop alternative methods of containing costs during declines in business and groups of stable and loyal workers began to emerge in leading firms. However, lifetime employment was never a matter of statutory law. Management and workers alike had an incentive internally to sustain practices that underpinned higher profits, efficiency and job stability. The government welcomed such a contribution to economic development and industrial peace at little cost to itself. Meanwhile, in the mid-1970s the courts severely curtailed the power of employers to dismiss at will. Subsequent institutional developments in the areas of state welfare, government subsidies, case law and the evolution of social norms helped to sustain and strengthen the system. Following the oil crises in the 1970s the Japanese government provided subsidies to enable struggling firms to retain or transfer workers. Further financial help was provided during the period from 1978 to 1983 to help workers from depressed industries and regions find new employment. For a discussion of the evolution of the lifetime employment system, see Chiaki Moriguchi and Hiroshi Ono, 'Japanese Lifetime Employment: A Century's Perspective', in Magnus Blomstrom and Sumner J. La Croix (eds.), *Institutional Change in Japan* (London: Routledge, 2006), 152–76. The evolution of the post-war employment system is discussed below. See pp. 154–65.

Such strategies and compromises forged in key industrial sectors transformed industrial relations from 'turbulence to order … from polarisation barely contained to cooperation carefully orchestrated.'[39]

In consequence, almost every Japanese firm had its own (often single) 'enterprise' labour union,[40] which negotiated wages with the company. Under the Shunto 'spring offensive', major firms and unions in four industries (steel, automobiles, shipbuilding and electronics) conventionally set wage rates that other sectors, including the public sector, used as a guide in their negotiations. Although such economy-wide wage setting enabled the wages won in sectors with high levels of productivity to lift the level of wage increases elsewhere and to reduce the conflicts that could have arisen from more fractious firm-level bargaining, it also effectively imposed wage restraints, since wages were set in line with productivity in order to preserve Japan's international manufacturing competitiveness.

These arrangements proved especially important in the aftermath of the inflationary oil price shocks of the 1970s. Dominant 'wage setters' in the steel and metals industries were aware of their vulnerability in export markets as well as the importance of their products as intermediate goods in other Japanese industries. They restrained wage increases during the decade, in line with the rate of productivity in the national economy rather than with the sectors showing the highest productivity in order to temper cost-push inflation and to protect jobs.[41] Management wanted to take wages

---

[39]   Gordon, *The Wages of Affluence,*3. See also Andrew Gordon, *The Evolution of Labor Relations in Japan: Heavy Industry, 1853–1955* (Cambridge, MA: Harvard University Press, 1962); John Price, *Japan Works: Power and Paradox in Postwar Industrial Relations* (Ithaca: Cornell University Press, 1997). The Japanese Trade Union Federation (RENGO) formally endorsed enterprise unionism in the mid-1970s, endowing it with even greater legitimacy. The labour presence was not emasculated. From the 1970s, and especially in the 1990s, representative unions at the national level, principally through RENGO, pressed for improvements in areas beyond the conventional concerns of enterprise unions, such as the protection of workers' real wages, and broader issues of lifestyle concerns, such as childcare. However, this did not reflect any strident lurch towards Japanese corporatism. See Toru Shinoda, 'Rengo and Policy Participation: Japanese-Style Neo-Corporatism?', in Mari Sako and Hiroki Sato (eds.), *Japanese Labour and Management in Transition: Diversity, Flexibility and Participation* (New York: Routledge, 1997), 187–214.

[40]   This was in direct contrast to the pre-war period, when horizontally organized industrial and craft unions prevailed.

[41]   Lonny E. Carlile, 'The Japanese Labor Movement and Institutional Reform', in Blomstrom and La Croix, *Institutional Change in Japan*, 177–201.

out of the competition so that they could recruit on equal terms and compete in markets with relatively stable wage costs, thereby avoiding costly inflation-provoking industry-level bargaining.

Post-war Japan embraced a system of corporate governance that favoured employees more than shareholders and which saw firms more as communities than as private market 'owners'. Its essence was the integration of management and labour, free from the control of shareholder capital. Management was charged with pursuing the interests of its employees and workers, assuming organizational responsibility for production, quality control and adaptability to technical change. Managers adopted various schemes, such as secondment (whereby a worker would remain on a sending firm's payroll), inter-firm transfer and early retirement with a premium bonus in order to reduce costs and ensure the survival of the 'lifetime employment' system during downturns in the business cycle.

Under these arrangements (kigyoism), managerial autonomy, at least within large and middle-rank corporations, was, according to Matsumoto, 'made possible by independence from capitalist control ... The structure of the corporate organization changed from one in which management, representing the interest of capital, controlled workers in a static, pyramid-shaped organization, to a dynamic organization that has process rather than structure as its essence, and that is dependent on the self-motivated teamwork of corporate employees.'[42]

With formal schooling biased towards a generalist tradition rather than to imparting specific technical skills, it was entirely rational for Japanese firms to conceive of a permanent workforce trained to a high level of performance and enjoying a raft of benefits. It was a way of ensuring stability of labour supply and a loyal workforce, one that was committed to quality, technological improvement, information sharing and high productivity. The rising competitiveness of Japanese manufacturing from the 1960s resulted in no mean part from the sharing of production information across occupations, from the development of on-the-job training and from 'quality control circles' that encouraged workers to share productivity-enhancing information.[43] Limited labour mobility meant that workers within a firm had to continually demonstrate their commitment to quality and success, a form of

---

[42]　Koji Matsumoto, *The Rise of the Japanese Corporate System: The Inside View of a MITI Official*, translated by Thomas I. Elliott (London: Kegan Paul International, 1983), 200–201.

[43]　Ryo Kambayashi and Takao Kato, 'The Japanese Employment System After the Bubble Burst: New Evidence', in Hamada et al., *Japan's Bubble*, 217–62.

contest that reduced free riding.[44] The fact that such company benefits were restricted to only around a quarter of the total working population (in practice, full-time male employees in large export manufacturing firms)[45] mattered less than the role that this distinctive pattern of industrial relations system played in supporting those government-business social values that were crucial to the developmental agenda. Carlile states:

> The labor movement began as a movement that was fundamentally hostile to the institutional status quo and devoted to altering the institutions of the Japanese political economy in a substantial way. The emergence of a 'productivity bargain' at the firm level, the institutionalisation of the Shunto wage bargaining system, and the employment security provided to the bulk of the unionized workforce through the Japanese employment system combined to moderate the stance and then to alter the thrust of the Japanese movement. In the late 1970s, this gave birth to a *de facto* social contract that brought the mainstream of the Japanese labor movement into the establishment as a 'social partner.'[46]

The government's emphasis on competition and market share during the high-growth period focused the corporate mind upon quality and productivity. These were enterprise-based concerns but it was easier to deliver them

---

[44]   That is, the ability to benefit from a situation without having borne any of its costs or responsibilities.

[45]   The term 'lifetime' was always something of a misnomer. Core workers in large firms were subject to mandatory retirement, usually at the age of 55. There is no agreed or precise definition of the term 'lifetime employment'. Abegglen described it as a lifetime commitment between worker and firm until mandatory retirement age. James C. Abegglen, *The Japanese Factory: Aspects of Its Social Organization* (Glencoe, IL: Free Press, 1958). Taira limited its scope to permanent unionized employees of high-wage, large firms employing 500 or more regular workers, thereby covering no more than one-fifth of all wage-earners in Japanese manufacturing. Koji Taira, 'Characteristics of Japanese Labor Markets', *Economic Development and Cultural Change* 10, no. 2 (1962): 150–68. Cole (1979), using the total labour force as the denominator in recognition of the fact that females were almost totally excluded from the experience, put the coverage at 32 per cent of all employees, or 20 per cent of those gainfully employed. Robert E. Cole, *Work, Mobility, and Participation: A Comparative Study of American and Japanese Industry* (Berkeley: University of California Press, 1979). In 1993, the Japanese Ministry of Labour focused on male regular workers in firms with over 500 employees and those employed in the government sector divided by the total number of workers employed in non-agricultural sectors. It estimated the coverage of 'lifetime' employment at 23.4 per cent in 1985 and 21.6 per cent in 1991. Hiroshi Ono, 'Lifetime Employment in Japan: Concepts and Measurements', *Journal of the Japanese and International Economies* 24, no. 1 (2010): 1–27.

[46]   Carlile, 'The Japanese Labor Movement and Institutional Reform', 198–9.

when collective bargaining and workplace practices were less contestable than they might otherwise have been.

The 'Dual Economy'

In concentrating resources on growth rather than on greater welfare, the post-war Japanese state constantly faced a trade-off between efficiency and stability. Japanese industrial policy provided preferential and discriminatory treatment to sectors believed to possess high value-added and potential for spillover, thus generally taking the lead from the farsightedness of the private sector.[47] Nonetheless, it also harboured 'pockets of conspicuous inefficiency'.[48] The advent of an essentially one-party political system in 1955, dominated by the Liberal Democratic Party, enshrined a determination by the ruling politicians to protect substantial swathes of inefficient sectors – agriculture, retail, distribution and services – whose disproportionate weight in delivering votes remained vital for the Party's political survival.

The authorities recognized from the outset that some promoted activities *would* fail or perform less well than expected, and that active intervention was likely to take one of two courses: either it would dwindle in scale and significance as assisted sectors gradually gained competitive strength and economic independence, or it would remain active in those sectors exposed to negative shifts in the competitive environment but which remained potential claimants to continued public support by virtue of their significant contribution to overall growth in the past.[49] This was the essence of Japan's 'bureaupluralism',[50] a process that was to cause Japan considerable difficulties in the decades that followed.

Industrial associations, parliamentarians and administrative bureaus that were responsible for particular industries colluded to both represent and arbitrate their particular interests. Elected officials of the ruling party

---

[47] Pekkanen, *Picking Winners*, 26.

[48] Okimoto, *Between MITI and the Market*, 223.

[49] For a robust defence of interventionist industrial policy which acknowledges the importance of costs, opportunities and the need for strategic cooperation between firms and the government see Dani Rodrik, *One Economics, Many Recipes: Globalization, Institutions, and Economic Growth* (Princeton, NJ: Princeton University Press, 2007), Chapter 4.

[50] M. Aoki, *Information, Corporate Governance, and Institutional Diversity* (Oxford: Oxford University Press, 2000), 156.

represented specific industrial interests to the bureaus under their jurisdiction, while the bureaus promoted their own special interests within the administrative process. Even though all concerned were aware that part of the profits of the efficient export sectors were being distributed among this broad range of interest groups, the system was not regarded as a threat to overall economic success so long as the efficient sectors remained successful in international markets. For their part, the efficient sectors acquiesced to the bureaupluralistic system because it supported the productive infrastructure and economic and political stability, enabling them to concentrate on their comparative advantage.

Banking, Finance and Corporate Governance

A crucial component of Japan's economic success down to the 1970s was its system of bank-centred finance. Ever since the Meiji period Japan's financial sector had been directed towards national economic development, though its component parts played different roles over time. Between 1911 and 1936 the greatest supply of new funds to large Japanese firms came from decentralized, competitive bond and equity markets rather than from bank loans.

A shift in emphasis from corporate external funding to private financial institutions (mainly banks) developed in the early 1930s. It grew more noticeable in wartime, once the government required banks to supply long-term funds to munitions industries.[51] The National Financial Control Association and the Wartime Finance Bank were established in 1942 to allocate funds to priority industries. Commercial banks responded to the demand for loans by forming lending consortia, whilst the government introduced a series of laws to influence fund allocations across the wartime economy.[52]

In the post-war period the government adopted a very similar system of channelling funds to specific sectors, first for the purposes of reconstruction and then to foster economic growth. Institutions inherited from the wartime

---

[51] Kent E. Calder, *Strategic Capitalism: Private Business and Public Purpose in Japanese Industrial Finance* (Princeton, NJ: Princeton University Press, 1993), 36–40.

[52] Okazaki and Okuno-Fujiwara, *The Japanese Economic System*. Lending to manufacturing, as a share of total lending by ordinary banks, increased from 22 per cent in 1933 to almost 52 per cent in 1945. Masahiko Aoki and Hugh Patrick (eds.), *The Japanese Main Bank System: Its Relevance for Developing and Transforming Economies* (Oxford: Oxford University Press, 1994), 66.

economy were reconfigured for the purpose of directing scarce capital towards companies likely to gain international competitive standing. During the war, large banks had become accustomed to lending to heavy industries and chemical industries and began to obey rules in the early post-war period to supply credit initially to the steel, coal and fertilizer sectors.[53] The Wartime Finance Bank continued lending until its demise in 1947. Thereafter, ordinary banks joined the government's Reconstruction Finance Bank (RFB) and the private Industrial Bank of Japan (IBJ) in sustaining the supply of funds to industry; the IBJ provided long-term funds to large firms in capital-intensive industries. Further lending by the RFB was suspended in March 1949, following the inauguration by the Occupying powers of a deflationary stabilization policy (the 'Dodge plan'). The establishment of the Japan Development Bank in 1951 and the Japan Long-Term Credit Bank a year later signalled government efforts to overcome any potential shortage of long-term funding for key industries, given the limited domestic financial market and official restrictions on access to international finance.

Equity and corporate bond markets in Japan were severely repressed after the war and remained so down to the 1980s. Banks rather than the capital market became the principal source of investment funds for the private sector, permitting firms to focus on growth rates over the medium term, without having to meet the dividend demands of possibly recalcitrant shareholders.[54] Spurning securities-based capital markets in favour of a concentrated banking sector incorporating a small number of efficient and profitable banks had obvious advantages. Experience of crises and panics in the banking sector during the 1920s had prompted the Japanese authorities to encourage bank mergers and acquisitions. The reduction in the number of banks and the emergence of directed banking during the war years strengthened these tendencies. Such concentration in banking reduced the risk of insolvency, promoted faster and less costly transactions, and encouraged

---

[53]   Aoki et al., *The Japanese Main Bank System*, 76.

[54]   Borrowings from private financial institutions incorporated not only city and regional banks but also long-term credit banks, trust banks and credit associations geared to the needs of small and medium-sized firms, and agricultural cooperatives lending to farmers. The government provided financial support, through its own institutions, to assist riskier sectors that were less likely to attract private investment. Subsidized preferential credit was channelled via the government-controlled Japan Development Bank (JDB) to a limited but strategic set of industries, such as electric power, ocean shipping, coal mining, and iron and steel.

discussion as to where and when capital might be deployed to spur productive investment.[55]

During the high-growth period official efforts to influence the flow of funds to dedicated industrial sectors relied upon the imposition of credit allocation policies through what was known as 'window guidance'. Favoured city banks received quarterly lending quotas and the BOJ instructed them to increase or reduce lending to particular industries on both a quantitative and qualitative basis. Banks were sanctioned for either undershooting or overshooting their quota or for paying insufficient attention to the uses to which credit was being put. It was the quota system – not interest rates – that essentially controlled the aggregate level of credit in the economy and its allocation to favoured sectors; funds went through the banking system to export producers rather than to consumers for domestic expenditure. The MOF restricted capital flows and regulated interest rates to below market-clearing levels. Financial institutions were not meant to pursue their self-interest but to serve the longer-term interests of the economy. Competition amongst banks was discouraged lest it undermine the stability of the system as a whole.

This credit allocation process was underpinned in turn by a 'convoy system' under which authorities would provide loans or devise merger plans to avoid the risk of any financial institution failing. Banking supervision and regulation were designed to sustain the viability of the weakest banks. It was commonly understood that the MOF, as the guardian of the banking system, would organize timely assistance for any troubled bank. In return for such protection, banks would act as financial intermediaries, channelling surplus household savings to the industrial sector in order to enhance the country's exports and its competitive standing in the world.

The BOJ's allocation of direct lending and MITI's influence on the sectoral direction of credit down to the 1970s provided hefty support to the government's developmental goals in textiles, shipbuilding, steel and, later, automobiles and electronics.[56] Given the commitment to mobilize national savings in order to sustain a stable supply of capital to the major city banks, which in turn were able to extend loans to manufacturers, often in excess of their deposits, there was a persistent risk of overlending and overborrowing. Firms had to meet explicit (often export) performance objectives to gain and

---

[55]   Aoki and Patrick, *The Japanese Main Bank System*, 44–5.

[56]   Richard A. Werner, 'A Reconsideration of the Rationale for Bank-Centered Economic Systems and the Effectiveness of Directed Credit Policies in Light of Japanese Evidence', *Japanese Economy* 30, no. 3 (2002): 3–45.

retain access to preferential finance. Since favoured firms were able to borrow at lower rates, they could also overborrow. There was thus, from the outset, a growth bias within the system as borrowers competed amongst themselves for larger market shares and export success.[57]

Such 'policy-based finance' was a key element in Japan's modernization and search for national competitiveness. The criterion of bank lending was more developmental than commercial, with loans frequently offered to firms not overtly profitable but thought likely to break into competitive markets abroad in time. In addition, directed credit assisted the funding of projects that might otherwise have been neglected because of uncertain returns or for want of high start-up capital. This in turn encouraged the private sector to finance activity in what were perceived as clearly favoured sectors.[58]

This system combined a high degree of financial stability with elements of moral hazard. Banks were willing to take risks because the 'convoy system' ensured that weaker banks would be guarded by stronger ones, but they were also able to finance high-risk investments through government support. Ozawa claims that bank-centred finance 'became the critical mechanism through which a policy of financial repression was implemented keeping interest rates low, controlling market competition (via entry regulations), and channelling capital to policy-prioritized sectors and projects, notably in capital-intensive heavy and chemical industries.'[59]

Although bank-centred finance was at the heart of the industrial funding process during the high-growth period, the government had always exercised considerable influence over the allocation of loans and over the operation of the banking system in general. In terms of catch-up, it was essential for Japan to reduce risk, to foster low transaction costs, and to mobilize its investible funds with the greatest speed and effectiveness. The financial regulatory regime that emerged during the high-growth period satisfied both the banks and the government authorities. The MOF, which enjoyed unequalled authority and prestige from the end of the Occupation until the early 1980s, put a high premium on stability. No single financial

---

[57]   Aoki, et al., *The Japanese Main Bank System*, 131–5.

[58]   The role of the government was to induce private bank lending through 'dialogue, persuasion ... and signalling'. Yujiro Hayami, 'Towards an East Asian Model of Economic Development', in Yujiro Hayami and Masahiko Aoki (eds.), *The Institutional Foundations of East Asian Economic Development: Proceedings of the IEA Conference Held in Tokyo, Japan* (Basingstoke: Palgrave Macmillan, 1998), 3–35.

[59]   Ozawa, 'Institutionally Driven Growth', 113.

institution was allowed to secure any destabilizing competitive advantage; competition was limited and the role of each class of financial institution proscribed.[60]

Through the subservient BOJ, the Ministry effectively managed the control of lending and deposit rates. Public savings could be channelled to favoured industrial sectors. Since control of interest rates was effectively a transfer of income from depositors, banks were able to earn excess profits. The Ministry, however, had leverage over the banks because it licensed the new branches that banks needed to build up their deposit base. Ministry officials would investigate and, where possible, conceal from the public any worrying cases of banking difficulties, arranging bailouts if absolutely necessary. It was very difficult for outside investors to monitor bank management. Traditionally, the Banking Bureau of the Ministry of Finance was responsible for monitoring bank portfolios and bank managers. Consequently, the system operated without deposit insurance funds or the need for public funds to settle bank failure. It was a system buttressed by the public's faith in the ability of the MOF and the BOJ to avoid major instability in the financial system.[61]

That ability rested in turn upon the operation of the main bank system. During the high-growth period most firms established connections with several banks; one would eventually emerge as the firm's main bank. Under the Occupation, banks had been limited to holding a maximum of 5 per cent of a client firm's shares. The limit was raised to 10 per cent in 1953 and reduced to 5 per cent again only in 1977. Within these limits, a main bank often became both the principal shareholder and the conduit through which firms could obtain funding from other lenders and government banks. Main banks exercising such a primary relationship were able (at least in principle) to gain important informational advantages over firms, to examine the viability of a firm's projects, and to monitor the performance of its management before committing funds, free of the pressure to deliver high dividends to outside shareholders.[62]

Although close bank-firm relationships increased the availability of capital to borrowing firms when access to capital markets was limited, the

[60]   Brown, *The Ministry of Finance*, 57–9.
[61]   Steven K. Vogel, *Japan Remodeled: How Government and Industry Are Reforming Japanese Capitalism* (Ithaca: Cornell University Press, 2006), 49.
[62]   This is adamantly disputed by Miwa and Ramseyer. See Yoshiro Miwa and Mark J. Ramseyer, 'The Myth of the Main Bank: Japan and Comparative Corporate Governance', *Law & Social Inquiry* 27, no. 2 (2002): 401–24.

cost of capital was often higher than that available to those without relational ties. Superior access to capital did not, however, ensure superior growth or improved productivity. Relatively high interest rates on bank loans suggested that banks were able to use their monopoly power to squeeze clients' profits. Firms affiliated with bank-centred groups did not always outperform those for whom capital was more restricted.[63] Young firms with less reputation in financial markets did benefit, however. They were often under financial constraints during the high-growth period and needed to save from their cash flow if they wanted to finance investments that might be abandoned if they had to depend upon costly external funds. However, young firms with a stable relationship with the main bank appear to have been able to save on cash flow, even in the face of financial constraints, because they could rely upon a supply of liquidity from that bank.[64]

Main banks were also expected to attempt (but not necessarily to guarantee) to rescue potentially productive firms that were suffering financial distress, either by providing additional loans or by refinancing existing debt. Failing firms would not be sold by managers; hostile takeovers would not be commonplace. Crossholding of shares was based on the understanding that shareholdings would not be sold in times of market downturn so as to provide a cushion against the unpredictability of stock markets.[65] According to Sheard, the system produced 'a quasi-internal capital market in which the main bank internalises the monitoring and control functions of the external capital market.'[66]

The government in turn provided various incentives to encourage the banks to bear the costs of such rescues. It controlled interest rates, restricted the bond market and limited new entrants to the banking system. The banks

---

[63] David E. Weinstein and Yishay Yafeh, 'On the Costs of a Bank-Centered Financial System: Evidence from the Changing Main Bank Relations in Japan', *Journal of Finance* 53, no. 2 (1998): 635–72; Iwao Nakatani, 'The Role of Financial Corporate Grouping', in Masahiko Aoki (ed.), *Economic Analysis of the Japanese Firm* (New York: North Holland, 1984), 227–58.

[64] Yasuhiro Arikawa, 'Financial Systems and Economic Development: The Case in Japan', in Hamada et al., *Miraculous Growth*, 44–7.

[65] Masahiko Aoki, Hugh Patrick and Paul Sheard, 'The Japanese Main Bank System: An Introductory Overview', in Aoki and Patrick (eds.), *The Japanese Main Bank System*, 5–8, 45–6.

[66] Paul Sheard, 'The Main Bank System and Corporate Monitoring and Control in Japan', *Journal of Economic Behavior & Organization* 11, no. 3 (1989): 399–422. See also Sheard, 'Main Banks and the Governance of Financial Distress', in Aoki and Patrick (eds.), *The Japanese Main Bank System*, 188–230.

themselves could not allow too many distressed clients to fail, since that risked damaging their reputation with clients, depositors and other financial institutions.[67]

These financial arrangements were enhanced by the prevailing system of corporate governance. Crossholding of equity enabled companies to develop stable, long-term relationships that shared business risk. The dense network of intragroup relationships further strengthened the tendency that bank-centred finance encouraged, namely the presumption of risk-free mutual support untrammelled by the discipline and monitoring of the free market. In the absence of any threat from powerful shareholders, owners of capital could spurn short-term profit maximization, accepting smaller profits and lower prices in world markets in order to gain a greater share of the market as a means of underwriting job security and enhanced long-term competitiveness.[68]

What was to prove so critical in later decades was that the financial and employment practices outlined above merged into a set of complex complementary institutions and practices (cross-shareholdings, bank-centred finance, lifetime employment, seniority wages and enterprise unions) that proved resilient to rapid or fundamental change. As long as such practices were customarily and firmly believed to be the bedrock of economic success, it was always going to be difficult to jettison conventional practice for largely untried Western, Anglo-Saxon (read American) norms.

---

[67]　Aoki, *Information, Corporate Governance*, 87–88.
[68]　Donald W. Katzner, 'Explaining the Japanese Economic Miracle', *Japan and the World Economy* 13, no. 3 (2001): 303–19.

2. Catch-up growth and maturity: developmentalism in retrospect

The principal features of the 'stylized developmental state' outlined in the previous chapter would appear, on cursory reflection, to explain the main-springs of Japan's post-war economic success. Nonetheless, retrospective analyses of the 'Japanese miracle' have become the staple diet of revisionist economists and historians. Not only have the certainties of earlier writing on Japan's post-war economic development become much more fluid but the criticisms of the 'developmental state' have deepened. It is not merely that the system faltered in later decades; it was, critics argue, always deeply flawed. Most economists and historians, it is alleged, have been living with a delusion created in part by Japan itself to cover the nakedness of its self-interest. We are now told that the developmental state of Japan's high-growth period was a fable, a myth, and that academics, especially in the West, have been judging a 'Japan that never was'.[1]

They have a case. Chalmers Johnson's classic description of a powerful and sophisticated bureaucracy judiciously deploying incentives and administrative guidance to steer the economy[2] has spawned counter studies that show a divided, ineffective and at times counterproductive political and bureaucratic apparatus.[3] It had always been a fallacy to regard the Japanese

---

[1] Yoshiro Miwa and Mark J. Ramseyer, 'The Fable of the Keiretsu', *Journal of Economics & Management Strategy* 11, no. 2 (2002): 169–224; Dick Beason and Dennis Patterson, *The Japan That Never Was: Explaining the Rise and Decline of a Misunderstood Country* (Albany: State University of New York Press, 2004); Chelsea C. Lin, 'The Transition of the Japanese Keiretsu in the Changing Economy', *Journal of the Japanese and International Economies* 19, no. 1 (2005): 96–109.

[2] Johnson, *MITI and the Japanese Miracle*, 242–74.

[3] Okimoto, *Between MITI and the Market*; Kent E. Calder, *Crisis and Compensation: Public Policy and Political Stability in Japan, 1949–1986* (Princeton, NJ: Princeton University Press, 1988); David B. Friedman, *The Misunderstood Miracle: Industrial Development and Political Change in Japan* (Ithaca: Cornell University Press, 1988); Richard J. Samuels, *The Business of the Japanese State: Energy Markets in Comparative and Historical Perspective* (Ithaca: Cornell University

state as a Weberian ideal, a cohesive entity in which rational and competent bureaucrats worked harmoniously to an agreed project. The factional politics and electoral impulses of the LDP spawned shifting relationships between the executive and the bureaucracy, whilst intra-bureaucratic dynamics encouraged horizontal rivalry and compartmentalization within different agencies.[4] It is acknowledged, for example, that during the early phases of its post-war modernization the Japanese government provided essential, costly and scarce information to firms through indicative planning and offered, through a highly developed consultative process, a 'vision' to guide private sector investment. However, the fact that there were clear divergences between private sector and public sector interests at the peak of MITI's influence in the early 1960s, sufficient to encourage some firms to defy state directives, has raised questions over the exact nature of the interface between the private sector and the Japanese government.

During the high-growth period, MITI tried and failed to restructure shipbuilding, the machine tool industry, the car industry in the 1960s and the petrochemicals industry.[5] Firms in the automobile industry, the steel industry and petroleum refining frequently ignored state overtures when their interests did not coincide with the state's intentions. State efforts to promote greater amalgamation in the machine tools industry foundered in face of opposition from private interests, who recognized – more than the government did – that the industry's international comparative advantage derived mainly from innovative small and medium-sized firms.[6] In the steel and electronics industries, government guidance was often opposed by maverick firms. There was resistance in individual sectors and family firms (Pioneer and Sony, for example). Sony failed to participate in any of the joint research projects in computers and semiconductors organized by

Press, 1987); Steven Tolliday, *The Economic Development of Modern Japan, 1945–1995: From Occupation to the Bubble Economy* (2 vols.) (Cheltenham, UK and Northampton, MA: Edward Elgar, 2001).

⁴   Chung-In Moon and Rashemi Prasad, 'Beyond the Developmental State: Networks, Politics, and Institutions', in Steve Chan, Cal Clark and Danny Lam (eds.), *Beyond the Developmental State: East Asia's Political Economies Reconsidered* (New York: St. Martin's Press, 1998), 12.

⁵   Friedman, *Misunderstood Miracle;* Okimoto, *Between MITI and the Market*; Ellis S. Krauss, 'Political Economy: Policymaking and Industrial Policy in Japan', *Political Science and Politics* 25, no. 1 (1992): 44–57; Etsuo Abe and Terence R. Gourvish (eds.), *Japanese Success? British Failure? Comparisons in Business Performance Since 1945* (Oxford: Oxford University Press, 1997).

⁶   Friedman, *The Misunderstood Miracle*, Chapter 4, 126–76.

MITI.[7] MITI granted permission for the transfer of transistor technology to what later became the Sony Corporation only when presented with a fait accompli by the company's management.[8] In later years, MITI lost out to other less powerful agencies, such as the Ministry of Posts and Telecommunications and the Ministry of Education in the development of high technology. It did little to spur the international standing of sectors such as aluminium and electric furnaces, preferring to retain cartels, and played only a modest role in the struggle for market share that high-tech industries were engaged in with US rivals by the late 1980s.[9]

Although Japanese bureaucrats have been afforded a positive role in providing the infrastructure needed to support important industries (especially the steel industry) in the 1950s, and in effecting rationalization in oil refining in the wake of the 1970s oil crisis, for example, they have been criticized for failing to support venture capital for emerging sectors, such as electronics in the 1960s and pharmaceuticals in the 1980s, largely because networks of benefit and obligation bound officials to established sectors at the expense of newcomers.[10] The LDP continued to provide guaranteed loans, tax deductions and safeguards against domestic and international competition to the construction industry, small businesses,[11] rural regions and farmers in order to garner votes. It sponsored countercyclical public works expenditure in rural areas during economic downturns, thereby facilitating a large-scale redistribution of wealth from urban areas to rural areas. At the same time, it subsidized declining sectors, such as coal and textiles, under the pressure of intense lobbying.[12]

When government licensing or restrained competition – via barriers to entry – were effective, private agents were more likely to follow official policy, if only because compliance and consensus were often easier to secure among a limited number of market participants. The government was not always able to control entry to the market, though, and was therefore

---

[7]   Gregory W. Noble (ed.), *Collective Action in East Asia: How Ruling Parties Shape Industrial Policy* (Ithaca: Cornell University Press, 1998), 179.

[8]   David Coates, *Models of Capitalism. Growth and Stagnation in the Modern Era* (Cambridge: Polity Press, 2000), 20.

[9]   Ibid.

[10]   Calder, *Crisis and Compensation*, 156–230.

[11]   Before the 1970s, severe restrictions were in place on, for example, the establishment of large department stores.

[12]   W. R. Garside, 'A Very British Phenomenon? Industrial Policy and the Decline of the Japanese Coal Mining Industry Since the 1950s', *Australian Economic History Review* 45, no. 2 (2005): 186–203.

vulnerable to non-compliance by the most efficient firms. It proved effective in limiting entry and competition in financial services, but at a cost. Haley writes:

> Developmental polices designed to produce economies of scale through concentration and stability through cartels failed in critical sectors of the economy to inhibit new entry and firm rivalry... . Yet, the combination of strong authority and weak power also enabled government-imposed barriers to succeed in other sectors – notably financial services, agriculture and construction – and thereby to set into motion countervailing economic and political trajectories that produced the stagnation and dysfunction of Japan's ... political economy.[13]

Sectors that had a close relationship with Japanese ministries did not always flourish (pharmaceuticals for example), while others that had avoided undue reliance upon the state did so, such as cars, consumer electronics, cameras, watches and other precision equipment.[14] Despite all the emphasis put upon industrial targeting, the greatest beneficiaries of developmental tariffs and quotas, subsidies, government low-interest loans and sectoral corporate tax breaks in Japan between 1955 and 1990 turned out to be the poorest performing sectors in terms of growth rates, such as mining and textiles.[15] The former gained the most in terms of Japan Development Bank loans, net subsidies and tax relief. Moreover, as industrial policies were pursued over the post-war period, connections between the regulators and the regulated in Japan became more intimate. While leading firms became more able to influence policy, the ability of bureaucrats to monitor the performance of enterprises grew more difficult.[16]

There were more factions and internal rivalries within the Japanese bureaucracy than were ever publicly acknowledged, and they frequently inhibited the exercise of authority and influence, especially in the economic

---

[13]   John O. Haley, 'The Paradox of Weak Power and Strong Authority in the Japanese State', in Boyd and Ngo (eds.), *Asian States*, 67–82.

[14]   Okimoto, *Between MITI and the Market*.

[15]   Richard Beason and David E. Weinstein, 'Growth, Economies of Scale, and Targeting in Japan (1955–1990)', *Review of Economics and Statistics* 78, no. 2 (1996): 286–95.

[16]   Barry Eichengreen, 'Capitalizing on Globalization,' *Asian Development Review* 19, no. 1 (2002): 14–67.

sections.[17] As we noted earlier, before 1945, wartime pressures had encouraged the Japanese government to make frequent use of industrial associations to foster planning and control. These were subsequently put under the jurisdiction of government Bureaus responsible for particular sectors of the economy. Cooperation and the exchange of information with industrial associations allowed Bureaus to speak with knowledge and authority within government about their particular 'charges'.[18]

In the 1950s and 1960s, such 'bureaupluralism' worked reasonably well to address the economic and political needs of both expanding and declining sectors. However, by fostering within the bureaucracy a clear sense of responsibility for particular industries, it posed a constant threat of jurisdictional struggles and the promotion of vested interests. For example, the Ministry of Posts defended the privileged position of the Nippon Telephone Corporation (NTT), which helped to keep telecommunication costs in Japan relatively high for a decade (from the mid-1980s) and delayed the development of computers and information technology.[19] Moreover, as the economy matured and the constraints on competitiveness gave way to robust competitive advantage in particular industrial sectors down to the 1970s, the array of informal sanctions that MITI had been able to deploy during the early high-growth period dwindled in scale and scope.

Historians are ready to accept that the Japanese economy required considerable state intervention in the 1950s in order to correct the distortions created by military-inspired policy during the 1930s and 1940s. Critics have asserted, though, that the Japanese state, far from being an integrated entity capable of orchestrating spectacular growth through its flexibility, professionalism and trustworthiness, was in reality far weaker than conventionally assumed.[20] Far more critical, it is argued, was the favourable international economic environment in which Japan operated, underpinned by the hegemony of US liberal capitalism during the years of high growth, the willingness of the USA and other industrialized nations to comply with Japan's highly protectionist strategies, and the competitive

---

[17] Bradley M. Richardson, *Japanese Democracy: Power, Coordination, and Performance* (New Haven, CT: Yale University Press, 1997).

[18] See above pp. 5–8.

[19] Tetsuji Okazaki, 'The Government-Firm Relationship in Postwar Japan: The Success and Failure of Bureau Pluralism,' in Joseph E. Stiglitz and Shahid Yusuf (eds.), *Rethinking the East Asian Miracle*, (New York: Oxford University Press, 2001), 323–42.

[20] Scott Callon, *Divided Sun: MITI and the Breakdown of Japanese High-Tech Industrial Policy, 1975–1993* (Stanford: Stanford University Press, 1993).

benefits Japan enjoyed from a low (and fixed) exchange rate during the period from 1950 to 1971. There was, in addition, the steely determination of Japanese politicians to ensure that official economic policy was fashioned for the benefit of those groups most likely to render caucus support.[21]

Moreover, while no one dismisses outright the effectiveness of Japan's corporate structures and complex inter-firm networks in fostering cooperation in research and development and in the formation of skills and competition, the influence of local-level lobbying and other interest-based associations as mediators and coordinators of inter-business and state-business relations may have been more significant than is customarily acknowledged. Even though there is mounting evidence of proactive managerial efforts down to the 1990s to experiment, to take risks and to encourage other entrepreneurs to follow suit for the sake of growth, the state's connivance with the very questionable corporate inter-financial links that ultimately gave rise to deception and bankruptcies on an unprecedented scale has undermined the benign view of the 'developmental state'. The main bank system may have played a significant role in mobilizing investment and facilitating information exchange but its record of monitoring client firms became suspect once growth slowed. Cross-shareholding allowed managers to focus on long-term business strategy, but its characteristic insider control was easily construed as a barrier to strategic change.[22]

Japan's experience of high growth from the 1960s to the early 1970s is not in doubt. By the start of the 1960s the economy had overtaken its pre-war potential trend. Its annual growth rate of real GDP averaged almost 10 per cent between 1960 and 1973. As Table 2.1 shows, the country's growth performance during that time exceeded that of other OECD countries, even though Japan's 'miracle' years were over by 1973. The US and British economies performed less well than the Japanese economy did from 1960 through to the end of 1989. In 1973 Japan's per capita GDP was only 55 per cent of that recorded in the USA. However, over the previous 10 years its annual per capita output had grown by 7.7 per cent compared with 2.7 per cent in the USA. At the 1963–73 rate of growth, Japan's total output

---

[21]   Beason and Patterson, *The Japan That Never Was*, 103–11.
[22]   Jackson and Miyajima, 'Diversity and Change of Corporate Governance in Japan', 8–9.

was destined to exceed that of the USA by 1998.[23] Between 1979 and 1990 Japan's annual growth rate was still almost 4%.[24]

Table 2.1 Real gross domestic product (GDP), 1960–89 (average percentage changes)

	1960–73	1973–79	1979–89
Japan	9.7	3.5	3.8
USA	4.0	2.6	2.4
Germany	4.3	2.4	2.0
France	5.4	2.7	2.1
Italy	5.3	3.5	2.4
UK	3.1	1.5	2.4
Canada	5.3	3.9	2.9

Source: Adapted from OECD, *Historical Statistics*, 1960–97, Organisation for Economic Co-operation and Development, 1999, 50.

Growth accounting methods decompose the growth experience of Japan and other Asian countries into factor accumulation and productivity components and have led pessimists to conclude that Japan's growth, though exceptional, leaves little to be explained. Krugman claimed that the rapid growth of East Asian newly industrializing economies (NIEs) in particular was principally because of a remarkable mobilization of resources, especially capital and labour with little improvement in efficiency, and that such growth was never likely to be sustained.[25] As Table 2.2 indicates, rates of growth in labour productivity in Asian NIEs in the three decades down to 1990 were almost twice as high as in developed economies (except Japan) but total factor productivity (TFP) growth rates were lower. The relatively small contributions of TFP within the NIEs resulted from a combination of relatively high elasticity of capital and high rates of growth in the capital-labour ratio. In Japan, the rapid growth in labour productivity was outstripped by the growth in the capital-labour ratio. The implied increases in

[23] Paul Krugman, 'The Myth of Asia's Miracle,' *Foreign Affairs* 73, no. 6 (1994): 73–4.

[24] Takatoshi Ito, 'Japan and the Asian Economies: A "Miracle" in Transition', *Brookings Papers on Economic Activity*, no. 2 (1996): 206.

[25] Krugman, 'Myth of Asia's Miracle', 62–78.

Japan's great stagnation

Table 2.2 Growth rates of labour productivity and total factor productivity in newly industrializing economies (NIEs) and developed industrial economies

	Output elasticity of capital ß	Average growth rate per year (%)			Percentage contribution of total factor productivity (G(A)/ G(Y/L))
		Labour productivity G(Y/L)	Capital-labour ratio G(K/L)	Total factor productivity G(A)	
NIEs					
Korea 1960–90	0.45	5.1	8.9	1.1	21
Taiwan 1953–90	0.49	6.2	9.6	1.5	24
Hong Kong 1966–90	0.40	5.2	6.1	2.8	54
Singapore 1964–90	0.44	4.5	6.6	1.6	36
Average	0.45	5.3	7.8	1.8	34
Developed economies					
France 1957–90	0.28	3.8	4.7	2.5	66
Germany (FR) 1960–90	0.25	3.6	4.9	2.4	67
UK 1957–90	0.27	2.3	3.0	1.5	65
USA 1948–90	0.23	1.5	1.6	1.2	80
Japan 1957–90	0.30	6.0	9.7	3.1	52
Average	0.27	3.4	4.8	2.1	66

Notes:
ß: Average estimates using the translog production function
Y: Real GDP per work hour
K: Reproducible capital (excluding residential buildings) adjusted for utilization rates
L: Work hours

Source: Eichengreen, 'Capitalizing on Globalization', 18, citing Kim and Lau, 'Sources of Economic Growth', Tables 3–1, 6–3 and 7–1.

the capital-output ratio correspond to Japan's relatively modest contribution of TFP, compared with France, Germany, the UK and the USA during roughly comparable periods.[26] Over the longer term, Japan, a late developer, appeared to rely more upon factor accumulation than upon increases in the efficiency with which those inputs were used. According to Beason and Patterson, the 'neoclassical model more than adequately accounts for Japan's post-war economic trajectory.'[27]

---

[26]   Hayami, 'Towards an East Asian Model', 5–9.
[27]   Beason and Patterson, *The Japan That Never Was*, 8.

During the high-growth period, keiretsu firms were supposedly so bound to one another in a web of obligation that, together with the support of their main bank, they were assured of sufficient financial assistance to promote growth and stability. However, as Table 2.3 shows, in 1965 the Mitsui Bank granted only 31 per cent of its loans to Mitsui group borrowers, and the Mitsui Trust Bank granted only 25 per cent to the group. Mitsui firms in turn borrowed only just over 14 per cent of their debt from the Mitsui Bank and just over 9 per cent from the Mitsui Trust Bank. In other words, keiretsu members appear to have had a much broader diversification of borrowings than conventional analysis presumes, and borrowed only a small portion of the loans they needed from the keiretsu bank.[28]

Miwa dismisses the idea of MITI and the MOF purposely directing the economy as 'a myth'.[29] In his view, the state's less than successful intervention in the agriculture, finance, distribution and the small business sectors, together with its particularly 'incompetent' role in the crucial machine tool industry, during wartime and in the high-growth period, undermines the notion that an elite bureaucracy made effective a 'plan rational' developmental state that was capable of overseeing the long-term growth and structure of the economy. On the contrary, he writes:

> Observers have drawn causal conclusions from toy facts ... Nobody has ever tested either the competence of the Japanese state or its active intervention and its contribution to development ... [The state] was not competent enough to do such a job and actually did not even try ... Ultimately it was the market that played by far the greater role in the achievement ... The notion that the Japanese government fostered economic growth through its intervention is instead a fable, a story we collectively tell and retell because we so badly wish it were true.[30]

Porter, Takeuchi and Sakakibara postulate in a similar vein:

> Conventional wisdom attributes the lion's share of Japan's post-war competitive success to the actions of its government; to the set of economic policies so prominently associated with Japan that they are universally known as the Japanese government model. But conventional wisdom is wrong.[31]

---

[28] Miwa and Ramseyer, 'Fable of the Keiretsu', 176–9.

[29] Yoshiro Miwa, *State Competence and Economic Growth in Japan* (London: RoutledgeCurzon, 2004), 221–2.

[30] Ibid., xxiii.

[31] Michael E. Porter, Hirotaka Takeuchi and Mariko Sakakibara, *Can Japan Compete?* (Cambridge, MA: Basic Books and Perseus, 2000), 18.

Table 2.3 Keiretsu loans, 1965–85

Keiretsu	Year	Number of firms	Borrowings (million yen)	Loans as percentage of								
				Financial-institution lending				Nonfinancial-firm borrowing				
				Bank	Trust Bank	Life Ins.	Marine & Fire Ins.	Bank	Trust Bank	Life Ins.	Marine & Fire Ins.	Total
Mitsui	1965	71	1 224 259	31.0	24.5	33.3	18.9	14.3	9.3	1.5	0.1	25.2
	1970	71	2 476 819	26.6	20.4	32.7	26.4	11.3	9.1	2.1	0.2	22.7
	1975	95	5 769 301	20.9	18.1	29.3	2.6	10.9	8.2	2.1	0.0	21.2
	1980	104	9 649 457	15.2	15.0	21.5	14.4	8.2	6.4	2.0	0.2	16.8
	1985	104	9 649 457	9.9	9.2	13.1	11.2	8.4	5.9	1.5	0.2	16.1

Source: Adapted from Miwa and Ramseyer, 'Fable of the Keiretsu', 177.

By the 1980s outside observers increasingly regarded the developmental system as the harbinger of rent seeking and crony capitalism. It had become costly in terms of the resources required to sustain subsidies, cut taxes, upgrade skill levels and finance industrial decline. Developments in the 1970s, critics argue, had merely intensified the interventionist agenda in directions that were to prove inimical to Japan's future economic flexibility.

The oil crisis of the early 1970s, for example, had posed a particular threat to Japan, given the country's high dependence on imported energy. The threat proved short lived. Japan avoided the stagflation that beset other nations. It drove inflation down from over 20 per cent in 1974 to only 3 per cent in 1975, effectively ending its post-oil crisis recession.[32] The institutions that had orchestrated growth in the 1950s and 1960s worked doggedly within the highly politicized policymaking regime to stabilize prices, establish and police domestic cartels, ration dollars and preserve energy through fuel-efficient practices in industry and elsewhere.[33]

Weak domestic firms and industries were sheltered from competition by a host of regulations and collusion among companies in order to protect jobs. In consequence, although competition between internationally successful manufacturing sectors remained intense, greater de facto protection was afforded both to sectors whose competitive advantage was eroding (textiles and metals) and to those that had never been efficient (wood, paper and chemicals). Firm-level data from the cotton-spinning industry suggested that although industrial policy had effectively controlled the output of firms and helped to establish a stable market structure during 1956–1964, it had also constrained the reallocation of resources from less productive large firms to more productive small firms, thus lowering the industry's overall rate of growth in productivity.[34]

During the 1970s, members of 'recession cartels' had been obliged to cut production in proportion to their market share to assist their weaker members. Laws designed to benefit 'structurally depressed industries' helped shipbuilding, cement, steel, chemicals and machinery. Japan's industrial policy had, however, never been fashioned to be ruthless. Cuts in capacity had always involved some compensation for losers, linking the

---

[32] Ibid. Inflation rates measured by the consumer price index.
[33] Pempel, *Regime Shift*, 176–86, 196.
[34] Kozo Kiyota and Tetsuji Okazaki, 'Industrial Policy Cuts Two Ways: Evidence from Cotton Spinning Firms in Japan, 1956–1964', *Journal of Law and Economics* 53, no. 3 (2010): 587–609.

developmental agenda with important distributive policies,[35] but this was harder to accept once growth slowed from the 1970s. The 'plan rational' state increasingly appeared less as a political entity driven by bureaucratic rationality and efficacious instrumentality and more as one whose primary concerns were 'politics and power'.[36]

The severe cost cutting that accompanied Japan's adjustment to the post-oil crisis recession powerfully altered sentiment within the business community, which 'contrasted the frugality, efficiency, and flexibility of the private sector with the profligacy, incompetence, and rigidity of government.'[37] Japan, it seemed, had moved from picking winners to protecting losers, switching from market-conforming 'accelerationism' to market-defying 'preservatism'. According to Katz, the system 'had soured', producing a dysfunctional hybrid of super-strong exporting industries (such as cars and machinery) and super-weak domestic sectors (such as food processing and textiles).[38]

This 'dual economy' had been sustainable because the revenue-earning capacity of productive exporters had cross-subsidized the less efficient ones. The embedded bureaupluralism[39] that had supported the dual economy came under strain once international competition threatened the profits of the efficient export manufacturing sectors. Globalization of trade began to erode Japan's previous cost and quality advantages in favour of lower-cost Asian countries in key sectors, such as electronics, machine tools and automobiles.

As large Japanese enterprises such as Toyota, Hitachi and Toshiba made strategic alliances with corporations overseas, they weakened their link with small and medium-sized businesses at home, threatening revenue,

---

[35] Ronald P. Dore, *Taking Japan Seriously: A Confucian Perspective on Leading Economic Issues* (Stanford: Stanford University Press, 1987). See below pp. 46–7.

[36] Richard Boyd and Tak-Wing Ngo, 'Emancipating the Political Economy of Asia from the Growth Paradigm', in Richard Boyd and Tak-Wing Ngo (eds.), *Asian States: Beyond the Developmental Perspective* (London: RoutledgeCurzon, 2005), 1–18.

[37] Lonny E. Carlile, 'Malleable Meaning, Shifting Practice, Lingering Rigidities: Postwar Japanese Industrial and Post-Industrial Policy in Historical Perspective', Paper presented at the Conference, 'Revisiting Postwar Japan as History: A Twenty Year Check-up on the State of the Field', Sophia University, Tokyo, 31 May 2009, 15.

[38] Richard Katz, *Japan: The System That Soured: The Rise and Fall of the Japanese Economic Miracle* (Armonk, NY: M. E. Sharpe, 1998), 6.

[39] See above pp. 28–9.

profits and jobs.[40] The shift of corporate activities offshore weakened the ability of MITI and the Japanese state to manage the direction of the Japanese economy as they had done in the past. There was now less assurance that corporate activities would provide the means whereby the government could continue to support the unproductive and heavily subsidized sectors at home; it was deemed too politically damaging to abandon industries such as cement, paper, glass, steel and petrochemicals.

The developmental system had worked well enough when corporate and government roles were clear, when the spirit of national consensus fostered collaborative relationships, when consumers were willing to bear the brunt of high domestic prices, when investment risk was small and could be financed from high savings and low domestic interest rates, when cross-shareholding fostered the pursuit of market share rather than short-term profit making, and when privatized social protection helped companies to retain skilled labour. However, by the 1980s the particular set of institutional arrangements crafted to achieve rapid catch-up growth in the post-war years, though essentially fit for purpose at the time, had to face new global pressures involving interlocking national economies, revolutions in technology and communications and a transformation in the dynamism of Japan's regional neighbours, for which these institutional arrangements had not been designed.[41] Although keiretsu ties had been particularly effective in reducing transaction costs and concentrating scarce resources in the high-growth period, they also created a quasi-guaranteed internal market for companies supplying each other with products and services in order to protect their cross-ownership of equity. Such stability-promoting activities frequently protected too many product lines and too many employees, stifling innovation.[42]

Lifetime employment may have delivered worker loyalty and low labour strife but it was increasingly blamed for low labour mobility and the inability of the business sector to respond flexibly to the very different technologies that globalization was spawning. These demanded highly specialized, knowledge-intensive capabilities rather than the firm-specific

---

[40] Between 1990 and 1994 the number of employees in Asian subsidiaries of Japanese firms increased from 500,000 to 1 million. Japanese domestic production declined as a consequence, and employment in manufacturing fell from 15.7 million in 1992 to 14.6 million in 1995. Ito, 'Japan and the Asian Economies', 220.

[41] Ozawa, 'Institutionally Driven Growth', 106.

[42] Marie Anchordoguy, *Reprogramming Japan: The High Tech Crisis Under Communitarian Capitalism* (Ithaca: Cornell University Press, 2005); Porter, *Can Japan Compete?*

skills so prized within the Japanese corporate sector. The post-war catch-up had relied upon large groups of workers with middle-level education working methodically in factories and upon a relatively small number of engineers and scientists who were focused upon adapting foreign technology for domestic use. Compared with the situation in the USA in particular, the government had neglected to develop higher (especially graduate) education in ways that would assist the country to move swiftly beyond the imitative technological frontier.[43]

It was the cruellest of ironies that the rapid growth of the 1950s and 1960s gradually eroded the foundations that had conferred legitimacy on the coalition logic of the developmental state.[44] Where consensus had emerged between bureaucrats and politicians it seemed to have disproportionately advantaged those constituencies important to the LDP rather than to the nation as a whole. For all its power, the bureaucracy had always realized that politicians established the pace and direction of policy. Interest groups unhappy with policies could always appeal to their political allies. Threatened thus with political intervention, bureaucrats had worked assiduously to resolve matters in ways that favoured industry, rural constituencies and small and medium-sized firms, at the expense of consumers.[45]

Pressure for change was mounting. It had been customary for government agencies and industrial associations within particular sectors to share information and to appraise and contain the demands of those seeking to advance their sectional interests. Economic and distributive conflicts within manufacturing were usually dealt with by MITI, while those within finance were handled by the MOF. As growth slackened in the 1970s, conflicts between ministries developed. MITI's protracted battle with the Ministry of Posts and Telecommunications and with computing and broadcasting interests over the division of the NTT reflected a growing tension between centralized coordination and pluralistic fragmentation.

Moreover, government/industry relations were being strained by growing conflicts between specific vested interests and regulators, even within traditional industries.[46] A formerly responsive national bureaucracy was being replaced by a system of patterned pluralism: 'multiple pockets of

---

[43]   Yujiro Hayami and Yoshihisa Godo, 'The Role of Education in the Economic Catch-Up: Comparative Growth Experiences From Japan, Korea, Taiwan, and the United States', in Hamada et al., *Miraculous Growth*, 112–34.

[44]   Pilat, 'Eyes Wide Shut', 170, 179, 184.

[45]   Brown, *Ministry of Finance*, 5.

[46]   Juro Teranishi, *Evolution of the Economic System in Japan*, 31.

highly specific power, many of them operating at cross purposes with one another'.[47] At the same time, the hitherto invincible electoral base of the LDP was under threat because of the very economic successes it had helped to create. Urban growth has spawned a more distinctive middle class that was conscious that the producer interests so close to the hearts of the bureaucrats had gained more from prosperity than had most Japanese citizens. As growth in wages peaked in the 1980s, coinciding with an appreciation of the currency, new middle-class urban workers, effectively excluded from lobbying within the government/industrial interface, demanded greater deregulation and consumer sovereignty.

With the rural population in decline and with politicians and non-bureaucratic groupings, including the courts and local governments, calling for greater clarity and detail in policy formulation, traditional lines of bureaucratic authority came under threat. One way of shoring up influence was to preserve traditional areas of support. The upshot, as Pempel puts it, 'was to drive a wedge into the business community and into ministries with close ties to different industries. One pull was that towards deregulation, liberalization, and rapid adjustment to international economics; the other was toward greater bureaucratic regulation, protection and the promise of efforts at structural readjustment.'[48]

Externally, the conservative elite faced growing criticism of its policy of economic mercantilism from the previously pliable USA, which began to adopt a far more defensive attitude towards the ever-increasing volume of Japanese imports. Pressure mounted for Japan to abandon policies that had led to the formation and maintenance of 'bastion markets'.[49] To the USA, Japan was no longer just different, it was dangerous; it was threatening, through 'unfair' practice and trading aggressiveness, to challenge American hegemony.

By the 1980s politicians were under pressure on numerous fronts: from the growing demands of new interest groups who were disenchanted with the ideological polarized politics of the past, from international competitors who demanded that Japan play a fuller and fairer part in international trade

---

[47]   T. J. Pempel, 'The Unbundling of "Japan, Inc.": The Changing Dynamics of Japanese Policy Formation', Special issue, *Journal of Japanese Studies* 13, no. 2 (1987): 292.

[48]   Ibid, 288–9.

[49]   Marcus Noland and Howard Pack, *Industrial Policy in an Era of Globalization: Lessons From Asia* (Washington, DC: Institute for International Economics, 2003), 32.

and exchange, and from those within the political system itself. Although decision making had for decades reflected a highly fragmented and compartmentalized structure, with political and bureaucratic interests overlapping, the development of 'autonomous pockets of power' during the 1970s had brought about greater diversity and division within the policymaking process.[50] These changes favoured those LDP politicians who had become experts in particular areas of policy and who were less willing to delegate power to leaders who had traditionally assigned discretion to the national bureaucracy.[51]

The government/business interface was also undergoing subtler transformations. By the late 1970s some industrial sectors (especially the automobile sector) were gaining independent marketing success while others were moving offshore. At the same time, sectors that were still facing competitive challenges – such as steel, aluminium and shipbuilding – and high-tech ones there were involved in integrated circuits and computers continued to seek support and protection from MITI. Private sector industrial interests had become recognisably more powerful and assertive, straining relations with state institutions.[52]

By the 1980s Japan was already aware that it had to rely more on technological innovation than imitation, which made profitable investment both costlier and scarcer. Despite such pressures, Japan had failed to develop institutions conducive to fostering small-firm initiatives or the financing of venture capital for research-intensive indigenous innovation. During the high-growth period, research and development had been geared largely towards those firms deemed to be potential winners in world markets. Successful catch-up had bred a degree of overconfidence and complacency, helping to preserve institutions and organizations more suited to the adaptation of already developed technologies. When innovation mattered, a cleavage occurred between those favoured firms that had customarily followed government intentions – biased as they were towards developing new production processes for existing products, using the informational advantages gained from more advanced countries, rather than

---

[50]   John C. Campbell and Ethan Scheiner, 'Fragmentation and Power: Reconceptualizing Policy Making Under Japan's 1955 System', *Japanese Journal of Political Science* 9, no. 1 (2008): 89–113.

[51]   Pempel, 'Unbundling Japan'; Campbell and Scheiner, 'Fragmentation and Power', 92.

[52]   Xiaoming Huang, *The Rise and Fall of the East Asian Growth System, 1951–2000: Institutional Competitiveness and Rapid Economic Growth* (London: RoutledgeCurzon, 2005), 188.

developing 'new' products with uncertain market prospects – and those that did not have such developed connections but to whom incentives and institutional support for innovation were often denied.

Japan succeeded when it came to processes, as distinct from product technology – in the steel, automotive, semiconductors and consumer electronics sectors, for example – but subsequently lagged in the development of computer software, personal computers and Internet rights.[53] Japanese firms in the information technology sector focused for too long upon propriety in-house production systems in which they had excelled (such as mainframe computer hardware and software). Although they subsequently became familiar with standardized and globalized computer production systems, they lagged behind international (especially American) rivals in underlying technologies. 'Ironically, the old Japanese criticism of U.S. industries such as automobiles and steel in the 1980s – that they were mostly run by financial and legal types with little understanding of manufacturing and technology – came to apply to Japan's leading IT firms.'[54] Given the dominant belief that development and production were inseparable, many firms clung to integrated rather than modular production systems, further restricting their ability to respond to new demands in a fast-changing market.

Once the path of state-led development had been embarked upon, it proved difficult for Japan to alter institutional developments and practices, at least not abruptly. On the road to economic maturity down to the 1980s, Japan had developed a set of institutional attributes that were well fitted for the purpose of catch-up but which were potentially likely to compromise its ability to sustain economic leadership without adequate or timely adaptation. Although Japan displayed a degree of flexibility in its responses to the oil crises of the 1970s, it had at the same time fostered a restricted domestic market and an underdeveloped transaction service sector. For many years this hampered the state's ability to connect consumer wants to effective demand or to link them to domestic production, since consumer financial services, laws and regulations concerning consumer protection, and the marketing of consumer goods, were relatively underdeveloped compared with the West. Domestic consumption had long been sustained by the

---

[53] Li Tan, *The Paradox of Catching Up: Rethinking State-Led Economic Development* (Basingstoke: Palgrave Macmillan, 2005), 102–6.

[54] Lincoln and Gerlach, *Japan's Network Economy*, 345.

income growth derived from export success. As a result, the country lacked the 'consumer-driven' dynamism seen in the USA during the early stages of the high-tech revolution.[55]

---

[55] Tan, *The Paradox of Catching Up*, 110–13.

3.   Developmentalism as ideology

Until the 1980s Japanese authorities were not unaware of the strains and contradictions embedded within their chosen form of political economy or of its ineffectiveness at times, despite headline success. There is still uncertainty about why the same authorities remained wedded to so many features of the post-war developmentalist agenda when a combination of domestic and international forces suggested that Japan needed to embark upon a fundamental rethink of its basic premises.

The priority accorded to export-led development, to defending the 'dual economy', to resisting any sustained appreciation of the yen, to retaining bureaucratic influence and prestige, and to eclipsing the full force of the free market in favour of the networked-relational state that embraced business, government and finance was to be a fundamental part of Japan's economic denouement from the 1990s onwards. Hindsight, economic 'rationality' and apparent common sense borne of Western economic values spurred criticism and sometimes outright denunciation of Japan's unfolding policies from the early 1970s onwards (as indicated in Chapter 2). Only by identifying the underlying rationale of Japan's post-war political economy can we begin to appreciate the fundamental premises that were to play such a distinctive and enduring role during subsequent periods of recession and deflation.

With the various parameters of the developmental agenda firmly in place during the period of stellar economic success down to the early 1970s, it is not surprising that the Japanese authorities came to believe that they possessed a workable and superior form of economic management. High growth practically insulated Japan from external pressure to adopt market-based strategies, encouraging the belief that the normal rules of market economics did not – and need not – apply.[1] Policy was pragmatic, fashioned by a government that worked assiduously to persuade business and labour interests that a collective national commitment to growth and international competitiveness were essential if Japan was to enjoy stability and security.

---

[1]   Hiromitsu Ishi, *Making Fiscal Policy in Japan: Economic Effects and Institutional Settings* (New York: Oxford University Press, 2000), 330.

The authority to plan was linked with the bureaucratic instruments and mechanisms needed to put plans into effect. Officials worked with industrial associations within specific industrial sectors to adjust the conflicting and self-interested demands that emerged, as we have noted, during the growth period.[2] Likewise, the Japanese bureaucracy worked deliberately to encourage industrial and private sector recipients of advice to regard such interference as part of a broader strategy for gaining and sustaining national competitive advantage or, as one observer puts it, to face the tension between 'rational individualism and collective compliance.'[3] The fact that this meant eclipsing the development of the domestic economy and setting limits on the growth of home consumption in order to forestall cost increases that might damage the export effort never caused major concern. It helped that most Japanese people regarded economic strength and performance as a definitive marker of national identity.

In spite of Western perceptions, the market in Japan was regarded as an integral mechanism for achieving sustainable growth, though one that had to be managed. The government's perceived role during the catch-up period had been to supply incentives to the market, by embracing a proactive industrial policy, developing a supportive tax policy, and controlling competition, foreign exchange, licensing and entry to industrial sectors; development was not to be left to the uncoordinated influence of market forces alone.[4] The state's relative autonomy from domestic classes enabled it to 'distort' prices – through cheap loans and subsidies, for example – but it also allowed it to counterbalance protection and incentives with punitive measures against inefficient firms; state authority aimed, in principle, to reinforce market principles within carefully chosen industrial sectors.[5]

Private agents were meant to respond where they perceived advantage. This was not displacement of the market but rather a 'state guided but privately owned economic system'; 'soft authoritarianism' designed to suppress rent seeking and to sustain enterprise.[6] Coalitions of government, financial and business interests allowed the state to embrace a form of

---

[2]   Teranishi, *Evolution of the Economic System of Japan*, 40.

[3]   Huang, *The Rise and Fall of the East Asian Growth System*, 98.

[4]   Mark Beeson, 'Japan's Reluctant Reformers and the Legacy of the Developmental State', in Anthony B. L. Cheung and Ian Scott (eds.), *Governance and Public Sector Reform in Asia: Paradigm Shifts or Business as Usual?* (London: RoutledgeCurzon, 2003), 25–43.

[5]   Pempel, 'The Developmental Regime', 173.

[6]   Chalmers A. Johnson, 'Japanese "Capitalism" Revisited', *Thesis Eleven* 66, no. 1 (2001): 58.

'embedded mercantilism' that provided 'institutionalized channels for the continual negotiation and renegotiation of goals and policies' in order to mobilize private business interests for production-oriented purposes.[7] Samuels describes the system as one of 'reciprocal consent' in which either side could take the initiative and where mutual agreement would be sought to move policy forward.[8] The focus was upon how government policy could be directed towards improving the ability of the private sector to overcome problems of market imperfections and problems of coordination, including elements of extra-market 'self-administration' at industry level.[9]

Neither the government nor the private sector possessed sufficient information upon which to construct an industrial order capable of meeting the challenges of competing nations. They were obliged to construct some form of ongoing relationship to reduce ignorance and to improve transaction costs and externalities. There was no inherent advantage in keeping the private sector at arm's length; one of the vital roles of government was to establish the rules that would govern interactions between private parties and the government, and among private parties.[10] Organizations in the private sector were the players in the game but it was state institutions that defined how economic activities could be coordinated for national economic development. In the West, state regulation tended to be specific and subject to impartial enforcement, whereas policies and regulations in Japan were formulated as a means of attaining the larger single goal of development.[11]

Under the politics of 'reciprocal consent' the state did not have to be 'strong' in a conventional sense or to 'force' its will on the public and private sectors. Negotiated 'governed interdependence'[12] permitted business dissent. Likewise, high-growth policy was not through diktat from bureaucrats. Of course, the pivotal economic and financial ministries wielded significant

---

[7] Evans, *Embedded Autonomy*, 12.

[8] Samuels, *The Business of the Japanese State*, 8–9, 260–62, 287–90.

[9] Masahiko Aoki, Hyung-Ki Kim and Masahiro Okuno-Fujiwara (eds.), *The Role of Government in East Asian Economic Development: Comparative Institutional Analysis* (New York: Oxford University Press, 1997); Ulrike Schaede, *Cooperative Capitalism: Self-Regulation, Trade Associations, and the Antimonopoly Law in Japan* (Oxford: Oxford University Press, 2000).

[10] Dani Rodrik, 'Understanding Economic Policy Reform', *Journal of Economic Literature* 34, no. 1 (1996): 9–41.

[11] Dore, *Taking Japan Seriously*, 85.

[12] Linda Weiss, *The Myth of the Powerless State: Governing the Economy in a Global Era* (Cambridge: Polity Press), 1998, 38–9.

influence over technology licences, access to raw materials, and the establishment of bank branches, for example, but they constantly galvanised and accommodated the private sector in its battle for competitive supremacy. Although, as Haley puts it, consensus was necessary to achieve compliance, 'compromise was necessary to achieve consensus.'[13]

From these perspectives, the 'violations' of preferences, tax breaks, industrial subsidies and so on, however imperfect they may have been in construction and execution, were regarded as necessary incentives to support growth. In this sense the Japanese developmental state reflected the views of Frederick List more than those of Adam Smith, extolling the virtues of economic nationalism and mercantilism rather than the purity of comparative advantage.[14] Development depended upon national effort and the subordination of individual interests and current consumption to the needs of heavy investment; this was a 'confederation of productive forces' to boost national power.[15] In the process the state fostered, liberalized, regulated and put boundaries around markets as a means of national empowerment.[16]

The government/business interface retained its own rationale. The high priority given to inter-firm harmony, the willingness to over-hire in good times and to retain labour in slack times, the subordination of short-term profit maximization in favour of growth of worldwide market share, the ability to alter bonuses and wages to meet cyclical fluctuations, and to conduct business to satisfy other members of an industrial group or bank that held a sizeable portion of one's equity, may have been 'inefficient' practices by Western standards but they underpinned Japan's distinctive political economy.

As we noted above, much is made of the fact that a considerable amount of the preferential aid available to industry was subsequently channelled to sectoral 'losers'[17]. During the high-growth period, however, the state was more concerned with sustaining economic development through a strategic

---

[13]   John O. Haley, 'Governance by Negotiation: A Reappraisal of Bureaucratic Power in Japan,' *Journal of Japanese Studies* 13, no. 2 (1987): 351.

[14]   Mark Metzler, 'The Cosmopolitanism of National Economics: Friedrich List in a Japanese Mirror', in Anthony G. Hopkins (ed.), *Global History: Interactions Between the Universal and the Local* (Basingstoke: Palgrave Macmillan, 2006), 106.

[15]   Chalmers A. Johnson, 'How to Think About Economic Competition from Japan', *Journal of Japanese Studies* 13, no. 2 (1987): 415–27.

[16]   Metzler, 'The Cosmopolitanism of National Economics', 119.

[17]   Garside, 'A Very British Phenomenon?' and see above pp. 17–18, 28.

allocation of resources and a steady supply of industrial capital, and with reducing investment risk so far as possible. It therefore developed a broad range of upstream and downstream activities to sustain profitable industries. It effected structural change within the parameters of the post-war 'social contract', and was supportive of employment and stability in large firms and of compensatory policy in less favoured or declining sectors.

Japan's post-war capitalism had always been subject to political and social pressures, despite the apparent organizational coherence and integration that descriptions such as the 'development state', 'reciprocal consent' or 'strategic capitalism' imply. One factor that strengthened Japan's commitment to its chosen development strategy was the manner in which the general population had, by the mid-1960s, come to identify with the country's programme of developing heavy industry.[18] Populist notions of economic nationalism as a means of strengthening Japan's industries' defence against the intense foreign competition – expected in the wake of the growing liberalization of trade and finance under the auspices of the General Agreement on Tariffs and Trade (GATT) and the International Monetary Fund (IMF) – were also embraced by business leaders who were only too glad to have state help in fending off hostile takeovers.

Until the early 1960s, there had been relatively little public engagement or identification with an economic policy that was biased towards heavy industry and exports, the weight of activity and influence residing within the bureaucratic ministries. With the formation of the LDP in 1955 and the subsequent regularization of ties between it and national level business and industrial associations, on the one hand, and mass producers in the agricultural and small business sectors on the other, new counterforces emerged to challenge and influence the formal bureaucratic machinery of policy formulation and administration.[19]

The publication of annual Economic White Papers repeated an argument from 1956: Japan had moved from a phase of post-war recovery to growth and prosperity precisely because of the state's developmental agenda. When the Income Doubling Plan was inaugurated in late 1960 it subtly focused the public's attention upon the benefits of state-directed industrialization in fostering generalized prosperity.[20] Moreover, the varied critiques levelled against the Japanese political economy in later decades – under the

---

[18]   The following remarks draw upon Carlile, 'Malleable Meaning'.

[19]   See above pp. 39–40.

[20]   Carlile, 'Malleable Meaning', 8–9. However, the Plan did not directly infer that an individual's income would double.

umbrella of the 'Washington consensus' – did not go unchallenged. Even at meetings of the World Bank and the International Monetary Fund in the early 1990s, the Japanese government was arguing that because markets were often dysfunctional under conditions of imperfect information, interventionist (and especially industrial) policies still retained an essential rationale.[21]

Reductionist claims and counterclaims over which agency or set of circumstances were at the heart of Japan's growth experience down to the 1990s have so polarized commentary that much of the country's pragmatic and faltering, but essentially holistic, approach to economic betterment, as we have described it so far, is often difficult to discern.[22] Growth accounting exercises, as we have noted,[23] demonstrate that factor accumulation was the most important component when explaining the growth experience of the newly industrializing ('tiger') economies (NIEs). However, although the percentage contribution of total factor productivity to growth in Japan compared less favourably with that of Western industrialized nations in the decades down to the 1990s, in the years before 1973 Japan benefitted from both a high rate of growth in input *and* high rates of growth in efficiency. Its experience at that time was closer to that of the more developed economies of France, Germany and the UK than it was to that of Korea, China, Hong Kong and Singapore.[24]

To argue that Japan merely engaged in an exercise of catch-up and convergence overlooks the fact that it did catch up when other countries with an opportunity to do so did not, and that in doing so it achieved spectacular success. Membership of the post-war convergence club was not automatic and it is too simplistic to view catch-up simply as a process of

---

[21]   For critical discussion of the neoliberal critique of East Asian development, see Dani Rodrik, 'King Kong meets Godzilla: The World Bank and the East Asian Miracle', in Albert Fishlow, Catherine Gwin, Stephan Haggard, Dani Rodrik and Robert Wade (eds.), *Miracle or Design? Lessons from the East Asian Experience* (Washington, DC: Overseas Development Council, 1994), 13–53; Robert Wade, 'Selective Industrial Policies in East Asia: Is the East Asian Miracle Right?', in Fishlow et al. (eds.), *Miracle or Design?*, 55–79.

[22]   For further discussion see Huang, *The Rise and Fall of the East Asian Growth System*, 6–47.

[23]   See above pp. 31–2.

[24]   Nicholas Crafts, 'The East Asian Escape from Economic Backwardness: Retrospect and Prospect', in Paul A. David and Mark Thomas (eds.), *The Economic Future in Historical Perspective* (Oxford, Oxford University Press, 2006), 209–30; Nicholas Crafts, 'East Asian Growth Before and After the Crisis', *IMF Staff Papers* 46, no. 2 (1999): 139–66.

mobilizing hitherto under-utilized economic resources. As Coates has pithily observed, mapping convergence is one thing, explaining it is another.[25]

From this perspective, the issue is less about whether market forces or government intervention should be credited with Japan's economic transformation, and more about how it was that institutions and policies were developed to help market forces sustain rapid rates of economic growth for a number of decades. The essential problem with evaluating the various factors contributing to Japanese economic success is that there is no robust way to determine what levels of growth might have been achieved had the laws, regulations and institutional and behavioural patterns that were generally supportive of Japan's post-war success not been in place.

Many of the revisionist perspectives outlined earlier are frequently based upon stylized presumptions about the roles of the state and the market in fostering economic growth. However, by emphasizing an arbitrary dichotomy between the state and the private sector and, by inference, between politics and economics, we compound our misunderstanding of how economies fare. The capitalist system is made up of a range of institutions, including markets. Institutional and evolutionary economists emphasize that the invisible hand of the market can work well only when the visible hand of state bureaucracy works equally well through a complex system of institutions. This comes as no surprise to economic historians who have repeatedly shown that markets came late in the development of capitalism and almost always as a result of state activity. To quote Karl Polanyi in the context of British experience:

> The road to the free-market was opened and kept open by an enormous increase in continuous, centrally organised and controlled interventionism ... Witness the complexity of the provisions in the innumerable enclosure laws; the amount of bureaucratic control involved in the administration of the New Poor Laws which for the first time since Queen Elizabeth's reign were effectively supervised by central authority; or the increase in governmental administration entailed in the meritorious task of municipal reform.[26]

---

[25] Coates, *Models of Capitalism*, 154–7.
[26] Karl Polanyi, *The Great Transformation: The Political and Economic Origins of Our Time* (Boston: Beacon Press, 1957), 140, cited in Ha-Joon Chang, 'An Institutionalist Perspective on the Role of the State: Towards an Institutionalist Political Economy', in Leonardo Burlamaqui, Ana Célia Castro and Ha-Joon Chang (eds.), *Institutions and the Role of the State* (Cheltenham, UK and Northampton, MA: Edward Elgar, 2000), 15.

What authors such as Evans and Block have emphasized is that states and markets are both limited in their ability to produce desirable results when they operate according to their own logic. What is required is a combination of their different views of logic to produce positive outcomes. This exercise – what Block calls 'disorderly coordination' – requires policies to undergo continuous adjustment, which in turn requires strong and effective central government. This is not a call for capitalism to be overcome by the force of the state but a recognition that since the capitalist system is not coherent but actually made up of multiple interlocking markets, each of which has itself been shaped by state action, the state can have a significant effect on how those markets work, even by exercising a small amount of leverage. Such leverage comes from governments interacting with the choices made by those operating within markets; that is, the interaction between state action and individual decision-makers.

From this perspective, the state can act as a network builder and strategist, exchanging information with firms in the private sector to assist cooperative structures within a competitive environment. This the more so since market signals can be a notoriously imperfect means of providing entrepreneurs with the information needed to determine, say, human resource management or choice of technology.[27]

Arguably, therefore, it was the recognition by the authorities in post-war Japan that what was required for potential success were institutions 'beyond market rationality' that could coordinate selective policies orchestrated by the state in cooperation with private sector agencies to cope with uncertainty, learning, structural transformation and instability, which fashioned and nurtured their distinctive approach to economic management.

Economic growth, in short, was the result of more than the simple decomposition of factor inputs. From a technical point of view, growth accounting models may have underestimated the combined effect of innovation (shifts in technology) and technical efficiency (the extent to which known technologies were applied to actual production). There is evidence

---

[27]   Evans, *Embedded Autonomy*; Fred L. Block, *The Origins of International Economic Disorder* (Berkeley, CA: University of California Press, 1977); Ha-Joon Chang, 'Breaking the Mould: An Institutionalist Political Economy Alternative to the Neo-Liberal Theory of the Market and the State', *Cambridge Journal of Economics* 26, no. 5 (2002): 539–59.

to suggest that the latter was important for countries imitating the frontier technologies of developed countries and that models which ignore such 'catching up' influences may have yielded estimates of productivity growth that were biased towards developed countries.[28]

More fundamentally, although North identified the important roles of property rights, efficient market structures and democratic and decentralized decision-making, he also acknowledged that we do not know what actually creates efficient markets. In their operation, such markets may produce low transaction costs and incentives to compete on price and quality, but they also require institutions to effect such outcomes. Path dependence will have an influence on the pattern of a country's development, depending on cultural heritage ('frugality, industry, honesty and fidelity' in the case of Japan) but there are often crucial opportunities to accelerate the process by structuring markets to achieve desired results.[29]

Abramovitz's focus on a nation's 'social capability' is relevant in this context. It is based on a somewhat vague and immeasurable term but one which nonetheless embraces:

> personal attributes, notably levels of education ... but ... also competitiveness, the ability to cooperate in joint ventures, honesty ... trust ... [and] ... a variety of political and economic institutions. It includes the stability of governments and their effectiveness in enforcing the rules of economic life and in supporting growth.[30]

In other words, the components of growth extend beyond resources such as capital, labour and technology. They incorporate institutional practices rooted in social systems of production, ideology, socio-economic pressure groups, the international economic order, historical accident and opportunity, external shocks, national economic policy and the competence of firms. How such influences interact over time is critical in determining whether economies forge ahead, fall behind or remain on a distinct

---

[28] Sangho Kim and Young Hoon Lee, 'The Productivity Debate of East Asia Revisited: A Stochastic Frontier Approach', *Applied Economics* 38, no. 14 (2006): 1697–1706.

[29] Douglass C. North, *Institutions, Institutional Change and Economic Performance* (Cambridge: Cambridge University Press, 1990), 107–17.

[30] Abramovitz, 'Catch Up and Convergence', 88.

growth trajectory.[31] At best, growth accounting can only indicate the proximate rather than the ultimate causes of growth.[32]

In the early 1950s expectations of high growth were not universal in Japan. There was an atmosphere of uncertainty and indecision. The obstacles to greater levels of investment and technical advance had first to be overcome. The subsequent programmes of high capital investment, first in heavy industry and later in other developmental sectors, which were orchestrated through pilot agencies such as MITI and the MOF, were meant to provide guidance to private firms, to lessen the risks of innovation and capital spending, and to encourage businesses to venture into new enterprises with a sense of purpose and confidence.

Japan's accelerated rate of technological convergence down to the 1960s was partly because 'private business was at first hesitant and went forward more boldly only as the growth potential of the post-war economy became apparent. It was government that provided the early impetus, and this was carried forward only later by the rising confidence of private business.'[33] Growth-promoting policies were always context specific and contingent, and influenced by the economic and political context in which they were formulated and executed. They relied upon the government identifying the most binding constraints and targeting policies to provide the best likely outcomes, even if that embraced what free marketeers would see as second-best interactions.[34]

The Distinctiveness of Japan's Post-war Institutionalism

Rather than being fearful of business links, the post-war Japanese bureaucracy created institutionalized channels for the negotiation and renegotiation of policies in cooperation with the private sector. The fact that relationships in some areas of activity became too cosy and less than transparent over time, and that conflicts of interest emerged to make the bureaucratic reach less embracing or effective than might commonly be assumed, cannot entirely erase the influence of the social and political setting in which institutions were embodied. In Japan, institutionalized

---

[31]   Michael Kitson, 'Measuring Capitalism: Output, Growth and Economic Policy', in Coates, *Varieties of Capitalism*, 29–46.

[32]   Angus Maddison, *Explaining The Economic Performance of Nations: Essays in Time and Space* (Aldershot, UK and Brookfield, VT: Edward Elgar, 1995), 103.

[33]   Abramovitz, 'Catch Up and Convergence', 104.

[34]   Rodrik, *One Economics*, 88–93.

relationships based on trust were unlike the more conventional legalistic enforcement of contracts but they reflected a particular set of social values that were not necessarily less effective.[35]

From the time Japan remodelled its domestic infrastructure to meet the challenges of the mid-nineteenth century imperialist order, it had accepted that the preservation and advancement of its national interests would require radical change. It drew upon important historical legacies, including profound respect for the pragmatic and opportunistic pursuit of power as a source of security and prestige that was grounded in the concrete and the particular rather than in the abstract. Japan's post-1945 economic institutions can thus be regarded as pragmatic adaptations to the liberal economic order, using distinctly illiberal means of achieving national ends, its mercantilist realism focused upon economic competition rather than on militarism.[36]

For Johnson, the processes inherent in the developmental state derived much of their legitimacy from the country's commitment to a 'widely-believed-in revolutionary project.'[37] Economic growth was fashioned as a national project that privileged GDP over domestic consumption, welfare and the environment. This was not a world of Schumpeterian 'creative destruction' – where economic dynamism was driven by bankruptcy and corporate reorganization in the interests of efficiency – but rather 'an economy mobilized for war but never demobilized during peacetime' in which the authorities intentionally altered incentives within markets in order to influence the behaviour of civilian producers, consumers and investors.[38]

Viewed thus, Japan's post-war economic endeavour was informed not so much by the search for efficiency – as an economist might define it – but by a set of social arrangements. This embraced, in Dore's words, 'the compromises made in favour of people who would lose out from the free working of market forces, the mobilizing of a sense of obligation and personal commitment in employment relations' together with 'customer market relations' generating 'a sense of fairness which enables people to work cooperatively, conscientiously, and with a will'. It is arguable from this

---

[35]   Beeson, *Reconfiguring East Asia*, 11.

[36]   Kenneth B. Pyle, 'Profound Forces in the Making of Modern Japan', *Journal of Japanese Studies* 32, no. 2 (2006): 406, 413.

[37]   Johnson, *MITI and the Japanese Miracle*, 52.

[38]   Chalmers A. Johnson, 'The Developmental State: Odyssey of a Concept,' in Woo-Cumings (ed.), *The Developmental State*, 41, 48.

perspective that Japan gained a form of 'x-efficiency' or 'production efficiency'. This is just as important as 'allocative efficiency' for explaining differences in national economic performance. If the incentive was to compromise and restrain the use of market power out of consideration for the bargaining partners engaged in the search for national competitiveness, that in turn required the incentive-providing, coordinating, conciliating and adjudicating role of government.[39]

Japan's high growth record stands alongside the 'consensual technocracy' and 'bargained compromise' and those other facets of relational contacts that neoclassical economists berate.[40] As a latecomer to industrialization, Japan had a compelling desire to catch up with the West, and this drove the post-war trajectory. With such a national rallying call, it was inevitable that the Japanese system would take on characteristics that were different to those found in earlier pioneering countries. The adoption and adaptation of new technologies required dedicated forms of capital finance, new corporate structures, and a stable and educated labour force; it also needed institutions for regulating product and labour markets and nurturing cooperation and competition.

If we are to understand the institutional foundations of the period of high growth in Japan, and in turn be able to delineate which features became sclerotic and the precursors of future economic malaise, it is necessary to see post-1945 developments as rather more than an evolutionary progression of inter-war and wartime trends, or even the culmination of the state's long-standing pursuit of modernization, dating back to the Meiji period. As Teranishi has argued, Japan's strategic post-war economic endeavour was a more complex and interrelated affair than this monotonic evolutionary approach might suggest. Much of the institutional and relational developments of this period of high growth were the result of a reaction against the vicissitudes and failures of the pre-1945 period rather than a natural outcome of its central premises.[41]

Although Japan had pursued a modernization and developmental strategy since the mid-nineteenth century, the roles of the principal economic agents and the institutional settings in which they operated were anything but monolithic. As Table 3.1 indicates, Japan's economic system up to the early 1920s was market based with limited government intervention. Workers were highly mobile between firms, distribution of income was unequal,

---

[39] Dore, *Taking Japan Seriously*, 18.
[40] Ibid.
[41] Teranishi, *Evolution of the Economic System in Japan*, 296–302.

corporate governance was dominated not by banks but by large share-holders, including regional merchants and large landlords, and the focus of economic activity and lobbying was not between the state and the private sector but rather within the regional economy, through which capital, resources, information and guidance were disseminated.[42]

Table 3.1   Characteristics of Japan's economic systems

Sub-system	Meiji-Taishô economic system	High-growth period economic system
(Peak time period)	Mid-1900s to early 1920	Mid-1950s to 1980s
Government–Market division of labour	Market mechanism	Government intervention
Government–Private sector interface	Inter-regional	Inter-industrial
Private sector	Large shareholders Banks finance indigenous industries	'Japanese-style' firms Bank-centred financial system

Source: Teranishi, *Evolution of the Economic System in Japan*, 29.

Direct intervention within the economy – for development, redistributive and planning purposes – grew steadily between the wars and during the Second World War. It was during the 1920s and 1930s, however, that direct efforts were made to alter the relationship between the government and the private sector and to promote particular industries. Industrial associations were developed to encourage greater representation of distributive interests between the state and the private sector, while embryonic forms of the much-lauded 'Japanese employment system', incorporating seniority wage systems and long-term employment, were developed within large zaibatsu firms.

The pre-1945 system stumbled badly between the wars, though, as Japan faced strong international competition in key industrial sectors, especially heavy industry and chemical industries. The foundations of the system also weakened. The agricultural sector slowed, the banking system grew increasingly unstable, and the impulse to preserve vibrant regional econo-mies faded because of disputes between tenants and landlords and because

---

[42]   Tomoko Hashino and Osamu Saito, 'Tradition and Interaction: Research Trends in Modern Japanese Industrial History', *Australian Economic History Review* 44, no. 3 (2004): 254.

of a broader desire by particular social classes and industrial interests to seek their own betterment rather than that of a regional community.[43] During the war, direct government intervention, economic planning, the control of employment and wage systems and the use of industrial associations to assist the flow of information and directives all intensified.[44] War-related financial lending was organized through financial syndicates, with bank lending under the direct control of the state. In short, politicians, bureaucrats and entrepreneurs had been challenged for decades before 1945 to establish an economic system compatible with both intensified government intervention and an active and potentially rent-seeking private sector.

None of this meant that Japan had necessarily to compromise the private sector to gain success. Various observers[45] see the relationship between the government and the private sector as zero-sum, whereas it was always a more complex affair. During the period from 1931 to 1940 the Japanese state on the whole delegated control to private industrial cartels (zaibatsu), which were run in response to state incentives. During 1940–52 state controls existed in the sense that state institutions were imposed onto the private economy, which displaced many private cartels. However, there was never complete self-control in the former period, when the steel, rail and communications industries had been run by the state, nor was there complete state control thereafter. Moreover, neither state control nor self-control had worked well.[46]

Faced with the shortcomings of earlier decades, the compelling imperative after wartime defeat was to build an economic system fashioned for national growth and security. If there was little faith that the free market would deliver this with certainty, efficiency or fairness, there was little evidence either that impulses from the past, be they cultural or modernizing, would be sufficient in themselves. The differing systems that emerged after 1945 were those consciously chosen for declared ends.

Economic warfare in peacetime was to embrace strategy, persuasion, compliance and direction. What is significant is that the Japanese state effected new relationships with labour and capital; on this occasion it

[43]   Teranishi, *Evolution of the Economic System in Japan*, 142–61.

[44]   Tetsuji Okazaki and Mashiro Okuno-Fujiwara, 'Japan's Present-Day Economic System and Its Historical Origins', in Okazaki and Okino-Fujiwara (eds.), *The Japanese Economic System*, 14–30.

[45]   See, for example, Calder, *Crisis and Compensation*; Friedman, *The Misunderstood Miracle*; Okimoto, *Between MITI and the Market*; and Samuels, *The Business of the Japanese State*.

[46]   Johnson, 'Odyssey of a Concept', 57–59.

succeeded, whereas it had faltered in earlier periods. These relationships were not fashioned according to Western profit-maximizing instincts. They were designed to encourage cooperation in pursuit of nationally sanctioned objectives and the preservation of national unity; as such they transcended ideological debates over liberal versus statist approaches to economic development.[47] The links between public and private, between the formal and the informal, and between government and market-driven activity were always blurred in Japan. As Johnson noted, state and civil society needed one another:

> The concept 'developmental state' means that each side *uses* the other in a mutually beneficial relationship to achieve developmental goals and enterprise viability. When the developmental state is working well, neither the state officials nor the enterprise managers prevail over the other. The state is a 'catalytic' agency ... and the managers are responding to incentives and disincentives that the state establishes.[48]

It was the pattern of state involvement – rather than its scale or 'strength' – that was critical to Japan's emerging post-war success.[49] National elites did not recognise a division between private and public enterprise in achieving national development but explicitly harnessed both state and private institutional capacity simultaneously. Strategic pragmatism drove them to use public institutions to develop the private sector's capacity to achieve long-term national development, utilizing both interventionist and market-oriented policies in key sectors, from railways to shipbuilding to microprocessors to computer electronics.[50]

Ever since the Meiji period Japan had recognised that the development of a market-oriented economy would succeed only after the government had provided the political, capital and industry institutions needed to secure national sovereignty and economic prosperity, but such institutions needed to adapt to changing circumstance in a timely way if they were to maintain

---

[47]   Ian P. Austin, *Common Foundations of American and East Asian Modernisation: From Alexander Hamilton to Junichero Koizumi* (Singapore: Select Publishing, 2009), 48.

[48]   Johnson, 'Odyssey of a Concept', 60.

[49]   The size of the state sector as measured by the total government budget as a ratio of GDP is never the best indicator of the degree of state intervention. In 1985 the ratio of government expenditure to GDP for Japan was 33 per cent, lower than in Germany (47 per cent), the UK (48 per cent), France (52 per cent) and Sweden (65 per cent). Chang, 'An Institutionalist Perspective', 22.

[50]   Austin, *Common Foundations*, 21, 108, 326.

their effectiveness. Japan's post-1945 strategy needed regular review and assessment if its ultimate objectives were to be met. Nonetheless, these post-war impulses add a rather more subtle interpretation of Japan's economic development than would be gleaned from a 'catch-up' based merely upon an opportunistic exploitation of cheap labour and capital in a benign national and international environment. They focus on a developmental state in which the government worked through various institutions to lower transaction costs as a way of encouraging an export-oriented growth process, spurred both by internal and by external competition.[51]

For the greater part of the post-1945 period Japan realized that the state could undertake selective intervention in growing, tertiary and declining industries, that it could shape taxation and expenditure on research and development, especially in high technology sectors, and invest in human capital accumulation. The cumulative effect of doing so would enable firms to maintain their competitive advantage in international markets to such a degree that, over time, they would be able to reshape the comparative advantage of the nation as a whole. During the critical catch-up years, the industrial, political and financial will was there to be exploited for the purpose of national growth and success. Japan was very willing to adapt, borrow and refashion past practice.

The semi-coercive manner in which MITI and the MOF exercised authoritative intervention was soon replaced by processes of regular consultation with business leaders and representatives of trade associations and academia. It was a process of consensual adjustment rather than diktat. The ability of MITI and the Economic Planning Agency, for example, to broker the interests of various interest groups who might otherwise engage in rent seeking, and thereby distort resource allocation for the greater part of the high-growth period, was conspicuous in its absence in other industrialized nations. This did not prevent conflicts arising between government and business, as the previous chapter indicated, nor failures of imagination or commitment on the part of the national bureaucracy. The pros and cons of direct government intervention, however, were always less critical than was the authorities' determination to permit market forces to work through the bureaucracy rather than in spite of it. It was a matter of balance, and always risky, but it was to prove a lasting legacy.

Japan's experience, therefore, was more the result of a pragmatic and urgent need to learn and borrow from the past, to adapt to circumstance and

---

[51]   Crafts, 'The East Asian Escape', 209–30.

opportunity, and to fashion and refashion relationships between the principal economic agents in a manner that was far from predetermined.[52] The amalgam of post-war policies, interventions, administrative interference and relational arrangements, which in their entirety offended many of the basic principles of neoclassical economics, emerged less as a natural post-war manifestation of Japan's economic building blocks – dating from the Meiji period – than as the means whereby earlier but unfulfilled attempts to establish working relations between government and business and to promote the private sector without aggravating distributive conflict could be enjoined for the urgent purpose of national economic reconstruction and security.[53]

---

[52] Etsuo Abe, 'The State as the "Third Hand": MITI and Japanese Industrial Development after 1945', in Abe and Gourvish, *Japanese Success, British Failure?*, 17–44.

[53] Teranishi, *The Evolution of the Economic System in Japan*, 200–261.

4. Economic and financial policy in a changing international environment: the origins and course of the bubble economy

Given the remarkable and relatively swift transformation in Japan's competitive and trading position within the industrialized world from the 1960s and the underlying rationale of its post-war political economy, to which we have just drawn attention, it is understandable that the country's elite remained wedded to forms of economic management and relational ties that had spurred and sustained catch-up growth. Japan's experience in the early 1970s indicates that the country was capable of adapting to changing international circumstance without undermining its particular comparative advantages. However, experience from the 1980s onwards severly tested that capacity.

To appreciate fully the drastic turnaround in Japan's economic and especially financial condition – from heady speculative fever during the mid-to-late 1980s to prolonged deflationary recession and stagnation during the ensuing decade – it is necessary to trace the country's policy responses to two major facets of ongoing globalization, one stemming from adjustments to the exchange rate and the other from the effects of financial deregulation.

Trade Surpluses and the Yen

During the high-growth period, as we have noted, Japan had ruthlessly and deliberately fostered competitive manufacturing for export and restricted imports. In this it was driven by interlocking monetary and industrial policies. The banking system, under pressure to lend, had financed productive capacity beyond immediate concerns of profitability; export vitality was therefore vital to sustain capacity utilization. In consequence, Japan's neomercantalist emphasis upon amassing huge dollar-denominated trade surpluses had never been seriously questioned within the Japanese bureaucracy. The dollar holdings held in US banks could not, however, be spent by Japan on imports without harming the country's domestic industries, nor could they be readily exchanged for yen without driving up its currency and damaging exports.

The favourable undervalued fixed exchange rate that Japan had enjoyed since 1949 was critical for this strategy of export-led growth. However, its continuance relied fundamentally upon the willingness of the USA to countenance regular balance of payments deficits to provide the liquidity for international exchange. Therein lay a crucial dilemma.[1] Although the USA had enjoyed the benefits of the dollar as a reserve and transaction currency during the post-war period, it had been responsible for sustaining confidence in the currency and was therefore unable to improve its trade competitiveness through devaluation.

In 1971 the USA called a halt. The 'Nixon shock' put considerations about US domestic policy ahead of maintaining the status of the dollar. The country's exchange rate was frozen, and a 10 per cent tax was imposed on imported goods. With the link between the US dollar and gold broken, the Bretton Woods system that had underpinned the post-war near-fixed exchange rate regime collapsed. However, even when faced with a new era of flexible exchange rates, Japan refused to rein in its policy of maximizing productive capacity for export. As we noted earlier, Japan recovered swiftly from the oil-crisis stagflation of the early 1970s, through a combination of anti-inflationary policies and a substantial increase in exports, aided by deliberate intervention in the money market to suppress the value of the yen.

Following the collapse of the fixed exchange rate system, the USA sought to redress trade balances through manipulation of the exchange rate. The surge in its economy during 1983–85 caused a major deterioration in its global current account, which turned from a surplus of US$5 billion in 1981 to a deficit of US$125 billion in 1985. As the USA underwent fiscal expansion in the early 1980s, the yen depreciated sharply against the dollar. It had averaged below 220/US$ between 1978 and 1981, but it depreciated to about 250/US$ in 1982 before averaging around 238/US$ during 1983–85.[2] Although these exchange rate movements renewed trade frictions between the USA and Japan, the MOF vigorously opposed trying to reduce

---

[1] Commonly referred to as the 'Triffin dilemma' after the American economist Robert Triffin, who drew attention to the contradiction in 1956.

[2] Maurice Obstfeld, 'Time of Troubles: The Yen and Japan's Economy, 1985–2008', in Hamada et al., *Japan's Bubble*, 53.

the country's mounting trading surplus by stimulating domestic demand through fiscal expansion. The volume of Japanese exports to the USA rose by almost 70 per cent during 1979–85.[3] The USA had already imposed voluntary export restraints on Japanese automobiles in 1981, and retaliatory pressure against the surge in Japanese imports intensified thereafter.

Circumstances changed dramatically in 1985. As domestic unemployment rose in the USA, it succeeded under the Plaza Accord of that year in persuading its major trading partners to engage in concerted policy intervention to appreciate their currencies to bring down the value of the dollar. In the aftermath, the yen appreciated considerably; it moved from 251/US$ in 1984 to 201/US$ a year later and to only 126/US$ in 1988, thus increasing the price of Japanese goods in international markets.[4] Within six months of the Plaza Accord, it was clear that the yen had appreciated more than policymakers had anticipated. Although the appreciation of G-5 currencies against the dollar after 1985 was halted for most affected countries by the Louvre Accord in 1987, which formally recognised that the slide of the dollar had destabilized global financial markets, the yen continued to appreciate, invoking a short-lived recession (endaka) in 1985–86.

Japan's response to these events proved fateful. It sought a ready escape from yen-induced deflation by boosting domestic demand, but its options were limited. Government deficit spending had increased substantially during the 1970s, as a result of the adverse effects of higher oil prices, a commitment to greater social security provision and reduced levels of tax revenue as a consequence of lower economic growth.[5] Weak aggregate demand and stagnant private investment in the wake of the oil price hike in 1973 had led to zero growth in real GNP in 1974, prompting Japan's first 'Keynesian fiscal expansion'.

---

[3]   David E. Weinstein, 'Historical, Structural, and Macroeconomic Perspectives on the Japanese Economic Crisis', in Magnus Blomstrom, Byron Gangnes and Sumner J. La Croix (eds.), *Japan's New Economy: Continuity and Change in the Twenty-First Century* (New York: Oxford University Press, 2001), 33.

[4]   It reversed direction in late 1988. It stood at 143 by end of 1989, compared with 126 a year earlier.

[5]   For details, see Kazumi Asako, Takatoshi Ito and Kazunori Sakamoto, 'The Rise and Fall of Deficit in Japan, 1965–1990', *Journal of the Japanese and International Economies* 5, no. 4 (1991): 451–72.

However, having just got its house in order after the fiscal looseness of the 1970s, the MOF was determined to restore fiscal rectitude from the mid-1980s.[6] Therefore, rather than undertaking government spending to effect industrial restructuring or to address the needs of housing, transportation, health and urban planning to boost the economy, the MOF used its entrenched organizational supremacy to ensure that monetary policy would be the default instrument of domestic economic stimulus. The 'Mayekawa' reports from the Bank of Japan – in 1986 and 1987 – called upon Japan to shift more to a market economy and to embrace structural reform in order to increase domestic demand rather than export demand, thereby reducing trade surpluses.[7] Nonetheless, growth through domestic demand came by an entirely different route.

The BOJ, at the behest of the MOF (to which it was subordinated) slashed the cost of capital. Interest rates were lowered from 5 per cent to 4.5 per cent in January 1986. Rates continued to fall: from 4.5 per cent to 4.0 per cent in March 1986, to 3.5 per cent in April, to 3.0 per cent in November and ultimately to a low of 2.5 per cent in February 1987, where they stabilized until May 1989. Only the first of the five reductions in the official discount rate (in January 1986) was instigated purely by the BOJ. The second through to the fifth (in February 1987) were influenced by considerations of international policy coordination, especially the prevention of external imbalances.

Raising interest rates would have been regarded by the BOJ as a violation of its post-Plaza responsibility.[8] Japan had long nurtured a special relationship with the USA and was not about to endanger it. It willingly accommodated the correction of the US budget and current account deficits by effecting a macroeconomic adjustment within its own borders. During the bubble years of 1987–90, Japan experienced the second longest period of economic expansion since the late 1960s, thanks to growing investment in

---

[6]   Though fiscal conservatism dominated the latter part of the 1980s, the government responded to the need to stimulate domestic demand and reduce trade surpluses by conducting expansionary fiscal policy during 1986–87, but this was a single exception. The budget was in balance by 1990. See below pp. 70, 77.

[7]   The 1986 report was issued by the Committee on Economic Adjustment, which was chaired by Haruo Mayekawa, a former Governor of the BOJ. Both reports argued for greater deregulation and for a shift in emphasis from export-led to domestic demand. However, faced with opposition from the MOF, neither argued for an explicit shift in fiscal policy to achieve such ends.

[8]   Takatoshi Ito, 'Retrospective on the Bubble Period and Its Relationship to Developments in the 1990s', *World Economy* 26, no. 3 (2003): 292.

business and housing, and rising expenditure on consumer durables.[9] Between 1986 and 1989 capital gains on land and stock assets surpassed the gross domestic output produced in the same period by more than 20 per cent.[10]

This is not to say that export-led growth was abandoned. Japanese manufacturers squeezed by the rising yen moved capital into the Asian tiger economies, courting customers and imports of cheaper components for struggling assembly sectors at home. Wage levels within Japan were too high to compete with Asian manufacturing costs but too low for Japanese consumers to absorb the country's excess capacity domestically. Although imports became cheaper in yen terms, Japan's continued protection of its highly-regulated distribution sector and its barriers to trade and inward foreign domestic investment created such price distortions that investment increasingly went overseas; this applied especially to the electronics, cars and metallurgy sectors. Japanese foreign direct investment into East Asia increased almost eight times in value between 1985 and 1989. Transnational corporations attempted to lower production costs in bases geared for export to the USA or to produce part-manufactured products and components to be exported for assembly in Japan and then re-exported to the USA and the West; this meant that although Japan's bilateral trade surplus with the USA may have been compromised, the export-led growth strategy that had dominated the high-growth era was sustained by regionalizing it elsewhere.[11]

---

[9] International Monetary Fund. World Economic Outlook: Financial Turbulence and the World Economy, Chapter IV Japan's Economic Crisis and Policy Options (Washington, DC: International Monetary Fund, 1998), 110.

[10] Rameshwar Tandon, *The Japanese Economy and the Way Forward* (New York: Palgrave Macmillan, 2005), 5.

[11] Lax monetary policy in the late 1980s reinforced the export of capital that was surplus to the needs of the Japanese domestic economy to East Asian manufacturing subsidiaries. The support of such subsidiaries as production bases for Japanese exports to the USA and Europe – as well as support for the keiretsu links between manufacturers and subcontractors – strengthened the development-state model of export. Japan refused to devolve economic control of vital technology to East Asian subsidiaries, thus keeping them dependent upon Japan for technology and for access to the US market. See Christopher W. Hughes, 'Japanese Policy and the East Asian Currency Crisis: Abject Defeat or Quiet Victory?', *Review of International Political Economy* 7, no. 2 (2000): 219–53.

The Impact of Financial Liberalization

It was particularly unfortunate for Japan that recourse to an easy money policy during the mid-to-late 1980s occurred in the wake of a period of financial deregulation and before the consequences of such liberalization were fully understood by its authorities. Increases in deposits and loans during the era of regulated interest rates in the high-growth period had invariably meant increased profits for banks, which had motivated banks to expand their balance sheets and their lending.[12] Since stability was equated, at the time, with no bank closures, banking overcapacity had been sustained, enabling banks to take risks with taxpayer insured deposits. However, once Japan's growth slowed – from the early 1970s – so did corporate demand for bank credit. Because corporations had been obliged to hold large compensating balances with lending banks as part of the banking/industry relationship during the high-growth period, they faced excess liquidity and clamoured for greater investment opportunities and fewer controls on the inflow and outflow of capital to Japan.

Moreover, during previous decades of much smaller deficits the government had relied on banks and securities companies to buy government debt at below market rates of interest to finance rising expenditure. Each party proved more reluctant to do so after 1973. As a consequence, 'the MOF permitted banks and securities companies to sell debt holdings in an unregulated secondary market. Once a secondary market was established with an unregulated interest rate, pressure to relax interest rate regulations in other parts of the financial system emerged.'[13] The government encouraged such liberalization because the controlled system of low interest rates had made it increasingly difficult for it to float bonds to finance what, at the time, were expanding fiscal deficits.

It was in these circumstances that Japan began a slow process of financial liberalization, which began in 1976. Its most potent symbol was the freeing up of foreign exchange transactions in 1980. From 1949 until the 1970s, as we noted earlier,[14] Japan had suppressed the development of money and capital markets, transferring funds through private and public banks in a highly regulated and internationally isolated framework. The difficulty that looser financial liberalization on an international scale posed for Japan was that it occurred without sufficient parallel progress having being made in

---

[12] See above pp. 18–24.
[13] Cargill and Sakamoto, *Japan Since 1980*, 71.
[14] See above pp. 10–11, 19–20.

the liberalization of its domestic financial institutions. Such liberalization proceeded only gradually during the 1980s and 1990s and was only really evident from 1998. Only in 2001 did the pace of Japan's international financial integration begin to track the trend of other major advanced economies.[15]

Once restrictions on borrowing from abroad were lifted (in 1980), it became easier for Japanese firms to raise funds in the securities market rather than from the banking system. They were often able to do this more cheaply, given that the cost of capital for firms with close banking affiliations had generally been higher than for non-bank firms during the high-growth period.[16] The benefits of relational banking now seemed rather less obvious. The proportion of new outside funds that corporations obtained from the capital market rather than from the banks tripled from 20 per cent in 1970–74 to 60 per cent in 1984.[17] By 1989 some 60 per cent of the total of bonds issued in Japan were raised outside the country.[18]

While the financial links between corporations and banks loosened, the deregulation of interest rates gathered pace. Deposit rates were more fully liberalized in 1985. The subsequent spread of short-term interest rates gave non-financial firms greater incentive to tap surplus funds from the capital market through securities, particularly from non-leveraged institutions such as life insurance companies. These surpluses were then deposited in the banking system as time deposits with liberalized interest rates; in effect, the non-financial firms became creditors to the banks.[19] Banks now faced pressure on both sides of their balance sheets: on the asset side they suffered the loss of traditional corporate borrowers to overseas funding sources,

---

[15]   For detailed empirical evidence of the nature and extent of Japan's foreign assets and liabilities, and estimates of its level of financial integration, see Philip R. Lane, 'International Financial Integration and Japanese Economic Performance', in Hamada et al., *Japan's Bubble*, 129–74.

[16]   Weinstein and Yafeh, 'On the Costs of a Bank-Centered Financial System'. See above pp. 20–21.

[17]   Shijuro Ogata, 'Financial Markets in Japan', in Suzanne Berger and Ronald P. Dore (eds.), *National Diversity and Global Capitalism* (Ithaca: Cornell University Press, 1996), 171–8.

[18]   Masazumi Hattori, Hyun Song Shin and Wataru Takahashi, 'A Financial System Perspective on Japan's Experience in the Late 1980s', Paper presented at the 16th International Conference hosted by the Institute for Monetary and Economic Studies, Bank of Japan, Tokyo, May 2009, 10.

[19]   Ibid., 37.

while on the liabilities side they came under pressure to lend out the funds they had newly acquired from non-financial corporate deposits.[20]

The problem was compounded by segmentation within the Japanese banking sector. Long-term and short-term banking had traditionally been separated according to the size of the client, with smaller banks lending to smaller businesses and long-term credit and trust banks caring for larger firms. It was the latter group that lost out to the developing bond and equity markets; however, because of segmentation, they were unable to move into other sectors, such as investment banking. One of the few avenues open to them was to expand into lending in the property market.[21] The limited development of the domestic corporate bond market restricted the range of investment opportunities available to absorb domestic savings, which increased the tendency for them to be funnelled into the property sector.

Exuberance, Cheap Money and Institutional Practice: the Emergence of the Bubble Economy

To anyone interested in the vagaries of economic and financial fortune, Japan's 'boom and bust' experience during the 1980s and 1990s remains mesmerizing. Japan Inc., the scourge of neoclassical purists for decades past, had seemingly taken on a kamikaze hue, capable of creating and sustaining a speculative mania that was sufficiently vibrant and protracted to leave in its wake a decade and more of deflation, low growth and financial hubris from which there appeared to be no escape. During this roller-coaster experience, it was easier to identify the supposed culprits – greedy short-sighted banks, self-serving bureaucrats and inept parliamentarians – than it was to discern the dynamics of boom and bust or to explain the rationale of contemporary action and inaction. We seek to do so, first in relation to the bubble economy.

By the mid-1980s banks were faced with declining returns from traditional commercial lending, and they responded with a surge of aggressive lending in order to find new borrowers and to increase their profit margins. Price competition began to place downward pressure on their risk-adjusted interest rate margins, tempting them to expand the riskier parts of their loan portfolios. Otherwise generally prudent banks drifted into soft budgeting,

---

[20] Ibid., 27.
[21] Kazuo Ueda, 'Causes of Japan's Banking Problems in the 1990s', in Takeo Hoshi and Hugh Patrick (eds.), *Crisis and Change in the Japanese Financial System* (Boston, MA: Kluwer Academic Publishers, 2000), 76–7.

extending the now expanded supply of credit from corporate depositors to marginal small and medium-sized enterprises (SMEs) that they might otherwise have declined. Before 1983 total lending to SMEs had been almost equivalent to total lending to large firms. By 1990 it was three times that volume, with the three long-term credit banks being the largest supplier of funds.[22] As Figure 4.1 below shows, large enterprises had accounted for more than 40 per cent of total loans to domestic corporations at the end of 1975. By the end of 1990, this proportion had fallen to around 20 per cent. In contrast, the share of loans to small enterprises almost doubled over the same period: from about 35 per cent to around 65 per cent.

Private consumption grew rapidly during the second half of the 1980s but there was much more marked growth in gross fixed investment, which expanded by about 10 per cent on average each year. Both large and medium-sized firms were able to tap into financial markets, using the rising value of land as collateral. It was the sharp rise in the *expected* return on specific categories of commercial land – especially central office space in Tokyo and luxurious resorts – that sparked feverish land-intensive corporate investment, largely by nonmanufacturing companies.[23]

Lending decisions by banks became increasingly based on collateral requirements rather than on cash flow analysis, tempting banks to loosen credit standards as property prices increased. With a premium on increased lending from the mid-1980s, banks competed feverishly to issue property-related loans to non-traditional customers without adequate assessment of risk, 'substituting estate-backed collateral for relational ties.'[24] The fact that tax rates were relatively low on land holdings but high on land transactions suppressed the supply of land. This accelerated the rise in land prices and

---

[22]   Kenneth N. Kuttner and Adam S. Posen, 'The Great Recession: Lessons for Macroeconomic Policy from Japan', *Brookings Papers on Economic Activity*, no. 2 (2001): 143; Yoshinori Shimizu, 'Convoy Regulation, Bank Management, and the Financial Crisis in Japan', in Ryoichi Mikitani and Adam S. Posen (eds.), *Japan's Financial Crisis and Its Parallels to U.S. Experience* (Washington, DC: Institute for International Economics, 2000), 57–100.
[23]   Hiroshi Yoshikawa, *Japan's Lost Decade* (Tokyo: International House of Japan, 2001), 60–67.
[24]   Jennifer A. Amyx, *Japan's Financial Crisis: Institutional Rigidity and Reluctant Change* (Princeton, NJ: Princeton University Press, 2004), 32.

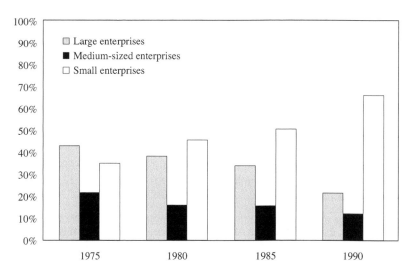

Note: Total outstanding loans used for calculations are outstanding loans and discounts to domestic corporate borrowers, excluding overdrafts. Large enterprises are corporations with capital of at least 1 billion yen and more than 300 regular employees. For the wholesale trade industry, the criterion for the number of regular employees is more than 100 persons. For the retail and service industries, it is more than 50 persons. Small enterprises are unincorporated enterprises as well as corporations with capital of up to 100 million yen or with up to 300 regular employees. For the wholesale trade industry, the definition is corporations with capital of up to 30 million yen or with up to 100 regular employees. For the retail trade and service industries, it is corporations with capital of up to 10 million yen or with up to 50 regular employees. Outstanding loans for medium-sized enterprises are calculated by excluding those for small enterprises and large enterprises from total outstanding loans.

Source: Hattori, Shin and Takahashi, 'Financial System Perspective,' 29.

Figure 4.1 Breakdown of corporate borrowers by size

the expectation that they would keep on rising, providing further support to the direction of bank lending.[25]

There were additional forces at work. Jusen companies – non-bank financial institutions acting as housing-loan companies – had been marginalized in the housing loan market in the 1980s by the subsidized loans available from the government's Japan Housing Loan Corporation. However, they also began to seek out riskier business, granting loans on the basis

---

[25] Kunio Okina, Masaaki Shirakawa and Shigenori Shiratsuka, 'The Asset Price Bubble and Monetary Policy: Japan's Experience in the Late 1980s and the Lessons', Special issue, *Monetary and Economic Studies* 19, no. 1 (2001): 416.

of second-rate collateral.[26] Moreover, the MOF remained wedded to fiscal reconstruction. Though the general government balance was in deficit down to 1986, the situation improved noticeably thereafter; the balance of the national debt fell from 42.7 per cent of GDP in fiscal 1986 to 38.1 per cent at the end of fiscal 1990. This resulted in a reduction in the issue of government bonds, which aggravated the portfolio difficulties of financial institutions, intensifying their need to compete to provide loans.[27] Not surprisingly, the share of lending to large manufacturing corporations fell from 60 per cent in 1985 to 40 per cent in 1991, while loans to the property sector as a percentage of total loans by Japan's city banks doubled from 6 per cent to 12 per cent between 1983 and 1989.[28]

Major corporations were able to raise money in the booming stock market and to use the funds to buy other financial assets offering high yields. Firms and households could just as easily acquire property with borrowed money. Given that land prices had been on a rising trend since the end of the war, bankers were rarely concerned about losses if loans were secured against property. The incentive was there: land prices in Japan had risen almost continuously during the post-war period and there was little reason to believe that they would not continue to do so.

Blaming the Bank

The surge in equity and property prices is commonly ascribed to the BOJ's laxity in providing excessive liquidity during 1986–89.[29] It is important, therefore, to determine why monetary policy remained so loose during that period. The argument that the BOJ should have reined in on easy money earlier in the bubble period has a certain ex-post rationality. Few in authority argued thus at the time. The financial authorities had not fashioned interest rate policy to pursue both core price and asset price stability. Since asset prices can fluctuate in response to economic fundamentals, they are

---

[26]   Mitsuhiro Fukao, 'Financial Crisis and the Lost Decade', *Asian Economic Policy Review* 2, no. 2 (2007): 276.

[27]   Yukio Noguchi, 'The "Bubble" and Economic Policies in the 1980s', *Journal of Japanese Studies* 20, no. 2 (1994): 298–9.

[28]   Mitsuhiro Fukao, 'Japan's Lost Decade and its Financial System', *The World Economy* 26, no. 3 (2003): 365–8.

[29]   See, for example, Hoshi and Kashyap, 'Japan's Financial Crisis'; Jinushi Toshiki, Yoshihiro Kuroki and Ryuzo Miyao, 'Monetary Policy in Japan Since the Late 1980s: Delayed Policy Actions and Some Explanation', in Mikitani and Posen, *Japan's Financial Crisis*, 115–48.

not customarily adopted as a monetary target.[30] Even when rates were reduced to the critically low level of 2.5 per cent in February 1987, the prevention of asset price inflation was not a major consideration for the BOJ.[31]

Though monetary policy was blamed for being too lax, authorities at the time found it difficult 'to say when the boom had to stop.'[32] The sharp rise in the exchange rate from 1985 had not brought about the recession many feared would occur. Moreover, there was a perceived need for international cooperation following the stock market crash in the USA in October 1987. Until 1989 the instinctive desire to avoid trade frictions through further appreciation of the yen remained dominant. In addition, self-confidence in Japan's government, financial and corporate nexus was high. Even if monetary policy had been tightened earlier – in, say, 1988 – it is doubtful whether it would have dampened expectations of a positive return on assets. It would have taken a substantial interest rate hike to have 'popped the bubble'.[33]

At the peak of the bubble – in the second half of 1989 – over 60 per cent of Japanese institutional investors did not believe that the Nikkei stock index was overvalued. 'In a period characterized by the arrival of news that [was] difficult to digest and subject to multiple interpretations',[34] many bullish investors believed that there was still a permanent component to the growth rate and were optimistic about economic fundamentals. It was never certain, of course, that growth would rise permanently (the lag in the rise of aggregate consumption over the bubble period indicates that the public were sceptical) or that BOJ-induced falls in interest rates would necessarily persist. Nonetheless, both GDP and corporate earnings picked up in 1986,

---

[30] Yoshikawa, *Japan's Lost Decade*, 72.

[31] Kunio Okina and Shigenori Shiratsuka, 'Japan's Experience with Asset Price Bubbles: Is It a Case for Inflation Targeting?', in William C. Hunter, George W. Kaufman, and Michael Pomerleano, (eds.) *Asset Price Bubbles: The Implications for Monetary, Regulatory and International Policies* (Cambridge, Mass. The MIT Press, 2003), 82–9.

[32] Ito, 'Japan and the Asian Economies: A "Miracle" in Transition', 215.

[33] Takatoshi Ito and Frederic S. Mishkin, 'Two Decades of Japanese Monetary Policy and the Deflation Problem', in Takatoshi Ito and Andrew K. Rose (eds.), *Monetary Policy with Very Low Inflation in the Pacific Rim* (Chicago: University of Chicago Press, 2006), 131–201.

[34] Robert Barsky, 'The Japanese Asset Price Bubble: A Heterogeneous Approach', in Hamada et al., *Japan's Bubble*, 48. Since the bubble was supported by heavy borrowing on the part of optimistic investors, it was always sensitive to any tightening of credit by the central bank, as later experience was to show.

at a time when the cost of capital was falling; this signalled to optimistic bullish investors that the check to growth and productivity that the country had experienced since 1974 was probably transitory and that higher equity prices could well continue into the foreseeable future. 'Rational or not, beliefs about fundamentals played a central role in generating the bubble.'[35] Optimistic investors faced few constraints on borrowing. In a world of heterogeneous beliefs, their attitudes and behaviour were able to prevail in the market.[36]

The government, the central bank and the general public did not have much appetite for higher interest rates. Increases in the money supply had resulted from the BOJ's determination (from 1985) to keep interest rates low to prevent the yen appreciating against the US dollar. The fiscal gap that had plagued the Japanese economy for two decades was being closed by increasing tax revenues. During the bubble years, the authorities were reluctant to engage in any contractionary policy that might be viewed by the outside world as a deliberate attempt to increase Japan's current account surplus.

Moreover, the orthodox rationale for monetary tightening is growth of inflationary pressure, but Japan's inflation rate was low in the mid-1980s. It had been above the average for the G7 countries during the 1960s and for most of the 1970s; but the trend was reversed from the early 1980s. The inflation rate had risen to about 8 per cent following the second oil crisis in 1979 but it had fallen to 3 per cent in 1982 and fluctuated at a low of 0 per cent to 3 per cent for the remainder of the 1980s.[37] The average annual percentage change in the consumer price index in Japan between 1983 and 1994 stood at 1.7, compared with 4.0 in France, 4.9 in the UK, 2.4 in Germany and 3.6 in the USA. The sharp appreciation of the yen had lowered import prices; and although the labour market was tight in the latter half of the 1980s, corporations had proved successful in persuading labour unions to moderate wage demands in order to maintain international competitiveness.[38] In the absence of inflationary pressure, it was not obvious to the BOJ that monetary policy needed to be tightened.

It was relatively easy, in other words, to sustain a lax monetary policy when economic fundamentals appeared to be sound. Japan had been able to grow in an environment of low inflation, in spite of an appreciated currency.

---

[35] Ibid., 37.
[36] Ibid., 35.
[37] Ito and Mishkin, 'Two Decades of Japanese Monetary Policy', 133–5.
[38] Noguchi, 'The "Bubble" and Economic Policies', 300.

This was largely because of an improvement in its terms of trade, which had resulted from falling energy prices and reduced yen prices on non-oil imports. This effective transfer of payments from oil-producing countries to Japan expanded its permanent income and worked through its distribution and transportation sectors to offset the unfavourable short-run effects of yen appreciation on competition in exporting and importing.

By the end of 1989 Japan's growth rate was approaching 5 per cent, exceeding the average of 4 per cent from 1975 to 1989. It was difficult to curb expectations, given the widespread but mistaken belief that asset prices, especially of land, would continue to rise. As Grimes puts it:

> The policy of easy money was popular… . Corporations and individuals were benefitting as their paper wealth increased, exporters appreciated the dampening effect it had on the value of the yen, MOF officials appreciated the opportunity to restrict fiscal policy and to start attacking the government's debt problem through the sale of assets at high prices, and politicians were happy with both the prosperity and the opportunity to expand political funds through stock-ramping deals or early purchases of new equity offerings.[39]

Regulation and Finance: the Dominance of Institutional Practice

The contemporary monetary circumstances that first encouraged and then helped sustain the bubble were only part of Japan's emerging difficulties. A more systemic problem was that the Japanese authorities, prompted by the 'one size fits all' framework of global governance that gave prominence to deregulated financial markets, had proceeded from the 1980s with a flawed and incomplete liberalization programme. They had undertaken the dual liberalizations of the capital account and the domestic financial system without any recognition of the transition risks involved.

The limited development of the domestic corporate market, whatever its contemporary rationale during the high-growth period,[40] had restricted the range of investment opportunities available to absorb domestic savings. An uncoordinated approach to external and internal financial liberalization thus enabled an excessive proportion of domestic savings to be channelled towards the property sector. Had there been a more open domestic financial system, allowing for a larger domestic securities market and permitting entry by foreign banks instead of the mismatched and uncoordinated

---

[39] William W. Grimes, *Unmaking the Japanese Miracle: Macroeconomic Politics, 1985–2000* (Ithaca: Cornell University Press, 2001), 141.

[40] See above pp. 19–22.

approach to external and internal financial liberalization that had long prevailed, there would have been less pressure on the property sector to be the funnel for domestic savings and compromised lending decisions.[41]

Accelerated deregulation had occurred without an appropriate adjustment in the regulatory framework.[42] It was conducted within the context of the well-established financial regime of the high-growth period, characterized by insider assessment of risk, lack of transparency and disclosure, mutual support and an implicit assurance that financial institutions would not be allowed to fail, thus shielding them from having to develop protocols of risk management. Financial liberalization had prompted modifications in the financial system to allow easier financing of government deficits, but 'the government viewed the current set of financial institutions as more than adequate. How could one argue with success?'[43] A well-developed capital market would have ensured more effective disclosure of information, and developed auditing and accounting procedures, shareholder sovereignty and an appropriate legal framework.

During the high-growth period, Japan had judged that open capital markets would be less likely to foster risk sharing, long-term maximizing behaviour and the incentives to enhance corporate growth. The contemporary financial system had been essentially opaque, however. As we noted earlier, regulatory control of bank behaviour had formerly been regarded as an adequate substitute for monitoring by shareholders and depositors. Controls had been enforced through the availability of cheap loans and the granting of licences for new branches to compliant banks. Lending was conducted within the framework of the keiretsu system, with financial decisions based upon information from the main banks, around which company groups were centred.[44] With the MOF's relational ties and informal networks grounded in and across organizations and intertwined within personnel systems, there had been little prospect of much institutional transformation over the years.

Such processes had worked reasonably well during the high-growth period, when the need for effective regulation was limited, when the domestic financial sector was insulated from international pressures and

---

[41]   Lane, 'International Financial Integration', 166–7.

[42]   Akihiro Kanaya and David Woo, *The Japanese Banking Crisis of the 1990s: Sources and Lessons*, Essays in International Economics No. 222, (Princeton, NJ: Department of Economics, Princeton University, 2001), 45–6.

[43]   Cargill and Sakamoto, *Japan Since 1980*, 72.

[44]   Ibid., 78.

when the self-regulation of the main bank system allowed policymakers to focus on stability rather than profit maximization. The MOF had been able to enjoy relative autonomy in decision-making and in the supervision of private-sector finance. Its informal ties with banks meant that their financial condition could be disguised, rescue mergers arranged and deposits guaranteed long after the market might otherwise have demanded higher rates for placing funds in weak banks or have denied funds to nonviable institutions.[45]

However, the use of inside knowledge and the lack of financial disclosure meant that monitoring increasingly became a matter of trust, prompted more by administrative guidance than by formal laws. Although the persistence of cross-shareholding among firms had helped companies to survive and stabilize during the catch-up years, it had also weakened the authorities' desire to review corporate governance. This had delayed the establishment of appropriate regulatory and supervisory frameworks for controlling risk. Relational banking had paid insufficient attention to the inspection of loan-to-value ratios. When capital shortage turned to capital surplus in the 1980s, the supervisory activities of the main banks weakened further, but without a Western-style stock market in place that might otherwise have demanded greater accountability.[46]

The persistence of weak accounting systems and inadequate measures to impose financial discipline or to force disclosure of unacceptable risk were only manifestations of a deeper malaise. During the catch-up period before the 1980s, financial regulation had come to rely upon informal relational ties between regulators and financial institutions and upon discretionary, rather than legal, coercive and rules-based procedures. The MOF had proved especially adept at retaining a monopoly over information affecting the macroeconomy and had managed resources to effect compliance with policy.[47]

---

[45]   Bai Gao, *Japan's Economic Dilemma: The Institutional Origins of Prosperity and Stagnation* (Cambridge: Cambridge University Press, 2001), 258.

[46]   As Stiglitz noted, the government deregulated the financial sector 'when it should have been asking what was the *appropriate* set of regulations, and it did not do enough to ensure good corporate governance which would have been necessary to create an effective stock market.' Joseph E. Stiglitz, 'From Miracle to Crisis to Recovery: Lessons from Four Decades of East Asian Experience', in Joseph E. Stiglitz and Shahid Yusuf (eds.), *Rethinking the East Asian Miracle*, (New York: Oxford University Press, 2001), 520.

[47]   Amyx, *Japan's Financial Crisis*, 29, 126, 257. See above pp. 5–8.

The influence of deep-seated coalitions of interests within state institutions, notably between the MOF and the BOJ, become only too apparent
as the bubble emerged.[48] As early as spring 1986 the BOJ had questioned
the extent to which the expansion of domestic demand should be borne by
monetary rather than fiscal policy; nonetheless, its major policy decisions
still came under the scrutiny of the MOF. It was the MOF that judged
whether the state of the economy warranted any change in the monetary
stance, making it in essence the final arbiter of the national interest.[49] The
BOJ called for interest rate rises in 1986 and 1987 but was obliged to extend
and maintain an easy monetary policy. Since the BOJ was not a Cabinet
Ministry with direct input into policymaking, it had little opportunity to
gain the support of either the MOF or the LDP to head off what it saw as
inflationary pressures. Nor was the presence of old-boy personnel from the
finance Ministry – via the system of amakudari – much of a deterrent. It
appears that the greater presence of ex-MOF personnel within the banking
sector was correlated positively with the magnitude of unsound investments, many of the transferees proving unfamiliar with, and unable to
properly monitor, branch-level decision making.[50] Nonetheless, the legacy
of mutual support dominated; should problems arise, it was still believed
that the 'convoy' system directed by the MOF would oblige stronger
institutions to assist weaker ones.

The loose monetary regime was also aggravated by the BOJ's continued
use of 'window guidance'. During the 1950s and 1960s, as we pointed out
earlier, money was not always available to banks willing to acquire it at the
ruling interest rate; it was allocated in specific amounts by the central bank
to selected banks. Window guidance was the process by which the BOJ
issued extra-legal nonbinding directives to banks, persuading them to
provide a ready supply of low-cost finance to targeted industries anxious to
gain and expand a foothold in global markets. Since banks faced high
demand for loans in the growth period, they were obliged to seek extended
liquidity from the BOJ, which in turn specified the net additional lending
each financial institution could make in each quarter. When the banks
visited the BOJ 'window' for loans, the BOJ could persuade them to
channel funds in preferred directions. In principle, the mechanism provided
a check on bank lending deemed inappropriate for national advancement.[51]

---

48   Grimes, *Unmaking the Japanese Miracle*, 3–6, 218.
49   Amyx, *Japan's Financial Crisis*, 101–3.
50   Ibid., 143.
51   See above pp. 20–21.

During the 1980s the BOJ continued the practice of dividing an overall economy-wide target of lending via quotas to commercial banks, which were in turn penalized for any overshooting or undershooting. But the system was not as benign as the growth-oriented focus of earlier decades might suggest. Banks that were reliant upon continued lending quotas from the BOJ were unwilling to undershoot the targets; they came to regard them as ones to reach rather than ones not to exceed, thereby fuelling the asset bubble.[52] Banks often 'struggled to meet sometimes outlandishly high quota imposed on them by the BOJ as they sought to avoid costly penalties for noncompliance.'[53] The quotas were increased during the 1980s, with lending to the property sector actively encouraged. As interest rates fell, window guidance was actually relaxed rather than tightened, so banks used their lending quotas to the maximum, directing their activities not to productive industry but to speculation in the property market.

Ever since the loose fiscal policies of the 1970s, and their associated deficits, the MOF had leaned towards fiscal consolidation.[54] Its actions allowed monetary policy to dominate in the years following the appreciation of the yen, and the Ministry made little effort to counter policy or to carefully monitor the BOJ's lending practices. However, despite the orthodox impression that the Ministry was engaged in tough retrenchment in the 1980s, it actually continued with substantial off-budget financing (of public works in particular) through the Fiscal Investment and Loan Programme (FILP), delivering budget deficits to the LDP.[55] The irony was that, in so doing, it stimulated even further levels of corporate investment that were now easier to finance. Corporations were able to head off the need to restructure Japan's 'dual economy' for the sake of greater efficiency and domestic stability, choosing instead to enjoy the expansion of revenues that contemporary circumstances and accommodating monetary policy permitted.

---

[52] Richard A. Werner, 'The Cause of Japan's Recession and the Lessons for the World', in Bailey, et al., *Crisis or Recovery in Japan*, 31–60; Richard A. Werner, *Princes of the Yen: Japan's Central Bankers and the Transformation of the Economy* (Armonk, NY: M. E. Sharpe, 2003); Vogel, *Japan Remodeled*, 24.

[53] Werner, *Princes of the Yen*, 2003, 87; Gary R. Saxonhouse and Robert M. Stern, 'The Bubble and the Lost Decade', *World Economy* 26, no. 3: (2003): 267–81.

[54] Amyx, *Japan's Financial Crisis*, 21–3, 117–8.

[55] See Maurice Wright, *Japan's Fiscal Crisis: The Ministry of Finance and the Politics of Public Spending, 1975–2000* (Oxford: Oxford University Press, 2002), 346–64, 461–84.

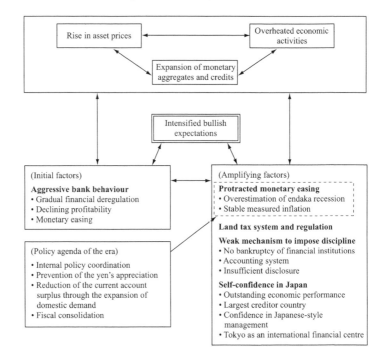

Source: Okina, Shirakawa and Shiratsuka, 'Asset Price Bubble,' 409.

Figure 4.2   Illustration of the bubble economy in Japan

These external, institutional and path-dependent influences help explain
why a loose monetary climate emerged in the mid-1980s and how elemental
features of the financial system sustained speculative pressure. On the basis
of output estimates at the time, the BOJ could have been expected to have
tightened monetary policy in 1987–88 without reference to asset prices.[56]
However, the fact that the bubble was still intact by early 1989 is not entirely
because such tightening did not occur. Experience of monetary easing in 15
OECD countries (including Japan) between 1970 and 2000 casts doubt on
the assumption that monetary laxity is either a necessary or a sufficient
condition for a boom in share and property prices, suggesting that other

---

[56]   Kuttner and Posen, 'The Great Recession', in Adam S. Posen, 'It Takes More
Than a Bubble to Become Japan', Institute for International Economics Working
Paper No. 03–9, Peterson Institute for International Economics, Washington, DC,
2003, 11. Available at http://ssrn.com/abstract=472962.

factors transformed the easy monetary conditions into a speculative boom.[57] Neither the BOJ nor any other major central bank at the time had had much experience in dealing with asset price inflation in the midst of generally low prices. It was by no means clear, in other words, that a temporary tightening of monetary policy would have had a measurable effect on the bubble process of Japanese stock and land prices.[58] Ex-post calculations suggest that interest rates would need to have risen to 8 per cent in 1988 to have had a noticeable effect, hardly something that either the government or the public would have countenanced.[59]

There is no monocausal explanation of Japan's bubble economy in the 1980s. The authorities' monetary stance during 1986–89 fuelled a 'euphoric expectation of protracted low interest rates'.[60] Some of the initial conditioning elements had arisen decades past, from changes in the internal and external environment facing Japan. They in turn were subsequently amplified, akin to a chemical reaction, into a 'process of intensified bullish expectations', as illustrated in Figure 4.2 above.

Once the *structural* shift towards greater supply of credit for lending on property and stock market speculation had taken hold, based on rising expectations of continued monetary easing, rising collateral values and deregulated shifts in lending practices, the bubble gained almost self-generated strength. Few called a halt; at least for the time being.

[57] Ibid, 6–9.
[58] Ito and Mishkin, 'Two Decades of Japanese Monetary Policy'.
[59] Okina, Shirakawa and Shiratsuka, 'The Asset Price Bubble', 429–30.
[60] Ibid., 409.

5.   'Losing a decade': economic and financial hubris in recessionary Japan, 1990–97

The effects of the explosion of land and stock prices between 1985 and 1990 and their subsequent dramatic collapse in the 1990s – the bubble that gave way to the 'lost decade' – was unprecedented in post-war Japanese experience. In a dramatic reversal of fortune, the Nikkei 225 stock index, which had peaked at 38,915 yen at the end of 1989, fell to only 14,309 in August 1992. In September 1990 land prices had stood at four times their September 1985 level. They started their decline only in September 1991, following MOF guidelines limiting bank lending to the property sector (Figure 5.1 below). The slide in prices thereafter was unabated; at the end of 1997, the average price of land in the six largest Japanese cities was about 40 per cent of the peak seen in 1990. By 1999 land prices more generally had collapsed to 80 per cent of their peak level.[1]

By May 1989 both the MOF and the LDP had become alarmed by the bubble in asset prices and the overheating of the economy. Monetary policy was tightened sharply to halt the rise in land prices. The BOJ raised interest rates some 18 months before the stock market peaked; it continued to raise them for a year thereafter, possibly because land prices continued to rise after the stock market collapse.[2] Interest rates rose from the 2.5 per cent level which had been sustained since 1987 to 3.25 per cent in May 1989, to 4.25 per cent in December and then to 6 per cent in August 1990, a cumulative increase of 3.5 percentage points in just over a year.

By 1990 there had been a need for some correction to the excesses of the bubble years, but hardly anyone expected that the subsequent decade would ultimately be dominated by protracted deflation and a deepening banking and financial crisis, and by an elite economic and political bureaucracy seemingly bereft of the strategic, interventionist prowess to initiate and

---

[1]   Okina, Shirakawa and Shiratsuka, 'The Asset Price Bubble', 399.
[2]   Hamada et al., *Japan's Bubble*, 7–8.

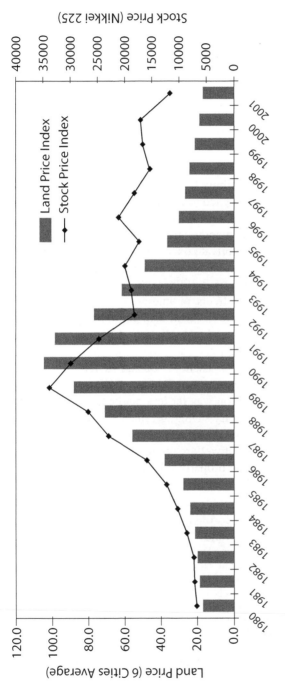

Notes: The land price index refers to commercial land in six metropolitan cities in September each year (calculated by the Real Estate Institute). The Stock Price Index is the Nikkei 225, annual average of daily close (provided by the Nihon Keizai Shinbun).

Source: Ito, 'Retrospective on the Bubble Period', 285.

Figure 5.1   Japanese stock and land price index, 1980–2001

sustain growth accorded to it in the past. As asset prices and spending declined in the early 1990s, the balance sheets of financial institutions and corporations deteriorated rapidly, setting in motion 'a regulatory and political response *wedded to the old regime* that ultimately became responsible for almost fifteen years of economic distress.'[3] It is to the nature and consequences of that response that we now turn.

Lending in a Recession

The interest rate tightening introduced at the end of 1989 had a draconian effect; it was more than merely curbing lending in the property sector. The swift about-turn in monetary policy led to dramatic deflation, first of stock and then of land values. Fluctuations in land values had a rapid and pervasive effect upon corporate income streams, profitability and stock market valuations. The decline in private fixed investment was particularly severe; on average it fell by over 2 per cent each year during the first half of the 1990s. The decline continued until 1998, with only a brief respite in 1996.[4] Until 1997 the negative effects of interest rate tightening upon private consumption was less severe in Japan than might have been anticipated, for a number of reasons. There had been no credit-fuelled consumption during the bubble (borrowing rates had been high relative to deposit rates), the portfolios of Japanese households contained relatively fewer holdings of equities than was the case in the USA or the UK, for example, so that the asset effect on consumption was far less marked; also, there was only muted recourse to precautionary saving, given that the bursting of the asset bubble had not initially led to any significant rise in unemployment or to doubts about the sustainability of welfare programmes.[5]

The drastic decline in stock and property prices seriously weakened the health of banks and other financial institutions. By 1992 it was clear that

---

[3]   Cargill and Sakamoto, *Japan Since* 1980, 99 [italics added].

[4]   International Monetary Fund. World Economic Outlook: Financial Turbulence and the World Economy, Chapter IV Japan's Economic Crisis and Policy Options. Washington, DC: International Monetary Fund, 1998, 110. The issue of falling investment is taken up later. See below pp. 108–9.

[5]   Ibid., 10–11. The negative effects of consumption were more noticeable amongst aged retirees and self-employed individuals with significant stock holdings, but they constituted only around 12% of total households. Hiroshi Yoshikawa, 'Japan's Lost Decade: What Have We Learned and Where Are We Heading', *Asian Economic Policy Review* 2, no. 2 (2007): 186–203; John, Muellbauer and Keiko Murata, 'Consumption, Land Prices and the Monetary Transmission Mechanism in Japan', in Hamada et al., *Japan's Bubble*, 175–216.

asset price deflation had led to deep falls in the value of bank capitalization and loan collateral, and that the banking sector was riddled with huge stocks of nonperforming loans (NPLs).[6] Because it was critical in the immediate term to stem even further depreciation of capital values, discount rates were lowered from 5.5 per cent in July 1991 to 3.25 per cent in July 1992, their lowest level since May 1989. Further reductions took rates to 2.5 per cent in February 1993, to 1.75 per cent in September 1993 and to only half of one per cent by September 1995.

Despite these repeated reductions of nominal short-term interest rates, the economy languished, suggesting that the authorities had seriously underestimated the influence of deflationary forces. As Table 5.1 shows, Japan's real GDP growth rate had averaged almost 4 per cent in the 1980s, better than that of the USA and the larger European economies. Compared with the 1980s, however, Japan's real GDP growth in the 1990s marked the largest decline among the G7 countries.[7] The average annual growth rate of per capita GDP between 1991 and 2000 was 0.5 per cent in Japan, compared with 2.6 per cent in the USA.[8] Signs of recovery in the 1990s quickly dissipated, with the economy little better fundamentally than it had been immediately after the bursting of the bubble.[9]

What distinguished Japan was not that it suffered a depression anything like that seen in the 1930s – GDP did not decline by 25–30 per cent over four years, as had happened in the USA between 1929 and 1933 – but the manner in which recession was transformed into extended stagnation. Japan suffered two distinct declines during the 1990s. The first lasted from 1990 to 1993; a mild recovery followed but the rate of GDP growth was lower than in earlier recoveries. The second recession occurred in 1997; it was deeper, and it deepened even more during the following two years.[10] A significant

---

[6] Kanaya and Woo, *The Japanese Banking Crisis*, 8. A loan was considered to be nonperforming when individuals or corporations that had borrowed from banks to fund the purchase of property or stock could no longer meet the payments (interest and principal).

[7] Naruki Mori, Shigenori Shiratsuka and Hiroo Taguchi, 'Policy Responses to the Post-Bubble Adjustments in Japan: A Tentative Review', Special issue, *Monetary and Economic Studies* 19, no. 1 (2001): 53–102.

[8] Fumio Hayashi and Edward C. Prescott, 'The 1990s in Japan: A Lost Decade', *Review of Economic Dynamics* 5, no. 1 (2002): 206–35.

[9] Ito, 'Retrospective on the Bubble Period', 283–8.

[10] Meltzer, 'Monetary Transmission at Low Inflation', 16; Michael M. Hutchison and Frank Westermann (eds), *Japan's Great Stagnation: Financial and Monetary Policy Lessons for Advanced Economies* (Cambridge, MA: MIT Press, 2006).

Table 5.1   Average annual growth rates of real GDP by decade

	1970s	1980s	1990s
Japan	5.2	3.8	1.6
USA	3.2	2.7	2.6
Germany	3.2	1.8	1.6
France	3.7	2.3	1.7
UK	2.4	2.4	1.8
Italy	3.7	2.4	1.3
Canada	4.4	2.9	2.0

Notes:
1. When calculating the average annual growth rates of the 1990s, data for 1999 are estimated by the Organisation for Economic Co-operation and Development, except for Japan, where the data are based on the quick estimates published by the Economic Planning Agency.
2. For Germany, real GDP is that of West Germany until 1991 and that of unified Germany from 1992 onwards; that is, comparison is made with aggregate East and West German GDP in 1991.

Source: Mori, Shiratsuka and Taguchi, 'Policy Responses', 54.

divergence developed between Japan's potential and actual real GDP (the output gap). The OECD estimated that Japan had 17 below-potential half years from 1980, 14 of them since the first half of 1992.[11]

Other countries, particularly the Nordic countries of Sweden, Finland and Norway, suffered collapses in asset prices and banking crises in the 1990s. The Nordic crises were associated with excessive consumer and commercial borrowing in the property market and poorly designed financial deregulation. Their banking sectors suffered considerable losses in the aftermath of the collapse in consumer spending and the failure of property companies. Real house prices fell by 30 per cent in Finland and by 25 per cent in Sweden during 1991–93.

Neither the duration of the crises nor the length of ensuing recessions in these countries was anything like as protracted as in Japan.[12] Swift corrective action was the key – a lesson that was lost on Japan. The Swedish government promptly nationalized failed banks and injected public funds

[11]   Kuttner and Posen, 'The Great Recession', 98–9.
[12]   International Monetary Fund, World Economic Outlook, 1998, 107–22.

into the system. In Sweden, the period when loan losses by banks exceeded profits before loan losses was limited to three years: from 1991 to 1993. In contrast, loan losses by Japanese banks consistently exceeded operating profits from 1994 until the end of the decade.[13] Whereas Sweden saw the banking crisis as a national crisis, Japan allowed financial instability and fragility to fester until a full-scale crisis materialized.[14] The output loss as a percentage of GDP – occasioned by banking crises and their effects – was substantially greater in Japan than in Norway, Sweden and Finland, largely because of the extended duration of its crisis, as Table 5.2 shows.

Table 5.2   Selected banking crises and their effects

	Date	Duration (Years)	Direct cost to taxpayers[a]	Output loss (% of GDP)
Japan	1991–2001	10	14.0	71.7
Norway	1989–1992	4	3.4	27.1
Sweden	1991–1994	4	2.1	3.8
Finland	1991–1994	4	10.0	44.9

Note: (a) per cent of annual GDP at end of episode.

Source: Barrel and Davis, 'Evolution of the Financial Crisis', 5.

The potential effects of interest rate reductions on aggregate demand in the early 1990s were blunted in Japan by the continuing appreciation of the yen; its nominal dollar value moved from 158/US$ to 84/US$ between April 1990 and April 1995, generating a 'high yen' (endaka fukyo) recession. With exports negatively affected, manufacturers reduced capacity utilization and worked their existing labour force less intensely, with adverse

---

[13]   Hiroshi Nakaso, 'The financial crisis in Japan during the 1990s: how the Bank of Japan responded and the lessons learnt', BIS paper no. 6, Bank for International Settlements, Basel, Switzerland, 2001, 30, available at http://www.bis.org/publ/bppdf/bispap06.htm.

[14]   Ray Barrel and Phillip E. Davis, 'The Evolution of the Financial Crisis of 2007–8', *National Institute Economic Review* 206, no. 1 (2008): 5.

effects on productivity. The strong yen down to 1995 'helped propel the Japanese economy into stagnation and deflation.'[15]

But there were other deep-seated influences. Although the direct effects of declining asset prices on corporate, household and banking balance sheets cannot be ignored, they were not in themselves the sole cause of Japan's post-bubble woes. These resulted from a series of policy 'mistakes' – much as did the excesses of the boom – or rather from policy decisions driven by the pervasive influence of past practice and time-honoured priorities that affected perceptions of the seriousness of the situation. Even after the collapse of asset prices, Japan was not self-evidently on the way to economic ruin, despite growing weaknesses within the banking and financial sector. Though monetary tightening induced a recession down to 1994, household and business confidence bottomed a year earlier. GDP growth was certainly nothing like it had been in the recent past, averaging less than 1 per cent during 1992–94 compared with 4–5 per cent during the 1970s and 1980s and conspicuously adrift from high-growth experience, but there were growing expectations of a return to better growth levels by the middle of the decade. Business investment turned positive in 1995.[16]

Much of the blame for the deepening recession of the first half of the 1990s has been put on the BOJ. Monetary easing began in mid-1991, at a time when both equity and property prices were declining. It was patently evident that the capital base of the commercial banks had been seriously eroded by the falling value of property and equity holdings, upon which their unrealized capital gains had been based. The continuous pressure that NPLs exerted on the balance sheets of banks meant that bank lending was curtailed for some potential borrowers, despite a loosening of monetary policy.[17]

Critics argue, however, that although the BOJ lowered interest rates in the aftermath of the collapse of stock and property prices, it failed to expand the supply of money sufficiently, allowing recession to set in early and to persist.[18] The unwillingness of the BOJ to take NPLs onto its own balance

---

[15]   Obstfeld, 'Time of Troubles', 98.

[16]   Posen, 'It Takes More Than a Bubble', 16.

[17]   Richard A. Werner, 'Bank-Centered Economic Systems', 25–8, 31; Tamim Bayoumi, 'The Morning After: Explaining the Slowdown in Japanese Growth in the 1990s', *Journal of International Economics* 53, no. 2 (2001): 241–59.

[18]   Saxonhouse and Stern, 'The Bubble and the Lost Decade'; Ito and Mishkin, 'Two Decades of Japanese Monetary Policy'; Mori, Shiratuska and Taguchi, 'Post-Bubble Adjustments'; Yoichi Arai and Takeo Hoshi, 'Monetary Policy in the Great Stagnation', in Hutchison and Westermann (eds.), *Japan's Great Stagnation*,

sheet, it is argued further, restricted lending. Whereas in the aftermath of the Second World War the BOJ had bought bad debts from banks and lent directly to the economy to boost recovery, in the 1990s it chose not to do so. To Werner, the BOJ singularly failed in its duty of working with the government to stimulate recovery and was thereby responsible for the prolongation of the recession of the 1990s. It failed to expand credit by either increasing open market purchases of government bonds or lending directly to corporations. This was not, according to this view, blatant ineptitude or short-sightedness. The BOJ abandoned the generous 'window guidance' practices of earlier years and curbed lending during the early 1990s in order to enforce a 'structural transformation which was unlikely to take place without sufficient pressure or a sense of crisis.'[19] The BOJ, by implication, was less interested in fashioning a short-term economic recovery than it was in sponsoring a form of 'creative destruction', with financial policy adapted accordingly.

It is doubtful, however, whether the reluctance of banks to lend was the major factor in slow growth and recession during the first half of the 1990s. Businesses that were very dependent upon bank lending certainly faced a much bleaker outlook than that of large exporters with access to international capital markets. Nonetheless, the effect of bank lending upon liquidity and the survival of firms is rather more complex than is frequently suggested.

The problem was that two differing forces were at work: one to cut back over-generous credit allocation that might, through imprudence, harm the capital bases of banks even more, the other to prevent any further damage to the credibility and financial stability of banks by shoring up those very firms whose bad loans had helped cause financial distress in the first place. As for the first, it is likely that the decline in new lending was more a reflection of the reduced *demand* for loans than of parsimonious banks. This decline in demand resulted in part from the severe stock adjustment that occurred

---

157–81; James Harrigan and Kenneth N. Kuttner, 'Lost Decade in Translation: Did the United States Learn from Japan's Post-Bubble Mistakes?', in Ito et al., *Reviving Japan's Economy*, 79–106; Adam S. Posen, 'The Realities and Relevance of Japan's Great Recession: Neither Ran Nor Rashomon', Institute for International Economics Working Paper No. 10–7, Peterson Institute for International Economics, Washington, DC, 2010, available at http://ssrn.com/abstract=1623828.

[19]   Werner, 'The Cause of Japan's Recession', 50–54.

within firms as a reaction to excessive investment during the bubble years. The corporate sector reined in borrowing, even from abroad.[20]

The consequences of the second influence were more damaging. During the first half of the 1990s Japan became embroiled in a misallocation of credit, which proved especially debilitating in its effect on productive investment. With collateral values falling, the capacity of the main banks – as primary lenders – to bail out distressed borrowers weakened significantly. Banks in general, however, were often reluctant to act too aggressively against borrowers, fearing that any exposure of their financial position would undermine their own financial standing. Proffering additional loans to help troubled borrowers meet interest payments already due helped to preserve the book value of bank capital and thereby forestall regulatory action.[21] It is questionable, therefore, whether business investment slowed from 1991 to 1997 primarily because of a credit crunch; indeed, regressions on bank capital and growth in bank lending among city banks, long-term credit banks, trust banks and regional banks over 1990–97 indicate little evidence of such.[22] Aggregate bank credit did not decline overall; moreover, between 1993 and 1999, credit extensions to poorly performing firms increased more from banks with weak balance sheets than from those with stronger ones.[23]

These developments exacerbated the problems of Japan's 'dual economy'. As we noted earlier, the country's success in protecting infant industries and in nurturing the competitiveness of sectors such as steel,

---

[20] Meltzer, 'Monetary Transmission at Low Inflation', 13–34; Yoshikawa, *Japan's Lost Decade*, 22–5. Corporations were also desperate to repair their damaged balance sheets. For further discussion, see below pp. 108–9, 114.

[21] See Zekeriya Eser, Joe Peek and Eric S. Rosengren, 'Secondary Bank Lending in Japan,' in Hutchison and Westermann (eds.), *Japan's Great Stagnation*, 129–56.

[22] Financial constraints do not appear to have adversely affected the investment decisions of large firms but they had a relatively greater negative effect on small firms. Taizo Motonishi and Hiroshi Yoshikawa, 'Causes of the Long Stagnation of Japan During the 1990s: Financial or Real?', *Journal of the Japanese and International Economies* 13, no. 3 (1999): 181–200.

[23] Joe Peek and Eric S. Rosengren, 'Unnatural Selection: Perverse Incentives and the Misallocation of Credit in Japan,' *American Economic Review* 95, no. 4 (2005): 1144–66; Joe Peek, 'The Changing Role of Main Banks in Aiding Distressed Firms in Japan', in Hamada et al., *Japan's Bubble*, 309–42.

shipbuilding, heavy machinery and chemicals, and later electronics[24] during the high-growth period had gone hand in hand with the regulatory protection of inefficient sectors within agriculture, food and beverage, wholesale and retailing, construction, telecommunications, transportation, healthcare, and banking, finance and insurance. It had long been recognised that although labour productivity had held up reasonably well in certain export sectors (such as chemicals, electrical machinery and transport equipment) from the 1980s, spurred by exposure to international competition, that had not been the case in the nontraded sectors (construction and wholesale/retail trade), where cartels and extensive government regulation still persisted.

Average annual growth in labour productivity in manufacturing as a whole declined from 4 per cent (1981–90) to 2.9 per cent (1991–2001). The declines in other sectors during the same periods were as follows: chemicals from 4.4 per cent to 3.2 per cent, transport equipment from 3.8 per cent to 2.9 per cent, electrical machinery from 11.3 per cent to 10.2 per cent, construction from 3.1 per cent to -1.6 per cent, and in wholesale and retail trade from 4.0 per cent to 1.5 per cent.[25] After 1950 Japan had decreased the productivity gap between it and the USA, converging to about 80 per cent of US per capita income levels by 1985, but progress slowed thereafter.[26]

Japanese total factor productivity (TFP) grew by only 0.6 per cent a year during the 1990s. It fell in manufacturing in general and in machinery, other electrical machinery and motor vehicles in particular. Expenditure on research and development also slowed, while the gap between Japan and the USA in the use of computers and the Internet grew noticeably.

Reflecting on these developments, Hayashi and Prescott claim that Japan's woes in the 1990s resulted more from falling TFP triggered by a decline in the pace of technological change and a reduction in the working week, rather than by misdirected financial policy.[27] Nonetheless, headline figures of declining TFP over the decade are likely to exaggerate the actual

---

[24]   Industries differed in the extent to which they relied upon state support. Some, such as consumer electronics, developed by exploiting foreign technologies under a licence agreement, while others (automobiles, for example) gained international market share with conspicuously less involvement by the government.

[25]   Alan G. Ahearne and Naoki Shinada, 'Zombie Firms and Economic Stagnation in Japan', *International Economics and Economic Policy* 2, no. 4 (2005): 366–7.

[26]   Diego A. Comin, 'An Exploration of the Japanese Slowdown During the 1990s', in Hamada, et al., *Japan's Bubble*, 375–98.

[27]   Hayashi and Prescott, 'The 1990s in Japan', 208–28.

decline in Japanese productivity because they do not account for the substantial decline in capital utilization over the period, a decline that was itself a reflection of low aggregate demand.[28] Where there was declining TFP, it was closely connected to banks extending loans to less efficient companies. The growth rate and levels of lending to the distressed construction and property industries, for example, exceeded the total of all other industries over the period from 1991 to 2002.[29] Such activities distorted the efficient allocation of resources and impaired restructuring among poorly performing firms.[30]

Large Japanese banks engaged in sham loan restructuring to keep credit flowing to otherwise insolvent borrowers ('zombies'),[31] a situation exacerbated by the tradition of banks holding shares in some of their principal distressed borrowers, who in turn held bank shares. In the face of regulatory weakness and the traditionally limited ability of shareholders to control bank activity, banks increasingly exercised forbearance. They renewed nonviable loans, extended loan maturity dates, increased the ratio of unsecured loans as a percentage of total loans (a reversal of the trend in the late 1980s) and opened new credit lines to allow borrowers to repay overdue loans (a process known as 'evergreening').[32] In other words, financial support from Japanese banks sustained a perverse allocation of market share, with resources directed at already inefficient, debt-ridden companies with low levels of productivity in the nontraded sector.[33]

---

[28]   See below, pp. 126–7, 146, 152.

[29]   Tokuo Iwaisako, 'Corporate Investment and Restructuring', in Ito et al., *Reviving Japan's Economy*, 285.

[30]   Naohiko Baba, Shinichi Nishioka, Noboyuki Oda, Masaaki Shirakawa, Kazuo Ueda and Hiroshi Ugai, 'Japan's Deflation, Problems in the Financial System, and Monetary Policy', *Monetary and Economic Studies* 23, no. 1 (2005), 56–7; Ricardo J. Caballero, Takeo Hoshi and Anil K. Kashyap, 'Zombie Lending and Depressed Restructuring in Japan', *American Economic Review* 98, no. 5 (2008): 1943–77; Yasuhiro Arikawa and Hideaki Miyajima, 'Relationship Banking and Debt Choice: Evidence from Japan', *Corporate Governance: An International Review* 13, no. 3 (2005): 408–18.

[31]   Caballero et al., 'Zombie Lending'; Toshitaka Sekine, Keiichiro Kobayashi and Yumi Saita, 'Forbearance Lending: The Case of Japanese Firms', *Monetary and Economic Studies* 21, no. 2 (2003): 69–92.

[32]   Kanaya and Woo, *The Japanese Banking Crisis*, 12–16; David C. Smith, 'Loans to Japanese Borrowers,' *Journal of the Japanese and International Economies* 17, no. 3 (2003): 283–304.

[33]   Ahearne and Shinada, 'Zombie Firms', 363–81.

It was precisely those sectors hardest hit by the bursting of the bubble in the early 1990s that continued to benefit from access to bank credit during the 1990s. Despite the fact that Japan's listed companies were better able to utilize the deregulated bond market during the 1990s, than they had previously, the share of Japan's largest firms that relied exclusively on bank financing rose from 28 per cent in 1990 to 47 per cent by the early 2000s, with the most dramatic increases in lending going not to profitable large companies but to long-term clients in underperforming industries.[34]

Until the 1980s, loans provided by the main banks had, on the whole, been beneficial to viable but troubled firms, helping them to meet temporary setbacks and to embark upon restructuring for the sake of long-term performance. During the 1970s and 1980s distressed firms that had obtained loans from their main banks revealed higher profit rates during the four years thereafter, but this link had disappeared by 1992.

Although deregulation of the bond market had allowed large firms to lessen ties with banks, smaller firms with already high levels of bank debt began to rely more upon loans from their main bank during 1993–99; in general, they tended to suffer slow growth and lower returns on assets.[35] Firms that had been very dependent upon bank loans during the bubble period suffered a worse return on stock and lower levels of investment once the bubble burst, compared with those that relied less on bank loans. They were less likely to engage in restructuring – than they would have been in earlier decades – because the main banks were themselves increasingly reluctant to force them to do so, lest their parlous condition revealed the banks' own financial imprudence.[36] Unfortunately, forbearance lending lowered levels of effort and productivity in inefficient firms as they anticipated banks bailing them out.[37]

During the 1990s the main banks increased lending to those clients least likely to pay them back. Japanese firms appear more likely to have received additional bank credit if they were in a parlous financial condition, since the banks were anxious to avoid the realization of losses on their balance

---

[34]   Yasuhiro Arikawa and Hideaki Miyajima, 'Relationship Banking in Post-Bubble Japan: Coexistence of Soft- and Hard-Budget Constraints', in Aoki, et al., *Corporate Governance*, 51–78.

[35]   For empirical evidence see Peek, 'The Changing Role of Main Banks', 318–40; Jun-Koo Kang and Rene M. Stulz, 'Do Banking Shocks Affect Borrowing Firm Performance? An Analysis of the Japanese Experience', *Journal of Business* 73, no. 1 (2000): 1–23.

[36]   Arikawa, 'Financial Systems and Economic Development', 48–9.

[37]   Sekine et al., 'Forbearance Lending', 71.

sheets.[38] Rather than seeking to help distressed – but viable – firms recover, the main banks focused on avoiding their own demise.[39] Such action was perfectly rational from their point of view. If NPLs could *appear* as performing loans, if the ratio of capital to risk-weighted assets could be maintained above minimum levels by lending firms sufficient funds to pay interest on their loans, and if banks could *appear* to have sufficient healthy capital to keep operating, these banks might continue to survive.[40]

If the main bank system had been weakened during the 1980s, because of the rise of alternative funding sources abroad, it found renewed strength and influence during the 1990s, through protecting banks and firms from having to face the harsh realities of imprudent lending and borrowing. Rolling over loans to client firms reduced the threat of bank intervention in poorly performing firms. However, it weakened the tradition of 'contingent governance' nurtured by the main banks during the high-growth period. As a result, overall corporate restructuring proved less frequent over the course of the 1990s than it had been in the 1980s or was to be in the early 2000s.[41]

The government itself provided the institutional setting to sustain 'evergreening'. With a voting public disinclined to support the funding of bank bailouts, the government could not face the political consequences of allowing major banks or large firms to fail. In the high-growth period it had provided incentives to the main banks to rescue potentially productive firms.[42] In the 1990s, however, the incentives shifted towards rescuing unproductive ones. Regulatory forbearance down to the mid-1990s disguised suspect accounting procedures, prevented adequate disclosure of the scale of bad debt and guaranteed bank management teams that their activities would not lead to bankruptcy.[43]

'Zombie congestion' at industry level exacerbated financial frictions by lowering collateral values, even for healthy firms. This stifled job creation, reduced the level of aggregate restructuring, and lowered industrial productivity, investment and employment growth, all to the detriment of rapid

---

[38] Peek and Rosengren, 'Unnatural Selection', 1162–3.
[39] Takeo Hoshi, Satoshi Koibuchi and Ulrike Schaede, 'Corporate Restructuring in Japan During the Lost Decade', in Hamada et al., *Japan's Bubble*, 343–73.
[40] Peek and Rosengren, 'Unnatural Selection', 1144–5, 1150–51.
[41] Arikawa and Miyajima, 'Soft- and Hard-Budget Constraints', 69–74. See below pp. 100–101.
[42] See above pp. 23–4.
[43] Dan W. Puchniak, 'Perverse Rescue in the Lost Decade: Main Banks in the Post-Bubble Era', in Nottage et al., *Corporate Governance*, 81–107.

economic recovery.[44] There was a particular irony in these developments. As we noted earlier, the scale of Japan's economic decline from 1990 was nothing like that suffered by the USA during the Great Depression. This was because the soft constraints on bankruptcy and asset liquidation that had kept funds flowing to firms with little prospect of quick recovery had helped Japan avoid the contagion and financial fragility that blighted the USA in the early 1930s. They worked instead to underpin a decade of low growth.[45]

The rate of firms exiting business in Japan declined from 1991, and the rate of new firms dropped noticeably.[46] The destruction of firms was least evident in those sectors receiving subsidized credit. An examination of large Japanese manufacturing firms between 1969 and 1996 indicates a fall in within-firm total factor productivity over two distinct periods: 1979–88 and 1988–96. There was a surprisingly low level of exits of inefficient firms before 1997, despite a marked slowdown in economic activity, suggesting that many had survived by virtue of extensions of bank credit.[47]

Although it is difficult to be certain, it is likely that the capacity of distressed firms to sustain market share because of preferential financial assistance prevented more productive firms from gaining ground in the market, to the detriment of the economy as a whole. The one positive counterweight was the growing ability of more competitive firms to seek out and gain funding from external sources rather than rely upon the vagaries of the internal banking system.

The fact that the BOJ – under the direction of the MOF – continued to bail out troubled banks and to keep marginal companies alive belies the notion that it pursued a limited, even negative, credit creation policy because it favoured structural reform. Even as the capital bases of banks shrank,

---

[44] Caballero et al., 'Zombie Lending', 1971; Arikawa, 'Financial Systems', 45. *The Economist* berated 'the unholy alliance between zombies and banks' as 'one of the most durable, distorting and debilitating compacts in modern economic history.' 'Dead Firms Walking: Japan's unproductive service industries are holding back its improving economy from achieving even better performance'. *The Economist*, September 23, 2004, available at http://www.economist.com/node/3219857.

[45] Franklin Allen and Hiroko Oura, 'Sustained Economic Growth and the Financial System', Discussion Paper No. 2004-E-17, Institute for Monetary and Economic Studies, Bank of Japan, August 2004, 19–20.

[46] Posen, 'It Takes More Than A Bubble', 33.

[47] Naomi N. Griffin and Kazuhiko Odaki, 'Reallocation and Productivity Growth in Japan: Revisiting the Lost Decade of the 1990s', *Journal of Productivity Analysis* 31, no. 2 (2009): 125–36.

outstanding loans continued to rise: from an estimated 443 trillion yen at the end of 1990 to at least 480 trillion yen in late 1995 and early 1996.[48] Lenders were fearful of writing off their bad loans or facing greater losses through the bankruptcy of borrowers, since any further depletion of bank reserve capital could prove fatal.[49] The government's guarantee of deposits allowed the banks to keep rolling over loans to some of its weakest borrowers. The corporate sector was disinclined to encourage too much financial restructuring, as it and its supplier companies might well have been the first to suffer.

The inability of banks to simply write off bad loans without suffering considerable losses served to deepen the problem of bank and commercial indebtedness. In earlier years, banks with holdings of stock purchased at prices much lower than their current market values had been able to use 45 per cent of such unrealized capital gains (hidden from balance sheets in accordance with Japanese accounting standards) to meet unexpected losses. However, the unrealized gains of the bubble years were based on stock and land portfolios that now threatened to expose the disastrous capital-asset ratios of banks.[50] Basel 1 capital asset requirements (introduced in 1988) had sought to establish risk-adjusted capital/asset ratios, but the outcome in Japan was not quite what was expected. The usual result was as follows:

> When banks wanted to call in a nonperforming loan, they were likely to have to write off existing capital, which in turn pushed them up against the minimum capital levels. The fear of falling below the capital standards led many banks to continue to extend credit to insolvent borrowers, gambling that somehow these firms would recover or that the government would bail them out. Failing to roll over the loans ... would have sparked public criticism that banks were worsening the recession by denying credit to needy corporations. Indeed, the government also encouraged the banks to *increase* their lending to small and medium-sized firms to ease the apparent 'credit crunch'... . The continued financing or 'evergreening' can therefore be seen as a rational response by the banks to these various pressures.[51]

---

[48]   Robert A. Madsen, 'What Went Wrong. Aggregate Demand, Structural Reform, and the Politics of 1990s Japan', Berkeley Roundtable on the International Economy (BRIE) Working Paper 162, University of California, Berkeley, September 2004, 35.

[49]   Ibid., 36.

[50]   Ito, 'Japan and the Asian Economies', 232; Amyx, *Japan's Financial Crisis*, 150.

[51]   Caballero et al., 'Zombie Lending', 1944.

By the mid-1990s the Japanese authorities were clearly in a dilemma. The BOJ, reflecting consistent priorities, had eased monetary policy by stages down to 1995 but had paid more attention to inflation than to evidence of a growing output gap. Monetary policy appeared incapable of affecting any expansionary impulse. The banking and corporate sectors were in dire need of restructuring but such action threatened further contraction in the immediate term. The BOJ feared that if it called for a more comprehensive safety net for the banking system, including more flexible ways of dealing with failed banks, using public money, it might trigger an even worse crisis by having to detail the existing fragility of the system as a whole. Addressing the problem of NPLs in a piecemeal fashion was infinitely more preferable.[52]

Meanwhile, the continuing power and influence of bankers made it difficult to nationalize insolvent institutions.[53] Vogel writes:

> As the economy weakened … the banking crisis grew beyond the ability of the authorities to manage with their traditional approach. They could not orchestrate private sector bailouts because the stronger banks were no longer able to bail out the weaker ones… . Their record of never using public funds to rescue banks came to haunt them, as the public opposed any form of taxpayer-funded bail out. And the post-war regime had relied so heavily on the ministry's own prestige and authority that when the ministry itself failed, market players lost confidence in the entire financial system.[54]

Japan had been obliged to live with troubled banks for years because of this standoff. By the mid-1990s the country was caught in the bind of short-term interest rates having fallen so much that they were unable to be driven below the zero-bound level, leaving the real interest rate too high to effect recovery. The central bank had little effective room for manoeuvre as long as the public and the markets remained convinced that monetary policy would never be sufficiently expansionary to stimulate activity.[55]

Driven by moral hazard, the banks continued to take risks with their lending; by 1997 rapidly accumulating loan losses had caused even large

[52]   Nakaso, 'Financial Crisis in Japan', 18.
[53]   Martin Wolf, 'Japanese Lessons for a World of Balance-Sheet Deflation', *Financial Times*, 18 February 2009.
[54]   Vogel, *Japan Remodeled*, 50.
[55]   Ito and Mishkin, 'Two Decades of Japanese Monetary Policy', 172.

banks to run out of capital base.[56] Little was done officially to arrest the decline of the banking system during 1990–95. Even when it became clear – by the middle of the decade – that problems in the banking sector were far greater than had previously been acknowledged, there was a reluctance to be too proactive in remedial policy lest it trigger public panic, given that there was no administrative or legal framework in place at the time for dealing adequately with a full-blown banking crisis.[57] The idea of bank closures, forced mergers or the acquisition of domestic assets by foreign banks hardly entered into official thinking.

Japan had managed to offend the basic principles of financial crisis management, first by failing to recognise its problems early enough to avoid further deterioration, second by failing to address problems swiftly once recognised, third by failing to engage in a comprehensive plan invoking public money for the disposal of bad debts and the recapitalization of the banking sector to ensure sustained profitable operation, and fourth by failing to provide sufficient incentives to immediately reduce excessive risk taking.[58] During the first half of the 1990s Japan had entertained an abiding faith that economic growth would soon be resumed. As a consequence, it postponed taking any painful decisions about restructuring finance. It was only when Japan was faced with a near collapse of the banking system in 1997 that more decisive action was taken.

Japan's problems were further compounded by a noticeable shift in corporate investment behaviour. During the high-growth period, Japanese corporations had been regarded as flexible non-hierarchical entities working to further Japan's competitive advantage. MITI's prejudice for promoting giant corporations at the expense of smaller firms, its approval of cartelization and increased industrial concentration, and its control of domestic competition had favoured the growth and expansion of corporate Japan. Over time, however, its ability to influence the direction of industry

---

[56]   Paul Krugman, 'It's Baaack? Japan's Slump and the Return of the Liquidity Trap', *Brookings Papers on Economic Activity*, no. 2 (1998): 137–205; Fukao, 'Financial Crisis and the Lost Decade', 273.

[57]   Kanaya and Woo, *The Japanese Banking Crisis*, 26; Mariko Fuji and Masahiro Kawai, 'Lessons from Japan's Banking Crisis, 1991–2005', ADBI Working Paper, no. 222, Asian Development Bank Institute, Tokyo, 2010, 9, available at http://ssrn.com/abstract=1638784; Masahiro Kawai, 'Reform of the Japanese Banking System', *International Economics and Economic Policy* 2, no. 4 (2005): 307–35.

[58]   See Claudio Boroi, 'Comment on "Financial Crisis and Lost Decade"', *Asian Economic Policy Review* 2, no. 2 (2007): 301.

in the public interest diminished, with economic power effectively being yielded to Japan's giant corporations.

Japanese corporations increasingly shaped the industrial structure to suit their own strategic interests, which were no longer necessarily compatible with those of the nation as a whole.[59] Until the 1970s MITI had strictly controlled foreign direct investment as a means of protecting the industrial structure. But it was the clamour to expand overseas, in the face of a saturated home market and low domestic demand, that led to the 'hollowing out' of the manufacturing base; transnational corporations diverted investment from Japan's industrial regions to overseas markets. The growth rate of Japan's overseas production between 1985 and 1995 was twice that of the USA and Germany.[60] Traditional links between firms and keiretsu networks weakened as corporations outsourced their supply chains or forced lower prices upon intermediate suppliers in the small business sector. Such hollowing out reshaped the subcontractor system away from long-term loyalty and cooperation and towards open price competition in components.[61] It was now much more difficult for the authorities to influence the investment and operating practices of firms in order to effect domestic economic revival.[62] The internationalization of Japanese capital thus weakened the fusion of interests between the government and industrial capital, upon which earlier success had been based.[63]

Financial Forbearance: the Political and Administrative Dimension

Japan's financial crisis during the first half of the 1990s was neither a random nor an inevitable consequence of a speculative bubble. Nor was it the result of a single regulatory or macroeconomic failure. It had its origins 'in a set of deficiencies deeply rooted in the country's post-war institutional and corporate culture.'[64] The high-growth strategy had ensured that banks

---

[59]   Keith Cowling and Philip R. Tomlinson, 'The Japanese Crisis – A Case of Strategic Failure?', *Economic Journal* 110, no. 464 (2000): 358–81.

[60]   Mireya Solis, 'Adjustment Through Globalization: The Role of State FDI Finance', *Japanese Economy* 28, no. 5 (2000): 27–49.

[61]   Ulrike Schaede, 'Globalization and the Japanese Subcontractor System', in Bailey et al., *Crisis or Recovery in Japan*, 82–105.

[62]   Teranishi, *Evolution of the Economic System in Japan*, 306.

[63]   Coates, *Models of Capitalism*, 238.

[64]   Mariusz Krawczyk, 'Changes and Crisis in the Japanese Banking Industry', in Janet Hunter and Cornelia Storz (eds.), *Institutional and Technological Change in Japan's Economy: Past and Present* (New York: Routledge, 2006), 121.

would play a central role in financial intermediation in Japan. This magnified the effect of the decline in asset prices upon the economy. Moreover, as long as the government insured bank deposits, there was insufficient constraint upon banks to abandon inherently risky investments, enabling them to continue to accumulate high levels of nonperforming loans. Weak enforcement and poor regulation, along with the government's steely determination to leave the resolution of the bad debt problem to the financial institutions themselves, almost ensured the emergence of an endogenous crisis.[65]

Part of the problem was that the economy was still growing, albeit at a much slower pace. In not a single year during the first half of the 1990s did it actually shrink. There was an enduring belief that asset prices and collateral values would eventually be restored, removing any major threat to the financial system. As a consequence, financial problems were dealt with in an ad hoc rather than a comprehensive fashion; sporadic problems were met with tailor-made solutions.[66] Thus, in the early stages of the developing financial crisis in the early 1990s, the obligations of failing banks were usually resolved by rescue mergers and injections of funds from the Deposit Insurance Corporation of Japan (DICJ) or the BOJ. In 1992 MOF officials arranged the merger of the Toho-Sogo Bank (a mutual bank) with the Iyo Bank, and the Toyo-Shinkin Bank (a credit union) with the Sanwa Bank, drawing funds from the DICJ. The Tokyo metropolitan government suspended the operation of two insolvent credit cooperatives, the Tokyo Kyowa Credit Cooperative and the Ansen Credit Cooperative towards the end of 1994, eventually fusing the two institutions into a new bank – Tokyo Kyoudou – with the BOJ subscribing 20 billion yen and the Deposit Insurance Corporation providing further financial assistance.[67] In July 1995 the Cosmo Credit Cooperative was ordered to cease operations; in August 1995 the Kizu Credit Cooperative was issued with the same order. In the same month, the MOF ordered the Hyogo bank, a regional bank, to suspend

---

[65]   Robert Dekle and Ken Kletzer, 'The Japanese Banking Crisis and Economic Growth: Theoretical and Empirical Implications of Deposit Guarantees and Weak Financial Regulation', *Journal of the Japanese and International Economies* 17, no. 3 (2003): 305–35; Yoshikawa, *Japan's Lost Decade*, 75.

[66]   Nakaso, 'The financial crisis in Japan', 1–3.

[67]   Ibid., 4; Sara Konoe, 'Financial Crisis, Politics and Financial Sector Restructuring: A Comparison Between Japan and the United States', *Journal of Asian and African Studies* 44, no. 5 (2009): 497–515.

taking deposits and lending.[68] Again the BOJ stepped in to support the liquidity bases of these institutions.

The authorities' limited response to the emerging financial crisis was assisted by the general public's continued belief in the MOF's celebrated 'convoy system'. The sporadic bank failures that had occurred since 1991 were among small financial institutions that did not seem to pose any systemic danger. It was still commonly believed that big banks would not – and could not – fail. This belief was sustained because the scale of the banking problem was hidden from view. Depositors, investors and the general public were certainly aware of the problems of particular banks but had there been more widespread awareness of the condition of the financial system as a whole, more decisive action might have followed.

As it was, the banks' financial statements down to the mid-1990s 'did not adequately capture even the past events that had already begun to be recognised, let alone expected losses, obscuring the general deterioration in asset quality of the banking sector.'[69] Public disclosure on NPLs was virtually non-existent before 1992, and disclosure requirements proceeded only incrementally down to 1997. Classifying loans as risky threatened to alienate members of industrial (keiretsu) groupings, which often included banks, so banking officials often failed to identify loans as nonperforming. Enforcement of more stringent regulatory standards would have obliged banks to recognise the deterioration in their balance sheets much earlier than they did. Creative accounting, however, allowed banks to value their holdings at purchase value and to disguise liabilities in order to meet imposed capital-to-assets adequacy ratios. Obscured capital ratios merely weakened the perceived need for recapitalization, delaying the timing of more substantial capital injections until later in the decade.

At the heart of the problem were the informal networks that had dominated banking regulation during the post-war period. The close relationships between the MOF and the private banks, the 'convoy system', and the unwillingness of politicians to monitor the actions of the regulatory authorities until a particular problem emerged had all been sustainable under conditions of high growth and bureaucratic-led regulation. In the straightened circumstances of the 1990s, though, they served to delay prudential regulation and undermined any credible commitment to enforcing strict capital adequacy standards, at least before 1997. The regulatory authorities had an incentive to prevent disclosure of inadequate banking reserves, since

---

68 Kanaya and Woo, *The Japanese Banking Crisis*, 24–5.
69 Nakaso, 'The financial crisis in Japan', 18.

any 'fire alarm' monitoring by Parliament threatened to invite political interference and a possible loss of autonomy.[70]

All too often, Japanese authorities met pressing and often rapidly changing economic and financial conditions without considering which policy instruments or priorities needed to be altered. The deterioration in the formal relationship between main banks and commercial banks in the high-growth years was important in this respect. During earlier decades, the main banks had played an important role in allocating capital to productive investment and facilitating industrial restructuring. As we noted earlier,[71] the essential purpose of the renowned 'convoy system' had been to prevent troubled banks from undermining financial stability and hence the long-run stability of the Japanese economy. The strength of the system was thought to be the willingness of the MOF to 'guide' financial institutions rather than leave them to the vagaries of the market.

In the event of a bank failure, the MOF was expected to encourage stronger, healthier banks to absorb weaker insolvent institutions. As large shareholders and principal lenders to companies, the main banks – such as Mitsubishi, Sumitomo, Mitsui, Fuji and Sanwa – had in previous years initiated bailout processes and/or the restructuring of debt within troubled firms, rescuing not only them but also the reputation of the banking sector as an integral and trustworthy partner in the developmental agenda. Troubled firms in which a main bank had a large equity share were more inclined to change their management structure rather than downsize or incur layoffs, often enjoying a better performance as a result. This system had functioned well in a growing economy where the MOF implicitly protected all deposits and where the BOJ provided liquidity assistance to prevent banking crises. Such implied safety nets sustained public confidence in the ability of the two key economic agencies to avoid major financial instability. Unlike in later years, the banks down to the early 1980s retained more diversified portfolios, and carried a much lower level of NPLs, relative to the total number of outstanding loans.

Even during the high-growth period, the monitoring standards of the main banks had been found wanting, especially in the steel and petrochemical industries, where the focus of the main banks appeared to be less on

---

[70]   Kentaro Tamura, 'Challenges to Japanese Compliance with the Basel Capital Accord: Domestic Politics and International Banking Standards,' *Japanese Economy* 33, no. 1 (2005): 44.

[71]   See above pp. 20–22.

profitability and more on growth through increased scale of production.[72] Later, the internationalization of fund raising and the shift to direct financing reduced the ability of the main banks to monitor lenders and shareholders, and made it harder for the bureaucratic authorities to control corporate behaviour through the banks. Moreover, as lending activity became riskier and less adequately monitored during the bubble years of the 1980s, banks were less able to play the role of independent arbitrator than they had in the past, being both the source of and the solution to the difficulties facing firms.

During the early 1990s corporate restructuring became less of a priority and timely main-bank-led corporate restructuring broke down, largely under the burden of NPLs.[73] It became increasingly difficult to persuade healthy banks to assist the growing number of troubled banks when even the relatively healthy were facing substantial declines in their balance sheets. The main banks were reluctant to allow borrowers to default, since they feared having to absorb some of the losses incurred by other creditors. Any default would reflect badly on their monitoring operations.

In the absence of adequate accountability there was little incentive for banks to acknowledge the scale of the NPL problem or to fashion policies to meet it. Given the continuing belief among most regulators and politicians that Japan would soon return to its growth trajectory, the dominant reaction of the financial authorities during the early 1990s was to protect ailing banks, pending a hoped-for recovery in asset prices.[74] Despite the failure of some smaller financial institutions during 1994–95 – credit unions, housing loan corporations and a regional bank in 1994[75] – the financial authorities continued to deal with the worsening crisis in conventional ways, rolling over bad loans and protecting deposits in the hope that prices would recover.

During previous decades, the MOF had neglected to undertake any meaningful review of its supervisory practices. Despite the activities of the Ministry's Banking Bureau in overseeing bank lending, there had been no effective early warning system in place to encourage banks to identify and

---

[72] Chikage Hidaka and Takeo Kikkawa, 'The Main Bank System and Corporate Governance in Post War Japan', in Robert Fitzgerald and Etsuo Abe (eds.), *The Development of Corporate Governance in Japan and Britain* (Burlington, VT: Ashgate Publishing, 2004), 124–40.

[73] Iwaisako, 'Corporate Investment', 287.

[74] Fuji and Kawai, 'Lessons from Japan's Banking Crisis', 4.

[75] See above pp. 98–9.

write off bad loans at an early stage.[76] Fearing widespread bankruptcies and unemployment, the Ministry acted too slowly to address the NPL problem, thereby delaying effective restructuring of the ailing banking sector.[77]

This should not have occasioned much surprise. Since 1927 it had been customary for Japan's financial institutions – especially the city banks – to be regarded as wards of the MOF. The Ministry was sovereign but did not operate as a regulator with explicit legal powers. Its regulatory system had served it well during the high-growth period. By the 1990s, though, the information requirements for effective regulation had become more complex, outstripping the Ministry's traditional – informal – style of regulation and control. Faced with the crisis of the 1990s, the Ministry strove to keep its wards alive and functioning, refusing in principle to let banks fail. It supported banks in their efforts to bolster margins and profits to disguise the nakedness of their financial indebtedness, and encouraged mergers and private-sector bailouts until the scale of the crisis rendered such traditional self-help redundant.[78] As late as 1997 the Ministry insisted that no public money would be needed to help ailing banks.[79]

The absence of reliable estimates of the scale of NPLs and the unwillingness of troubled institutions to declare the need for public assistance, lest it undermined public confidence, only made the situation more intractable. Full disclosure of the scale of nonperforming assets and the health of individual banks threatened a collapse of public and overseas confidence in the sector as a whole. In the absence of adequate procedures to deal with a troubled financial sector, save for the timeworn precept of burden sharing, the authorities simply bought time.[80] Yoshimasa Nishimura, director general of the Banking Bureau of the MOF between 1994 and 1996, explains: 'Because we did not think seriously enough about the decrease in land prices or the future of the economy, we believed that a conventional Japanese approach to the problem would suffice; that is, we thought it

---

[76]   Michael M. Hutchison, Takatoshi Ito and Frank Westermann, 'The Great Japanese Stagnation: Lessons for Industrial Countries', in Hutchison and Westermann (eds.), *Japan's Great Stagnation*, 10–11.

[77]   Amyx, *Japan's Financial Crisis*, 162, 257.

[78]   Vogel, *Japan Remodeled*, 49; Andrew DeWit and Tobias Harris, 'Japan's Twenty Year Response to Economic Crisis', *Asia-Pacific Journal: Japan Focus* 7, no. 3 (2009); Thomas F. Cargill, 'Central Banking, Financial, and Regulatory Change in Japan', in Blomstrom, et al., *Japan's New Economy*, 145–61.

[79]   Ito, 'Retrospective on the Bubble Period', 287.

[80]   Mori, Shiratsuka and Taguchi, 'Policy Responses to the Post-bubble Adjustments', 56.

would work out if the main banks just *gave more time* to companies that were experiencing problems.'[81] The MOF was content to keep banks afloat, even with bad debts, if it avoided bankruptcies and layoffs, especially since many NPLs were concentrated in the politically sensitive sectors of property, construction, retail and the service industries. In other words, the balance of interests between the banks, parliamentarians, bureaucrats and business people favoured procrastination.

This troubling situation was affected by subtle shifts in the bureaupluralism of earlier decades. The LDP briefly lost control of government in 1993, after almost 40 years of political supremacy. Elected officials now feared for their political survival in the midst of the country's relatively poor economic performance and in the aftermath of high-profile financial scandals following the collapse of the bubble. New electoral rules added to the pressure. Japan adopted a mixed voting system, including proportional representation, in place of its single non-transferable voting system. Under the latter scheme, between two and six parliamentary representatives had been elected from a single district. Many of them came from the ruling LDP party and therefore competed amongst themselves, waging candidate-centred campaigns rather than policy-centred ones. This mobilization of personal votes was time consuming and costly but it had enabled the LDP to garner sufficient representation to form single-party governments without coalition partners.

The revised system in place from 1993 penalized smaller parties in favour of large major political groupings with whom aspiring politicians wished to be associated. Although the LDP regained power in 1994, in coalition with the Social Democratic Party, politicians thereafter became increasingly embroiled in electoral and power concerns and intraparty conflict rather than in addressing pressing economic and financial concerns. It was easier to rely upon conventional and familiar policies than to attempt policy innovation to spur economic recovery.[82]

What worsened matters was that the LDP, traumatized by its loss of political majority, sought desperately to preserve its influence and authority among the domestic interests it had long safeguarded, namely farmers, the construction industry and small retailers. It swiftly distanced itself from the criticisms of the regulatory incompetence being levelled against the MOF.

---

[81]   Nishimura Yoshimasa, 'Reasons for the Failure of the Financial Administration Tokyo 1999', cited in Tamura, 'Challenges to Japanese Compliance', 37 (emphasis in the original).

[82]   Cargill and Sakamoto, *Japan Since 1980*, 150–55.

The LDP was willing to rescind the authority of the MOF if that helped to convince the public of the Party's political competence.

With the rise of 'public interest politics', the MOF's influence as the organizer of political bargains declined while that of the LDP increased as it strove to procure public support.[83] As Johnson puts it, the LDP 'no longer much cared about the LDP's chief domestic function: giving the economic bureaucracy enough autonomy for it to cultivate growth industries for the future.... [It] increasingly indulged in 'bureaucrat-bashing' in an attempt to shift the blame for the recession.'[84] The MOF, threatened with a loss of power and prestige, became increasingly balkanized. Greater transparency and measured reform threatened to expose its paltry regulation of bank solvency and to deepen criticism of its operational efficiency.

With a well-developed instinct for survival, the MOF ruptured the flow of information, stalled regulatory reform and systematically disguised the full extent of the country's fragile financial condition for fear of being called to account for its failures in financial supervision. In the high-growth period, it had been assumed that the Ministry would rescue failing financial institutors in order to protect national, rather than strictly financial, goals. The same Ministry was now more concerned with disguising past supervisory neglect than it was in insisting on better accounting procedures and the management of financial distress.

Only in 1995 did the MOF admit that the consortium of seven (jusen) housing-loan corporations was insolvent and that the scale of NPLs was worse than previously acknowledged. Although the MOF had earlier restrained the flow of funds to property business, the financial channels operating from agricultural cooperatives through jusen into property had been left unrestrained.[85] At first, the Ministry tried to dissolve insolvent jusen mortgage companies and to spread the cost of closures amongst their owners. It assumed that, with all the weight of its accumulated prestige, it could resolve the financial difficulties being suffered by mortgage companies through administrative channels, unaccountable to either the judiciary or the public. However, some of the creditor banks refused to participate in the conventional (convoy) support, while the politically powerful agricultural credit associations (which had supplied almost half of the jusen

---

[83]   Tetsuro Toya, *The Political Economy of the Japanese Financial Big Bang: Institutional Change in Finance and Public Policymaking*, edited by Jennifer A. Amyx (New York: Oxford University Press, 2006), 220–48.

[84]   Johnson, 'Japanese "Capitalism" Revisited', 74.

[85]   Konoe, 'Financial Crisis', 500.

mortgage funding during the bubble period) sought the help of the LDP to release them from any obligation to pay their share. After a bitter political struggle, the government eventually absorbed the 685 billion yen losses arising from insolvency in the jusen sector. The public, viewing such action as a clear sign of administrative failure, stiffened their hostility to any further use of public funds to aid non-bank financial institutions.[86]

For all its manoeuvring, the MOF had suffered a considerable blow to its prestige. Moreover, public criticism of the MOF hastened political demands for organizational restructuring of the Ministry, an agenda that figured prominently in the reform programme of the LDP Hashimoto administration, which took office in November 1996. Bruised by the experience of the MOF and fearing further public antagonism, the administration became ever more reluctant to use taxpayers' money to address problems with bank balance sheets, thereby prolonging the life of troubled financial institutions. Efforts were directed instead towards strengthening deposit insurance schemes as a more palatable way of containing the problems faced by the banking sector. By 1997 the immediate prospects for financial stability were bleak. The prospects for the macroeconomy were little better, as fiscal policy became subject to the same short-sightedness and political sensitivities that had bedevilled monetary policy during the first half of the 1990s.

---

[86]   The matter only worsened. In 1996, a Housing Loan Administration Corporation was created to buy up the nonperforming loans from the seven loan firms. Its activities were subsequently transferred to the Resolution Collection Corporation in 1999; this organization sought to sell the property that had earlier been put up as collateral for loans. However, property values declined substantially during the prolonged slump that occurred later in the 1990s. By September 2010 the RCC had racked up 1,212 trillion yen of secondary losses, which the government and the private sector had agreed (in 1996) to meet in equal shares. *The Japan Times*, 31 January 2011.

6. Funding a recovery: the impact and fate of fiscal policy, 1990–97

Japan's recession during the early 1990s was – and is – commonly regarded as being rooted in the troubled financial sector. An article published in the *Nihon Keizai Shimbun* newspaper on 6 December 1993 stated: 'The current recession is a combination of the cyclical downturn following the collapse of the bubble and a structural slump due to anxiety regarding the financial system. The source of the problems lies in banks' bad debts. The banks that are burdened by these nonperforming loans are adopting a cautious lending attitude. While the banks deny it, there is a strong discontent concerning the credit crunch, especially among small and medium enterprises.'[1]

Such explanations are, however, insufficient to account for either Japan's continuing recession during the early 1990s or the more worrying slide into stagnation and deflation from 1997.[2] Fluctuations in investment and aggregate demand played a determinant role. The duration and amplitude of rises in investment in Japan in the 1990s were smaller and the declines much deeper and longer than in earlier cycles, as Figure 6.1 below shows. In consequence, average investment for the decade was much lower and a cause of slower growth.[3]

From our perspective it is the link between growth, investment and aggregate demand from the mid-1980s that is particularly important. By then Japan had reached the technological frontier, as defined by activities in the USA, the UK and elsewhere. Opportunities for rapid profitable investment slowed as the focus shifted to the incremental improvement of existing products and the search for new, innovative ones. Corporations had the opportunity to lower their reliance upon capital expenditure and to improve salaries and earnings to allow consumption to have a greater role in driving aggregate demand, especially since middle-aged citizens had begun to save

---

[1] Cited in Yoshikawa, *Japan's Lost Decade*, 50. We examined the issue of an alleged credit crunch in the early 1990s above. See above pp. 80–87.

[2] Compare above pp. 97–105.

[3] Meltzer, 'Monetary Transmission', 17–18.

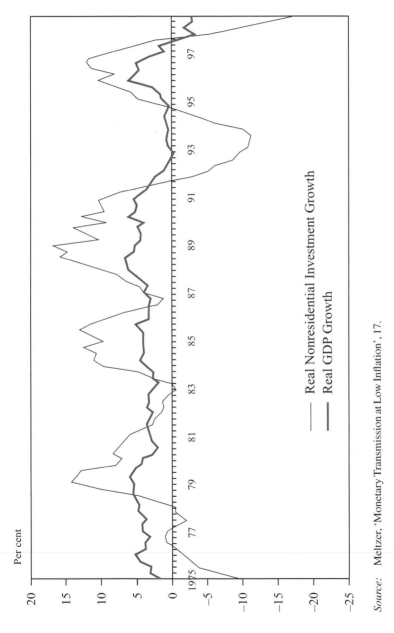

Source: Meltzer, 'Monetary Transmission at Low Inflation', 17.

Figure 6.1   Real nonresidential investment growth and real GDP growth, Japan, 1975/I-1998/IV

more for their future. Depreciation of the currency to help funnel the excess savings abroad was ruled out, since it threatened politically sensitive import-dependent industries and possible international retaliation. Politicians, bureaucrats and banks feared the ramifications of comprehensive structural change. Japanese corporations therefore continued to expand capacity and to invest; the structural surplus of savings was mopped up by increased capital expenditure.[4]

Private sector capital investment had grown in real terms at an average of 12 per cent a year between 1987 and 1990. It declined on a quarterly basis for over 15 consecutive months, between the second quarter of 1991 and the fourth quarter of 1994, as companies engaged in 'balance sheet adjustment'. The share of investment in real GDP, which had averaged 19 per cent during the boom of the late 1980s, declined to 7.2 per cent in 1992 and to 10.4 per cent in 1993. Falling land prices severely curtailed capital spending in the non-manufacturing sector.[5] When the growth rate of GDP fell from 3.8 per cent to 0.3 per cent during 1991–93, the contribution of investment fell from 1.2 per cent to -1.9 per cent, accounting for nearly 90 per cent of the fall in the growth rate. When GDP growth accelerated between 1993 and 1996, over 80 per cent of the recovery was accounted for by movements in investment.[6]

One of the critical manifestations of the ineffectiveness of *falling* interest rates to boost economic activity was the significant reduction in the demand for loans by the corporate sector. Rather than seeking out opportunities to gather cheap funds for profitable investment, in the early 1990s companies began to shift their attention from profit maximization to the minimization of debt in order to repair their balance sheets, thereby nullifying the potential effect of reductions in short-term rates.[7] Whereas corporate and household bank deposits increased in parallel during the 1980s, corporate

---

[4]	Madsen, 'What Went Wrong', 6–11, 61–3.

[5]	Osamu Narai, *Exploring the Japanese Economy: Historical Background, Current Topics and Japan's Role in the Global Integration* (Kashiwa, Chiba: Reitaku University Press, 2005), 75–6.

[6]	Motonishi and Yoshikawa, 'Causes of the Long Stagnation', 183–4.

[7]	Richard C. Koo, *The Holy Grail of Macroeconomics: Lessons from Japan's Great Recession* (Singapore: John Wiley & Sons, 2008), 88–9. See also Richard C. Koo, *Balance Sheet Recession, Japan's Struggle With Unchartered Economics and Its Global Implications* (Singapore: John Wiley & Sons, 2003). This is not to deny the positive contribution of fixed investment in computers and telecommunications, especially during 1995–97, but the generalization still holds. See Giovanni Dell'Ariccia, 'Banks and Credit in Japan', in Callen and Ostry, *Japan's Lost Decade*, 43–61.

deposits from the 1990s declined as firms focused on reducing long-term debt whilst the level of household deposits steadily increased.[8] High levels of corporate leverage caused a reduction in investment, leading to a contraction in aggregate domestic demand.

The effect of this reduction in investment on Japan's struggling economy might have been far more dramatic had it not been for countervailing fiscal policy. During the first half of the 1990s the government introduced six stimulus packages. Public works packages were implemented in August 1992 and in April and September 1993, though this early fiscal spending was stifled by a parallel contraction in the money supply. Tax cuts were introduced in November 1994, and in 1995 there was the first relatively large combination of tax cuts and public spending. The overall fiscal balance shifted from a surplus of 1.5 per cent of GDP in 1991 to a deficit of almost 3.5 per cent in 1996.[9]

This fiscal activity has attracted almost universal derision. It is frequently regarded as little different from previous bouts of fiscal spending and as ineffective as they were judged to have been. Determined to retain a stable, undervalued exchange rate and to preserve unlimited access to the US market, the government during the 1970s had organized extensive public works spending in rural areas and fiscal support to small businesses, not only to garner political support but also to spur a build-up of deposits in the banking system to offset growing dollar holdings.[10] Since the 1980s Japan had purposely resisted financing deficits through higher taxes, choosing bond issues instead because it made it easier to countenance public works expenditures in favoured constituencies.

Critics are therefore almost predisposed to condemn the flurry of fiscal activity in the early 1990s as little more than 'the distributive predisposition

---

[8]   Yoshikawa, *Japan's Lost Decade*, 67.

[9]   Kenneth N. Kuttner and Adam S. Posen, 'Fiscal Policy Effectiveness in Japan', *Journal of the Japanese and International Economies* 16, no. 4 (2002): 537. Such actions were contrary to normal practice. Traditionally, Japan had followed a balanced budget policy. Budget deficits only began to expand in the wake of the first oil crisis in 1973. The subsequent slowdown in economic growth reduced tax revenue. This coincided with a burst of new spending on social welfare programmes in the first half of the 1970s and on public investment in the second half, leading to a widening gap between government expenditures and revenue. In consequence, in 1975 the MOF embarked upon 'fiscal reconstruction' – synonymous with the elimination of fiscal deficits – imposing severe spending constraints on departments. See above pp. 62–3.

[10]   Murphy, 'A Loyal Retainer?'

of the LDP'.[11] According to Cargill and Sakamoto, stimulus packages 'had little positive impact on the economy and wasted valuable resources'; they merely represented 'a rapid growth of government gross debt without too much to show'.[12] Such fiscal activity, it is alleged, crowded out private spending in favour of pork-barrel expenditures of low multiplier effect because they were concentrated in unproductive rural agricultural areas rather than being focused upon education, social services or sustainable growth areas, such as energy or food resources.[13] Macroeconomic public works policies, it is alleged, encouraged the private sector to seek out 'easy money' from the government rather than engage in riskier high technology ventures that might have stimulated new consumer and industrial demand.[14] The economist Milton Friedman put it succinctly in 2001: 'Does fiscal stimulus stimulate? Japan's experience in the '90s is dramatic evidence to the contrary. Japan resorted repeatedly to large doses of fiscal stimulus in the form of extra government spending ... the result: stagnation at best, depression at worst, for most of the past decade.'[15]

Such misgivings distort the influence of fiscal activity during the first half of the 1990s. Investment spending during the second half of the 1980s had been excessive, stimulated by the boom in asset prices and the lax lending policies of the banks. In the wake of the collapse of asset prices, firms burdened with investment overhang had cut back abruptly, especially in the small and medium-sized sectors. With the private sector acting thus, it is

---

[11]   Cargill and Sakamoto, *Japan Since 1980*, 174.

[12]   Ibid., 113, 144. The same authors bemoan the fiscal austerity of 1997 as a major policy error that worsened Japan's situation. Ibid., 104, 113–14.

[13]   Representative of these views are Bayoumi, 'The Morning After'; Toshihiro Ihori, Toru Nakazato and Masumi Kawade, 'Japan's Fiscal Policies in the 1990s', *World Economy* 26, no. 3 (2003): 325–38; Toshihiro Ihori and Atsushi Nakamoto, 'Japan's Fiscal Policy and Fiscal Reconstruction', *International Economics and Economic Policy* 2, no. 2–3 (2005): 153–72. Fiscal spending might have been directed more productively towards quality-of-life and/or environmentally friendly developments in the infrastructure. However, as one observer puts it, 'fresh vision was rare among a political leadership that tended to see only the colorless alternatives of old "Japan Inc." and the new U.S.-style neoliberalism.' Metzler, 'Toward a Financial History', 665.

[14]   Gerard F. Adams, Lawrence R. Klein, Yuzo Kumasak and Akihiko Shinozaki, *Accelerating Japan's Economic Growth: Resolving Japan's Growth Controversy* (New York: Routledge, 2008), 19.

[15]   Milton Friedman, 'No More Economic Stimulus Needed', *The Wall Street Journal*, 10 October 2001, quoted in Kuttner and Posen, 'Fiscal Policy Effectiveness', 537.

doubtful that government fiscal spending was crowding out much latent investment. Some public sector spending was at least better than leaving resources locked, unused, in the banking sector.[16]

Sweden faced growing budget deficits in the 1990s but had intentionally raised taxation to improve revenue flows. By contrast, taxation and expenditure policies in Japan had been structured to provide support for policy preferences. A low level of tax revenue had become an institutionalized feature of fiscal policy. As a result, spending increases quickly ballooned into rising deficits because the prospective gap between revenue and expenditure was not adequately addressed.[17]

Although growth was unspectacular down to 1995, in the midst of a weakened financial sector, Japan did not suffer outright collapse. Its fate might have been much worse, however, had fiscal spending not provided critical support to aggregate demand. 'Without the lift from higher government spending', writes Yoshikawa, 'the economy would certainly have posted zero or negative growth from 1992 through 1994.'[18] Between 1990 and 1997 corporate demand slumped to an estimated 20 per cent of GDP. Fiscal spending proved to be a critical antidote to the decline in corporate investment, restraining any more substantial downward movement of the economy after the bursting of the bubble.[19]

The relationship between private (Ip) and public (Ig) investment since the start of the bubble economy is illustrated in Figure 6.2 below. The brisk levels of private investment from 1986 reflect the bubble experience; see Figure 6.2 (a). By contrast, in 1991 public investment began to expand to compensate for the slowdown in private investment and it increased substantially in the wake of pump-priming expenditures in the mid-1990s; see Figure 6.2 (b). The combined trends shown in Figure 6.2 (c) indicate that public investment played a major role in compensating for the decline in private investment and triggered successive rounds of fiscal expansion. This in turn restrained the further downward movement of the economy, even if it did not stimulate full recovery.[20] Although the announced cut in personal income tax in November 1994 was declared to be temporary, and would

---

[16]   Koo, *The Holy Grail*, 92.
[17]   Junko Kato and Bo Rothstein, 'Government Partisanship and Managing the Economy: Japan and Sweden in Comparative Perspective', *Governance: An International Journal of Policy, Administration, and Institutions* 19, no. 1 (2006): 75.
[18]   Yoshikawa, *Japan's Lost Decade*, 17.
[19]   Ibid., 21–6; Ishi, *Making Fiscal Policy*, 197.
[20]   Ishi, *Making Fiscal Policy*, 196–7.

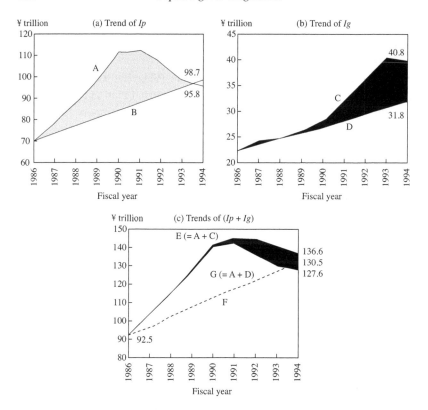

Note:
Ip includes private investment and residential investment; *Ig* is government capital formation.
The lines A, C and E indicate actual expenditure. The lines B, D and F indicate trends,
extrapolated using nominal GDP growth rates.

Source: Ishi, *Making Fiscal Policy*, 196.

Figure 6.2   Trends of private investment and government investment

have to be paid for by a rise in consumption tax in April 1997, its effect
nonetheless proved stimulative, raising private consumption by 1 per cent of
GDP in 1995 and by 1.7 per cent of GDP in 1996.[21]

   Although broad structural reform continued to be regarded as a necessary
requirement for Japan's long-term recovery, it was no substitute for a
macroeconomic response in the face of a short-run crisis and a severe
decline in aggregate demand. As we noted above, in the 1990s Japan

---

[21]   Posen, *Restoring Japan's Growth*, 50; Wright, *Japan's Fiscal Crisis*, 504–21.

suffered more from the under-utilization of the factors of production than from any marked decline in their supply or productive use, rendering actual growth lower than its potential.[22] Major structural adjustments, even if it had been possible to implement them quickly, were more likely to result in short-run unemployment and excess capacity, thereby fuelling uncertainty and damaged expectations.

The effect of fiscal spending was felt especially from 1995. A downward correction of the yen[23] was accompanied by a substantial fiscal stimulus, made even more effective by an accommodating monetary policy (interest rates were not increased). Despite the major setbacks of the first half of the 1990s – low GDP growth, stalled domestic demand (compounded by a sharp appreciation of the yen during 1990–95), reduced business investment and persistent fragility within the banking sector – the effects of fiscal stimulus, interest rate cuts and an exchange rate correction led to a brief resurgence of confidence and growth in the economy during 1996 and early 1997.

The September 1995 stimulus package actually exceeded 50 per cent of its announced level (rare for the time) and included 8 trillion yen of new spending during fiscal 1995–96. In addition, as we noted above, the effects of a cut in personal income tax proved effective in increasing spending on consumer durables.[24] Ishi notes that Japan's real growth of almost 4 per cent in 1996 reflected 'strong fiscal stimuli and an easing of monetary policy [during] the past five years'.[25] In an important sense, Japan's experience demonstrated Keynes's predilection that contractions are contractionary and expansions expansionary; even wasteful public spending has a clear multiplier effect.[26] Kuttner and Posen judge that fiscal policy 'provides an

---

[22]   See above pp. 88–91.

[23]   In 1995, the American Treasury and the MOF agreed to work together to depreciate the yen against the dollar. The aim was to enhance Japan's export competitiveness and to sustain, in return, a continued supply of capital from Japan to the USA to enable it to keep interest rates low. The yen began to depreciate against the US dollar in April 1995 and continued to do so during the following three years. Its nominal dollar rate moved from 84/US$ in April 1995 to 145/US$ in August 1998. Obstfeld, 'Time of Troubles', 66.

[24]   Tomomi Miyazaki, 'The Effects of Fiscal Policy in the 1990s in Japan: A VAR Analysis with Event Studies', *Japan and the World Economy* 22, no. 2 (2010): 80–87; Kuttner and Posen, 'Fiscal Policy Effectiveness', 543–50. The tendency for taxes to rise in response to positive spending, however, reduced the effect of spending increases.

[25]   Ishi, *Making Fiscal Policy*, 87.

[26]   Kuttner and Posen, 'The Great Recession', 157.

... explanation for a surprisingly large amount of the variation in Japanese economic growth over [the 1990s]'.[27]

During the first half of the 1990s, but particularly from 1995, fiscal activity helped to reduce the gap between potential and actual GDP by compensating for declining private sector investment and preventing a major debt-deflation crisis; as such, it has been judged to have been 'one of the most successful economic policies in human history' and to have 'kept Japan's Great Recession from becoming another Great Depression'.[28] Even allowing for exaggeration, there is little doubt that in an environment where monetary policy was rendered almost useless because those with negative equity were reluctant to borrow, where the private sector was seeking to minimize debt, following the collapse of the debt-financed bubble in asset prices, and where there were few lenders so long as banks remained preoccupied with repairing their balance sheets, it was the willingness of the government to borrow and spend that prevented the emergence of a possibly prolonged deflationary spiral.

Conventional assessments of the ineffectiveness of fiscal activity in the 1990s commonly draw attention to the co-existence of rising budget deficits and persistent slow growth over the decade. However, contrary to conventional wisdom, the deterioration in Japan's structural budget deficit over the decade arose more from declining tax revenue and increases in social security spending, as a result of changing demographics, than it did from increases in government stimulus packages.[29] The increase in public investment over the course of the 1990s contributed only 1 percentage point to the decline in the structural balance between 1990 and 1998.[30]

Official claims of the scale of public investment spending were notoriously exaggerated; this is clear if allowance is made for the actual amounts

---

[27]   Kuttner and Posen, 'Fiscal Policy Effectiveness', 539.

[28]   Koo, *The Holy Grail*, 25, 27. A point reiterated by Koo in 'A Different Kind of Crisis', *The Economist*, Vol. 400, Issue 8747, 20 August 2011, and contemplated by Metzler, 'Toward a Financial History', 666.

[29]   Spending on social security was generally estimated to have had a lower effect on output than other government spending or tax cuts did. S. Kalra, 'Fiscal Policy: An Evaluation of Its Effectiveness', in Tim Callen and Jonathan D. Ostry (eds.), *Japan's Lost Decade: Policies for Economic Revival* (Washington, DC: International Monetary Fund, 2003), 164–76.

[30]   Martin Muhleisen, 'Too Much of a Good Thing? The Effectiveness of Fiscal Stimulus', in Tamim A. Bayoumi and Charles Collyns (eds.), *Post-Bubble Blues: How Japan Responded to Asset Price Collapse* (Washington, DC: International Monetary Fund, 2000), 109.

of *new* spending that were undertaken. The effective tax cuts and public works components of the stimulus packages – the 'discretionary' elements of fiscal policy – were much smaller than the headline figure of overall spending (some 136 trillion yen between 1990 and 2000) might suggest. Stimulus packages frequently included large 'private investment incentives'; these were in effect loan programmes offered by institutions such as FILP or the Japan Development Bank to affect the allocation of funding among investment projects but they had little effect on the total level of investment undertaken. Similarly, many packages included elements of 'front-loading', which merely moved forward already planned spending on public works.[31] The 'real water' content of the stimulus packages – that is, the proportion that had a direct effect upon activity – was quite small over the greater part of the 1990s, often less than 50 per cent of the total.[32] This suggests that a more aggressive fiscal policy might have moderated the recession even further had the levels of new spending been greater than they actually were, given the predilection of both central government and local governments to spend less than headline figures suggested.[33]

The comparison frequently drawn between the substantial public outlays undertaken in Japan during the 1990s and the meagre economic growth that the country registered rarely considers what growth might have been in the absence of such spending. The real multiplier of fiscal spending lies in the difference in GDP in an economy already in recession before and after stimulus measures have been taken, and in the face of a massive drop in national wealth.[34] It is arguable that monetary policy should have been used to prevent the Japanese economy from suffering prolonged recession; however, once the economy was faced with excess capacity, collapsed confidence and low interest rates, monetary policy had become reduced, as Keynes would have it, 'pushing on a string'.

Even critics accept that deficit spending after 1993 may have been 'marginally effective in resolving the economic distress' and may even

---

[31]   Posen, *Restoring Growth*, 43.

[32]   Kuttner and Posen, 'The Great Recession', 127–8.

[33]   The situation was worsened by the fact that over the period from 1992 to 1996 local governments failed to spend an estimated 10 trillion yen of the discretionary fiscal resources allocated to them. Hiroko Ishii and Erika Wada, 'Local Government Spending: Solving the Mystery of Japanese Fiscal Packages', IIE Working Paper, no. 98–5, Peterson Institute for International Economics, Washington, DC, 1998. Available at http://www.piie.com/publications/wp/wp.cfm?ResearchID=146.

[34]   Koo, *The Holy Grail*, 146.

'have kept Japan from falling into an even deeper recession.'[35] Risk aversion and home bias on the part of the investing public worked in the country's favour, enabling 'captive savings' to be translated 'into fiscal power'.[36] When the government applied deficit finance, the economy improved; when it stopped, it deteriorated.[37] That the fiscal spending did not achieve more in Japan during the 1990s had less to do with its composition, wastefulness or misdirection than with the fact that it was not sustained long enough. By 1996 economic recovery and inflation were anticipated; fiscal austerity was not, even given the fall in asset prices.[38]

Nonetheless, despite growth having risen to 3 per cent only a year before, government concerns over the rising budget deficit led it to commit a major policy error: a sharp reversal in fiscal policy in 1997. The reasons are not difficult to discern. With the yen then falling against the dollar and in the belief that the economic recovery in 1995 was self-sustainable rather than partly the result of the public spending that had taken place during the previous three years, the government felt that the worst of the bubble years were behind it. Insolvent financial institutions within the jusen sector, and elsewhere, had been closed and a deposit guarantee system introduced to calm public nerves.

Controlling the growing deficit had become a priority. The share of taxes and social security contributions in national income (the 'national burden ratio') was rising in the face of an ageing population. Growing debt was seen as a threat to existing and future generations. The budget deficit of 4 per cent of GDP had unsettled the MOF. Perversely, the Ministry entertained the notion of 'expansionary fiscal contraction', believing that easing fears over the level of public debt would lead to lower interest rates and more consumption.

The authorities took the disastrous step of raising taxes and cutting fiscal spending shortly after signs of economic revival in 1996, despite having had to grapple with a deficiency in demand over the previous five years. Consumption taxes were raised from 3 per cent to 5 per cent in April 1997, the individual income tax cuts of the previous two years were terminated, and a 10 per cent rise in employees' healthcare co-payments was introduced. The combined effects eroded consumers' disposable income by an estimated 2.25 per cent in 1997 alone, denting overall spending.

---

[35]   Cargill and Sakamoto, *Japan Since 1980*, 173, 187.
[36]   Kuttner and Posen, 'Fiscal Policy Effectiveness', 555.
[37]   Wolf, 'Balance-Sheet Deflation'; Posen, *Restoring Growth*, 29.
[38]   Posen, 'More Than a Bubble', 26–7.

Far from improving the deficit, the rise in taxes and the cuts in public expenditure during 1997 merely worsened it as continued economic contraction reduced tax revenue. The about-turn in fiscal spending was rapid and damaging. Total public works expenditure as a percentage of GDP – which had risen from 6.0 per cent in 1991 to 7.9 per cent in 1993 and had stood at 7.5 per cent in 1995 – fell to 6.4 per cent in 1997.[39] The effects of the fiscal contraction were felt over the next two years. Growth rates shrank during five consecutive quarters in 1997 alone, GDP declining by at least 2.5 per cent.[40]

The fall in output between 1997 and the last quarter of 1998 reflected the worst recession that Japan had experienced over the entire post-war period. From the early 1990s Japanese nominal GDP had continued to rise; after 1997, though, deflation outstripped real GDP growth, causing a nominal contraction in the economy.[41] Real GDP declined by 1 per cent during 1998 – the largest decline since 1974 – and unemployment rose to just over 4 per cent (high by Japanese standards).[42] Business investment remained weak; during 1997–98, the peak to trough fall was almost 20 per cent, a contraction far more severe than in previous recessions.

Declines in consumption, investment, public expenditures and exports contributed to negative growth in 1998, as Table 6.1 below indicates. Real exports fell from an annual increase of 15 per cent in the spring of 1997 to negative values one year later, principally because of the collapse of several Asian economies.[43] The eight smaller East and Southeast Asian economies most affected had accounted for 35 per cent of Japanese exports in 1997.[44]

---

[39]   International Monetary Fund, Japan: Economic and Policy Developments: IMF Country Report No. 01/221 (Washington, DC: International Monetary Fund, 2001), 34.

[40]   Kuttner and Posen, 'Fiscal Policy Effectiveness', 550; Ito and Mishkin, 'Monetary Policy in Japan', 143.

[41]   Hamada et al., *Japan's Bubble*, 3.

[42]   Cargill and Sakamoto, *Japan Since 1980*, 192.

[43]   Meltzer, 'Monetary Transmission', 20–21.

[44]   Andrea Boltho and Jenny M. Corbett, 'The Assessment: Japan's Stagnation – Can Policy Revive the Economy?', *Oxford Review of Economic Policy* 16, no. 2 (2000): 3. It was a recovery in export growth during 1999–2000 that helped Japan emerge briefly from recession.

Table 6.1 Contribution of demand components (per cent)

	GDP growth	Consumption	Housing investment	Fixed investment	Inventory investment	Public consumption	Public investment	Exports	Imports
1990	5.1	2.6	0.3	2.0	-0.2	0.1	0.3	0.7	-0.8
1991	3.8	1.5	-0.5	1.2	0.3	0.2	0.3	0.6	0.3
1992	1.0	1.2	-0.3	-1.1	-0.5	0.2	1.0	0.5	0.1
1993	0.3	0.7	0.1	-1.9	-0.1	0.2	1.2	0.2	0.0
1994	0.6	1.1	0.4	-0.9	-0.3	0.2	0.2	0.5	-0.8
1995	1.5	1.2	-0.3	0.8	0.2	0.3	0.1	0.6	-1.4
1996	5.1	1.7	0.7	1.8	0.4	0.2	0.8	0.8	-1.3
1997	1.4	0.6	-0.9	1.2	-0.1	0.1	-0.9	1.4	-0.1
1998	-2.8	-0.6	-0.6	-2.1	-0.1	0.1	-0.0	-0.3	0.9

Source: Adapted from Motonishi and Yoshikawa, 'Causes of the Long Stagnation', 184.

In 1997 the government had taken the excessively optimistic view that the private demand-led recovery, which had already been sustained for almost three years, would continue and that it could proceed with cutting the deficit without inflicting much harm. During the first quarter of 1997 economic activity had been supported by depreciation in the value of the yen and by rising household consumption in anticipation of announced rises in taxation. Thereafter industrial production declined, at first in the consumer durables sector (especially the automobile sector), the one most affected by the consumption tax hike, and then more generally in the intermediate and capital goods sectors (chemicals and electric machinery, for example), as the effects of declining domestic and regional demand took hold.

In 1997 Japan had tightened fiscal policy before private demand was strong enough to sustain the recovery, thereby entrenching deflation. The reductions in public works spending were introduced only shortly after the positive effects of fiscal support had registered within the economy. It had been the absence of an appropriate macroeconomic response to the financial crises of the early 1990s that had initially turned a cyclical recession into a prolonged economic decline. Thereafter, macroeconomic austerity had combined with financial laissez-faire to put the country in greater trouble than many were willing to concede.[45] By 1997 Japan faced falling demand, negative investment and declining profits, effectively ruling out any recourse to recession-driven structural reform.[46] Worse still, the lurch towards fiscal orthodoxy came at a time when Japan was about to suffer the outbreak of a major financial crisis, which was to further damage confidence and deepen deflation.

---

[45] Posen, *Restoring Growth*, 2.
[46] Kuttner and Posen, 'The Great Recession', 171; Posen, *Restoring Growth*, 157.

7. Banking crises, monetary policy and deflation, 1997–2000

In the half-decade leading up to 1997, the Japanese authorities' responses to financial distress, low growth and laggard demand had been limited, uncoordinated and essentially ad hoc.[1] As we have noted, there had been some timely shifts in policy stance, as witnessed, for example, by the shift in political relations with the MOF during the mid-1990s and by the government's willingness for a while to embrace a deepening fiscal deficit in the face of falling corporate investment. Until 1997, though, few in authority fundamentally questioned the capacity of the bureaucratic, business and political nexus to ride out the consequences of an albeit prolonged but bounded cyclical downturn.

The Crisis in Banking, 1997

What changed matters was the emergence of a systemic banking crisis in late 1997. Until then the funds and the resolve needed to deal adequately with weakened financial institutions had simply not been in place. Banks had been allowed to understate the value of their bad loans (until 1995, only major banks disclosed the actual figures) and had even continued to pay dividends when it was clear that retained earnings were needed to strengthen their capital base. Capital requirement rules, normally an important regulatory instrument, had been leniently applied by the supervisory authorities, which had tended to intervene only when distressed banks had already become insolvent. Loan-classification rules were lax compared with international best practice.[2]

Both the MOF and the BOJ had been aware that a number of large financial institutions were either undercapitalized or close to insolvency. As late as 1995, though, the MOF was continuing to guarantee all deposits in the sector as whole, whilst declaring that no major bank would fail. We

---

[1]   See above pp. 97–105.
[2]   Kanaya and Woo, *The Japanese Banking Crisis*, 31–2.

have seen how it joined the banks in denying the severity of the bad loan problem; however, by understating the scale of loan losses it merely postponed the costly resolution of financial insolvency. Until 1997 there was hope that weak banks might survive long enough to be saved by an upturn in economic activity; full disclosure of the banking sector's woes, it was feared, would threaten bank runs and lead to a collapse of confidence.[3] With neither the public nor the politicians allowed to become sufficiently alarmed, there was little support for fiscal injections to recapitalize the banks.[4]

Matters changed abruptly in 1997. Although a number of small financial institutions – including credit cooperatives and regional banks and, most notably, seven of Japan's home mortgage (jusen) companies[5] – had failed during the first half of the 1990s, it was the collapse of major financial institutions in 1997 that signalled the end of the banks' celebrated 'convoy' safety net; these institutions had previously been seen as too big to fail. It also put paid to the government's reluctance to commit public funds to address the financial crisis.[6]

On 3 November 1997 Sanyo Securities, a mid-sized securities company, failed; this significantly reduced the liquidity available in the interbank market. A fortnight later the Hokkaido Takushoku bank, one of the country's largest regional banks, was declared bankrupt, the first closure of a major bank in Japanese history. A week later (on 17 November) Yamaichi Securities, one of Japan's largest brokerage firms, suspended operations, burdened with large balance sheet liabilities. Five days later a small regional bank, Tokuyo City Bank, in the northeastern city of Sendai, collapsed. This was the fourth banking collapse in the month of November.

With bank failures occurring against the backdrop of the July Asian financial crisis, unprecedented disruption threatened. Many financial institutions were going bankrupt simultaneously, bank share prices were tumbling, several commercial banks were cut off from access to the interbank

---

[3]   Japanese banks lost an estimated 96.8 trillion yen because of bad loans between March 1992 and March 2006. Fukao, 'Financial Crisis', 273–6.

[4]   Ito and Mishkin, 'Two Decades of Japanese Monetary Policy', 138.

[5]   See above pp. 98–9.

[6]   Earlier, the government had made efforts to contain problems in the banking sector without using public funds. In 1996 it amended the Deposit Insurance Law to strengthen the insurance system but its efforts were targeted mainly at credit cooperatives rather than large banks (securities houses were excluded).

market, and some smaller banks faced depositor runs.[7] Ever since the early 1990s, Japan had needed a more transparent regulatory regime, greater injection of public funds into the banking system, and a more universal and less ad hoc system of rescue mergers for troubled financial institutions; nonetheless, the authorities had vacillated in the hope that fundamental reforms could be delayed or even avoided.[8] By late 1997 it was clear that if further and deeper financial instability was to be avoided the government would have to act far more decisively than it had done in the past.

LDP politicians, alarmed by the effect that credit restrictions were having upon small and medium-sized firms, a critical section of the party's electoral base, backed an explicit injection of public funds into the ailing financial system in February 1998 to help ease the credit crunch. The assistance proved inadequate, even though capital adequacy regulations were openly ignored.[9] Only 13 trillion of the 30 trillion yen made available was actually allocated for capital injection into banks.[10] The response was neither sufficient nor properly targeted.[11]

Because banks were generally reluctant to be singled out as sufficiently weak to require special assistance, all major banks applied collectively for a capital injection. Funding was therefore allocated uniformly, irrespective of the condition of the recipient bank and without any formal requirement that banks should undertake restructuring. As a result, all major banks received a capital injection in March 1998; this amounted to a combined total of 1.8 trillion yen. For most banks the assistance offered was far short of what was required to restore capital levels (at the time the MOF's estimate of bad debt was 77 trillion yen).[12] In any event, small and medium-sized enterprises remained strongly opposed to any rigorous implementation of capital/asset ratios, since that threatened to reduce new lending and encourage further

---

[7]   Masahiro Kawai, 'Reform of the Japanese Banking System', *International Economics and Economic Policy* 2, no. 4 (2005): 311.

[8]   Amyx, *Japan's Financial Crisis*, 147, 208.

[9]   Tamura, 'Japanese Compliance', 46. The financial crisis further weakened the profile of the key financial institutions. Several MOF bank examiners were arrested in January 1998, causing the finance minister and administrative vice-minister to resign. The Governor and Deputy Governor of the BOJ also resigned. Six officials in the MOF and BOJ committed suicide during the first three months of 1998. Metzler, 'Towards a Financial History', 660.

[10]   The remaining 17 trillion yen was to be used for dealing with bank failures down to March 2001. For details of the capital shortage during the 1990s see Hoshi and Kashyap, 'Japan's Financial Crisis', 15–18.

[11]   Cargill, 'Central Banking', 156.

[12]   Amyx, *Japan's Financial Crisis*, 184.

calling in of NPLs. Instead of fully capitalizing the financial sector to encourage healthy banks to resume lending, the government dithered. Moreover, since banks had generally been understating the scale of NPLs, both insolvent banks and weak but solvent banks continued to co-exist. 'The whole endeavour', writes Nakaso, 'appeared to be a remnant of the convoy approach.'[13]

Such relative timidity did not last the year. In the autumn of 1998 the government was forced to intervene and effectively nationalize two major banks, the Long-Term Credit Bank of Japan and the Nippon Credit Bank. The public bailout of banks was now more firmly on the agenda. A second, larger, round of capital injections was made in December 1998 in order to boost capital adequacy ratios, assist in the writing off of NPLs, increase lending to small and medium-sized enterprises and encourage bank restructuring. The policy was broadly successful, at least within the international banking sector, which received up to fifty times more capital than was allocated to domestic banks.[14]

Although the banking system received a further capital injection in March 1999, a fundamental problem remained. Economic stagnation continued to create new NPLs, which only depleted bank capital further.[15] Since 1993 striking progress had been made in writing off bad loans; however, in March 1998 the overall total of bad loans[16] among the top 20

---

[13]   Nakaso, 'The financial crisis in Japan during the 1990s', 12.

[14]   Heather Montgomery and Satoshi Shimizutani, 'The Effectiveness of Bank Recapitalization Policies in Japan', *Japan and the World Economy* 21, no. 1 (2009): 1–25. There is evidence that the availability of public capital had a favourable effect in redirecting the loan portfolios of banks away from unproductive industries and towards more productive industries, a reversal of the situation during the first half of the decade. Fuji and Kawai, 'Japan's Banking Crisis', 6–10; Wako Watanabe, 'Does a Large Loss of Bank Capital Cause Evergreening? Evidence from Japan', *Journal of the Japanese and International Economies* 24, no. 1 (2010): 116–36.

[15]   Watanabe, 'Does a Large Loss of Bank Capital Cause Evergreening?', 112.

[16]   The issue of the scale of NPLs is complicated by the many changes in the definition of 'bad loans' over the years. Banks had a considerable amount of discretion in defining what constituted a nonperforming loan. For a fuller discussion, see Takeo Hoshi and Anil K. Kashyap, 'The Japanese Banking Crisis: Where Did it Come from and How Will it End?', in Ben S. Bernanke and Julio J. Rotemberg (eds.), *NBER Macroeconomics Annual 1999, Volume 14* (Chicago: University of Chicago Press, 1999), 129–221.

banks, using the same definition as in 1993, was higher than it had been five years earlier.[17]

It was not that banks were very keen to lend. If there had been doubts about the scale and effect of a 'credit crunch' in the early 1990s,[18] there was far greater concern from 1997. For some years Japanese banks had been under pressure to maintain their capital ratios but by 1997 low profitability, limited access to capital markets and exposure to greater regulatory scrutiny made them determined to preserve their capital base.

Regulatory forbearance in the past had been guided by a 'too big to fail' strategy to help forestall a full-blown crisis, given the absence of an adequate legal framework for bank restructuring. Nevertheless, government action to tighten banking regulation and to acquiesce in the failure of high-profile financial institutions (from 1997) made weak banks aware that they too could face closure if they did not act more prudently to reduce their indebtedness and review their lending practices.[19] The result was a 'regulatory driven capital crunch,'[20] the effects of which are estimated to have reduced Japan's growth rate of investment and GDP by 10 per cent and 1.6 per cent respectively in 1998 alone. Even that ignores the further additional negative effects of the corporate bankruptcies, falling consumption and labour displacements that followed in its wake.[21]

Banks, which were now seriously undercapitalized, proved reluctant to deplete their diminishing capital stock by making further advances, risky or not. Rather than expand advances, they began to absorb the funds channelled to them by the BOJ.[22] Bank loans showed virtually no growth in 1997 and then fell sharply in 1998. Although capital injections by the government in 1998 reduced the capital constraints on banks, the positive effects on

[17] For further discussion, see Nobuyoshi Yamori and Narunto Nishigaki, 'Japanese Banks: The Lost Decade and New Challenges', in Rien T. Segers (ed.), *A New Japan For the Twenty-First Century: An Inside Overview of Current Fundamental Changes and Problems* (New York: Routledge, 2008), 46.

[18] We noted earlier that during the early 1990s weakly capitalized banks appeared to increase their lending more rapidly than strongly capitalized ones did. See above pp. 88.

[19] David Woo, 'In Search of "Capital Crunch": Supply Factors Behind the Credit Slowdown in Japan', *Journal of Money, Credit and Banking* 35, no. 6 (2003): 1019–38. For a discussion of the developments in banking regulation, see below pp. 134–9.

[20] Watanabe, 'Does a Large Loss of Bank Capital Cause Evergreening?', 641.

[21] Yoshikawa, *Japan's Lost Decade*, 76–9; Motonishi and Yoshikawa, 'Causes of the Long Stagnation of Japan', 198–200.

[22] Arai and Hoshi, 'Monetary Policy in the Great Stagnation', 176.

lending were insufficient to improve the overall situation.[23] The tightening of credit was particularly apparent among those small and medium-sized firms that relied most heavily upon it.[24] As the banks became more cautious, so did the public. Households increasingly transferred their funds from bank deposits to the Postal Savings Scheme, whose liabilities were guaranteed by the government.[25]

The essential problem, however, was more endemic. Because the Japanese authorities had failed to adopt a comprehensive strategy to address banking problems in the early 1990s, harbouring the expectation that renewed growth would restore asset values, banks' balance sheets had been allowed to deteriorate to such an extent that by the late 1990s the conventional monetary transmission system had broken down. Even if the BOJ had adopted a more expansionary policy, there was no guarantee that banks would have increased lending merely because of an increase in the supply of base money.[26] Although the introspection and caution that emerged within banking after 1997 were welcome improvements on past practice, they came at a time of continuing economic weakness. Nakaso writes:

> The capacity of banks to extend new loans was constrained by the deterioration in their capital positions. The tightened credit conditions discouraged business fixed investment by the corporate sector. Medium and small-sized corporations were hit most severely as their alternative sources of funding were limited. The resultant economic contraction further undermined the asset quality of banks, thus entrapping the financial system and the real economy in a vicious circle that dragged the economy into recession. This mechanism may have been significantly underestimated at the time. As a consequence, the recession became

---

[23]   Wako Watanabe, 'Prudent Regulation and the "Credit Crunch": Evidence from Japan', *Journal of Money, Credit and Banking* 39, no. 2–3 (2007): 640.

[24]   Constraints on bank capital were eased in subsequent years, once public funds were injected into the system. Nevertheless, bank lending continued to show negative year-on-year growth down to 2000. Nakaso, 'The financial crisis in Japan during the 1980s', 35.

[25]   Woo, 'In Search of "Capital Crunch"', 1034.

[26]   Kawai, 'Reform of the Japanese Banking System'. Reflecting these concerns, the government expanded its existing loan guarantee programme for SMEs in October 1998 to encourage greater lending by regional banks (SMEs still accounted for 75 per cent of non-agricultural employment). Under the scheme, the government took on the credit risk inherent in lending to such firms. Unfortunately, as in previous years, such guarantees undermined the banks' incentive to adequately assess credit quality and the incentives for these firms to make good use of the borrowed funds.

deeper and longer than had been widely anticipated and the cost and time for overcoming the financial crisis grew that much larger and longer.[27]

Monetary and Fiscal Policy midst Deflation: Japan in the Late 1990s

The weakening of the real economy during 1997–98 briefly shifted the political consensus towards expansionary fiscal policy in order to stimulate domestic demand.[28] The Hashimoto cabinet had initially been constrained by its commitment to fiscal consolidation, under the terms of the Fiscal Structural Reform Law. By April 1998 the mood had changed. Fiscal consolidation was put on hold. 'The economy is in a very serious state', premier Hashimoto declared, 'and while still upholding structural reforms, I have decided that we will take the steps seen as both necessary and sufficient to regain trust both at home and abroad.'[29]

A comprehensive 16.6 trillion yen set of stimulus measures – the seventh economic policy package since the collapse of the bubble in 1991 and equivalent to 3.2 per cent of GDP – was announced that month. It embraced tax cuts, public works spending (on a broader range of social infrastructure projects than customarily deployed) and support to SMEs. The package, however, was less expansionary than the headline figure implied. Spending on public works by central government totalled 3.8 trillion yen and a temporary tax cut accounted for 2 trillion yen, the totals therefore amounting to less than 60 per cent of announced spending. Even if matching local government expenditures were undertaken as the central government demanded (highly unlikely given past experience),[30] actual spending would have amounted to some 1.1–1.6 per cent of GDP, short of what was estimated as needed (2.0–2.5 per cent of GDP) to raise Japan's growth rate above its potential.[31] In July 1998 Japan's *Monthly Economic Report* noted ruefully that '*the effect of stagnant final demand* on production, employment and the real economy as a whole is strengthening, the stagnation of the economy is becoming prolonged, and business conditions remain harsh.'[32] Hashimoto's cabinet resigned in July 1998, following the LDP's loss of a majority in the upper house of the Diet. Incoming premier Obuchi invoked a further 40 trillion yen worth of nominal fiscal stimulus during the second

---

[27] Nakaso, 'Financial Crisis', 20.
[28] Ishi, *Making Fiscal Policy*, 150–53.
[29] *The Japan Times*, 9 April 1998, cited in Ishi, *Making Fiscal Policy*, 150.
[30] See above pp. 15.
[31] Posen, *Restoring Growth*, 53.
[32] Quoted in Yoshikawa, *Japan's Lost Decade*, 37. Emphasis added.

half of 1998, equivalent to about 10 per cent of GDP; this was followed by an additional fiscal package in November 1999.

By the end of the decade Japan had the highest gross debt to GDP ratio among OECD countries. The 1998 stimulus packages were expected to turn fiscal policy from somewhat contractionary to neutral.[33] Japan's average budget deficit from 1995 to 2001 was about 5.1 per cent of GDP. Although one can criticize fiscal policy for not being consistently expansionary, Hoshi and Kashyap claim that it was 'by conventional measures ... highly expansionary.'[34] Nevertheless, although fiscal stimuli after 1995 had helped to neutralize the fall in corporate investment, to bolster aggregate demand and to generate some growth before fiscal consolidation reversed the process, any potentially positive effects of fiscal expansion in the later 1990s were muted by a growing mistrust of the likely success of government economic policy. Financing 'zombie' firms had helped perpetuate low productivity and to stifle new investment. As growth stalled, the government continued to suffer a reduction in revenue, 'sticky' expenditure commitments almost ensuring that the fiscal situation would deteriorate. Macroeconomic conditions, including a tightening of monetary policy and rises in real interest rates and in the real exchange rate from 1998, dampened the influence of fiscal policy.

More fundamental was the fact that the gap between the country's actual and potential output had widened so much that even the revitalization of fiscal policy proved unable to sustain any sizeable recovery. Bald figures of the level of real gross domestic product did not adequately reflect the output losses generated by the protracted economic slowdown. Even when growth had slowed from the 1980s to the end of 1991, Japan registered an increase of nearly 3.8 per cent a year in real GDP. Between the end of 1991 and the end of 1999, however, the rate of growth of real GDP had fallen to less than 0.9 per cent a year. Had Japan grown by even 2.5 per cent a year, its real GDP in 1999 would have been almost 14 per cent higher than the level recorded.[35]

The essential problem was one of continuing price deflation, growing uncertainty and stagnant final demand. Nominal GDP (taken as a proxy for the growth of nominal aggregate demand) grew by less than 1 per cent a

---

[33] Ben S. Bernanke, 'Japanese Monetary Policy: A Case of Self-Induced Paralysis?', in Mikitani and Posen, *Japan's Financial Crisis*, 149.

[34] Hoshi and Kashyap, 'Japan's Financial Crisis', 8.

[35] Bernanke, 'Japanese Monetary Policy', 153–4.

year in every year from 1992 to 1999 (except for 1996) and declined by
nearly 3 percentage points in 1998.[36] As Table 7.1 indicates, standard
measures of price inflation (the GDP deflator, personal consumption
expenditure, the consumer price index, and the wholesale price index) all
reflected increased deflationary pressure between 1992 and 1999, and
especially from 1997, pointing to a deficiency in aggregate demand as the
fundamental issue rather than inflationary supply-side problems or inadequate structural reform.[37]

Table 7.1   Measures of inflation in Japan, 1991–99 (per cent change)

Year	(1) GDP deflator	(2) PCE deflator	(3) CPI deflator	(4) WPI deflator	(5) Nominal GDP	(6) Monthly earnings
1991	2.89	2.13	2.30	–1.29	5.30	2.84
1992	0.94	1.44	2.08	–1.69	1.09	1.78
1993	0.44	0.96	0.91	–4.07	0.91	1.82
1994	–0.62	0.60	0.50	–1.25	0.04	2.70
1995	–0.38	–0.90	0.07	–0.06	0.79	1.87
1996	–2.23	0.34	0.30	–0.33	2.43	1.87
1997	1.00	1.91	2.23	1.42	0.39	0.81
1998	0.17	–0.02	–0.32	–3.64	–2.78	–0.10
1999	–0.79	–0.14	0.00	–4.12	0.12	0.84

PCE = personal consumption expenditure
CPI = consumer price index
WPI = wholesale price index

Note: Growth rates are measured fourth quarter to fourth quarter, except for 1999, which is
third quarter over third quarter; the CPI measure excludes fresh foods.

Source: Bernanke, 'Japan's Monetary Policy', 152.

The experience of deflation had been bad enough, but expectations of
continued deflation posed a serious threat. Sustained falls in prices had left
real interest rates at relatively high levels, which worsened the burden of
firms' debt and choked off consumers' desire to spend. There was a

[36]   Ibid., 152.
[37]   Yoshikawa, 'What Have We Learned', 30.

noticeable rise in precautionary saving after 1997, as fears about growth prospects, employment and fluctuations in income grew. The public became alarmed at rising unemployment and were especially concerned that the prevailing level of national debt might compromise the government's ability to meet its pension and healthcare obligations. They protected themselves by increasing their savings (the amount of cash held by the public is estimated to have risen from 35 trillion yen in 1994 to 70 trillion by 2001). The more households tried to restore their personal wealth, the smaller was the effect of fiscal expansion on GDP. This further exacerbated the problem of low aggregate demand.[38] The worries over mounting public debt were genuine, even if slightly misplaced. In 1997, the ratio of gross financial liabilities to GDP stood at 87 per cent but net debt was only 18 per cent because of offsetting government assets.[39] Japan was not insolvent but public perceptions and fears were both paramount and determinant.

Despite the government's use of public funds to recapitalize banks during 1998–99, consumers continued to face high real borrowing costs, which left banks struggling to obtain sufficient profit margins on their lending activities. Moreover, the rise in savings reduced the supply of loanable funds to the banks. The decline in credit supply finally outpaced the drop in demand from corporations, both of which made the situation worse in the immediate term. At the same time, government revenue was being squeezed just as the budget had to cope with increased social security payments in the face of rising unemployment.

In short, prolonged unanticipated deflation constrained monetary policy, hampered corporate profitability and raised the real burden of public and private debt, thereby weakening the impulses to recovery that monetary easing, fiscal spending, bank recapitalization and regulatory reform were designed to encourage. As deflation deepened, so did deflationary expectations; this only intensified shrinking demand in the macroeconomy. Japan had fallen into a process of almost self-sustained deflation, and that is what hobbled fiscal policy. Although there was a case for continued fiscal stimulus from 1997, there was still a fear that such outlays might be needed for an indefinite period, mainly because of the public's excess desire for savings beyond levels required for domestic investment. This structural savings surplus added a constraint that could plausibly have been solved by

---

[38]   Martin Wolf, 'Saving Japan, A Permanent Cure', *Financial Times*, 7 April 1998.
[39]   Fukao, 'Financial Crisis', 273.

increased net investment abroad but that ran the risk of courting unwelcome international reaction from countries fearful of Japan building up greater surpluses.

Japan had been overwhelmed by three separate crises: the secular decline in long-term growth, partly as a result of technological catch-up and demographic slowdown; a banking crisis in the wake of the bursting of the asset bubble; and perverse macroeconomic policy which had reversed tax and fiscal policy at precisely the wrong time in 1997. Because Japan delayed getting its expansionary macroeconomic policy right, especially when it came to tackling deflation and low aggregate demand, it was never able to deal effectively with either its structural problems or the condition of its financial institutions.

The Argument over Inflation Targeting

In hindsight it is arguable that the BOJ, aware that persistent deflation increased the cost of servicing government debt and continually threatened further bankruptcies in the commercial sector, should have adopted inflation targeting in the 1990s to boost demand, a policy subsequently urged upon it.[40] Historically, low consumption in Japan had created a high structural saving rate; in earlier years that had been offset by high levels of investment. As growth slackened, an imbalance between saving and investment occurred, so that the equilibrium rate of real interest became negative. As a result, the monetary authorities were unable to reduce the real interest rate to a level sufficient to restore the economy, despite record low nominal short-term and long-term interest rates. In other words, Japan faced a classic liquidity trap, where aggregate demand fell short of productive capacity, despite the move to essentially zero short-term nominal interest rates.[41] Individuals had become indifferent about holding money and other financial assets because of very low interest rates.

For monetary policy to stimulate demand, the authorities needed to induce inflationary expectations in order to reduce the real rate of interest. If the BOJ had countenanced an explicit price level target sufficient to encourage a low but positive inflation rate, it might in theory have helped to

---

[40] Most notably by Paul Krugman; in 1998 he suggested that the BOJ should set an inflation target of 4 per cent a year for 15 years. See Krugman, 'It's Baaack'.

[41] Deflation is not necessarily harmful to an economy if it results from favourable shifts in productivity, but this was not the situation facing Japan in the late 1990s. See Paul Krugman, *The Return of Depression Economics* (London: Allen Lane, 1999).

restore financial and non-financial balance sheets, encourage investment and raise demand to levels high enough to cushion the effects of much-needed industrial restructuring.[42] However, the BOJ took a benign view of deflation and opposed inflation targeting. It argued that falling prices, far from being harmful, reflected beneficial technological progress, deregulation and efficient methods of production; together, these would work to encourage the structural adjustments necessary to stimulate economic recovery.[43]

This was a view shared by most of the mass media. As late as 1999 BOJ Governor Hayami was praising the virtues of 'good deflation' and rejecting the call for 'irresponsible' inflation targeting. There were academic economists in Japan who fundamentally disagreed and who called for a highly expansionary monetary policy, but they found it difficult to mobilize support for their ideas. They were daubed the spokesmen of unhealthy inflation.[44] Only in 2002 could a significant shift in the emphasis of official thinking towards the defeat of deflation be detected.[45]

The past cast a long shadow. For decades the BOJ had cosseted price stability. Even though it had gained greater discretionary power after becoming independent in 1998, by the late 1990s it was in no mood to weaken its authority or to damage the reputation it had built during the high-growth period.[46] It remained sceptical of its ability to influence inflationary expectations in the manner implied by inflation targeting. Given the BOJ's anti-inflationary reputation, expectations of future inflation were traditionally low. Past experience led the BOJ to judge that the public and the corporate sector would expect it to rein in the money supply if prices started to rise, thereby nullifying any effort on its part to engage in short-run monetary expansion. In any event, when faced with *falling* prices

---

[42]   Ito and Mishkin, 'Monetary Policy in Japan', 111–39.

[43]   This argument ignored the fact that such influences would affect prices only in particular sectors; it was the decline in the overall level of prices that was the principal concern of contemporary critics.

[44]   Koichi Hamada and Asahi Noguchi, 'The Role of Preconceived Ideas in Macroeconomic Policy: Japan's Experiences in Two Deflationary Periods', *International Economics and Economic Policy* 2, no. 2–3 (2005): 101–26.

[45]   Deflation appeared in the agenda of the Council of Economic and Fiscal Policy (CEFP) – the Cabinet body that sets the basic goals of economic policy – only once in 2001 but increasingly so thereafter. This shift in emphasis was also reflected in the editorial opinions of Japan's major newspapers. Ibid., 122.

[46]   Japan had adopted a policy of raising inflationary expectations in the 1930s, but it operated a low inflation policy for the greater part of the post-1945 period.

why would the public believe in a policy that promised future inflation? Trying to find a route out of recession by fostering inflationary expectations was, in its view, futile.[47]

The BOJ argued further that even if an inflationary policy were launched, forward-looking households would be more likely to increase savings rather than raise consumption in order to maintain the real value of future purchasing power. If domestic demand failed to respond in a period of uncertainty, it would be difficult to sustain the expectation of future inflation. Moreover, inflation targeting offered no guide as to how to achieve a given target. If the BOJ announced a target and missed it, its credibility would suffer. And there were attendant risks. Commercial banks might absorb any increase in liquidity merely to balance their own books rather than lend in order to spur recovery.[48] A policy of targeted inflation might be regarded by the public as a strategy to inflate away NPLs, enabling indebted problem firms to survive longer than they should, thereby delaying necessary structural 'cleansing'.[49]

In retrospect the BOJ's stance seems especially perverse. It focused on the dangers of inflation when deflation was the core problem. It was clear to the markets and the public, however, that the BOJ was fundamentally unwilling to consider any sustained expansionary policy for the sake of reviving the economy. It was unwilling to stimulate the economy until the government tackled the problems of bad loans, low productivity and structural reform. Such an approach served only to dampen expectations further and to deepen deflation. Despite the need for a more aggressive monetary policy, the BOJ rebuffed calls for any substantive easing until the spring of 1999, when a zero interest policy was adopted. Even then the BOJ was hesitant and circumspect; in September 1999 it announced that its monetary policy would be formulated independently and not in response to pressure from the government or the market.

---

[47]   Yoshikawa, *Japan's Lost Decade*, 234–5.
[48]   Vogel, *Japan Remodeled*, 28.
[49]   Ito and Mishkin, 'Japanese Monetary Policy', 166.

8. Reform without salvation: Japan 1997–2000

The financial and economic crisis that engulfed Japan in 1997 provided the country with an opportunity to effect radical policies for economic revival, ideally incorporating both macro and micro (structural) reforms that would, in earlier years, have been difficult to implement because of their distributional implications.[1] Japan had already proved capable of change when moved to act. It had bailed out financial institutions as diverse as housing loan companies to the once powerful Long-Term Credit Bank of Japan and the Nippon Credit Bank, both of which were subsequently nationalized. City banks had been recapitalized from public funds and measures had been taken to enhance the protection of deposits and claims against failed institutions.[2]

However, until 1997 there was no clear or dominant consensus within Japan as to whether an alternative and more radical political economy was required to remedy its prolonged stagnation beyond the financial and political fixes that that hitherto been implemented. This was partly because sectoral interest groups and their political allies had a vested interest in forestalling reform and partly – indeed more fundamentally – because politicians, industrialists, bureaucrats and the public at large were ambivalent about what should be reformed, at what cost and in whose interest.

Ryutaro Hashimoto, who was Prime Minister from 1996 to 1998, had been unequivocal in his rejection of 'Japan Inc.' as a model for the immediate future, and urged reforms in finance, education and social security. 'The Japanese socio-economic system which has sustained the country over the 50 year post-war period, has revealed serious limitations', he stated in 1997, 'Wide-ranging reforms are needed [to] create a new

---

[1]   Rodrik, 'Understanding Economic Policy Reform', 29; Nicholas Crafts, 'Implications of Financial Crisis for East Asian Trend Growth', *Oxford Review of Economic Policy* 15, no. 3 (1999): 110–31.

[2]   See above pp. 121–2.

system suitable for the twenty-first century.'[3] Likewise, in 1997, a former President of the Japanese Business Federation (Keidanren) declared that 'staying with the status quo will cause the economy to stagnate further.'[4]

Nonetheless, because the responses of agents – to decline, deflation and uncertainty – differed in scale, scope and urgency, what emerged during the late 1990s was a mix of continuity and change within corporate governance, public policy and labour market employment patterns. Lifetime employment continued alongside strategic lay-offs;[5] supply chains and industrial 'losers' remained protected, even as competitive pressure was enhanced; consensual networking and accommodating banking continued; and in many businesses stakeholders continued to reign over shareholders. As we shall see below, later in the 1990s existing core institutions acted in selective and differentiated ways to leverage the benefits of prevailing practice to foster 'patterned' innovation. Solutions to pressing problems were forged by drawing upon the rich resources of the Japanese model rather than abandoning it wholesale.[6]

A flurry of reform activity did occur within the financial sector from 1997, spurred essentially by the desperate need for both the LDP and the MOF to restore their battered reputations. Scandals and performance failures had seriously eroded public trust in both organizations. It seemed the time had come to abandon partial fixes in the financial sector. Within the banking sector, objective risk assessment had long struggled with a tradition of informal relational interactions and conflict avoidance. The Japanese public urged greater transparency and political and bureaucratic leaders responded, at least in part. They elevated efficiency and competition above stability and cooperation (in the financial arena if not elsewhere) and sought to meet the needs of the public rather than regulatory constituencies.

Having committed itself (in 1997) to using public funds to aid troubled banks, the government subsequently imposed a more defined regulatory and supervisory framework upon the financial sector. It was anxious to free policy formulation from the established reliance upon informal networked ties and opaque, exclusionary relationships and to place it within a more

---

[3] Cited in Austin, *Common Foundations*, 129.
[4] Ibid.
[5] See below pp. 155–8.
[6] Toya, *The Political Economy of the Japanese Financial Big Bang.* See below pp. 179–86.

objective and transparent rules-based environment, incorporating greater monitoring and prudential oversight.[7]

The Financial Reconstruction Law of 1998 allowed failed banks either to be placed under formal reorganization administration or to be temporarily nationalized. In the same year the Financial Supervisory Agency (FSA) was established under the guidance of a newly created Financial Reconstruction Commission (FRC). The FSA oversaw the rehabilitation of the financial sector, largely through improved inspection and supervision of banks, tasks that had previously been the responsibility of the Ministry of Finance but which experience had shown had been only cursorily undertaken. Restructuring thereafter focused upon private capitalization, branch closures, stricter loan classification and more deliberate assessment of the solvency of individual banks, especially with regard to their NPLs.[8]

This reallocation of bureaucratic authority over financial policy was a clear sign that the government wished to improve national and international confidence in the conduct of financial policy. There were constraints, however. The FSA was obliged to consult the MOF in any decision to declare a financial institution insolvent, but the MOF proved reluctant to allow the FSA to cast judgement on the asset situation and financial condition of banks, since it risked being accused further of having supported essentially insolvent institutions.[9]

From April 1998 banks became subject to 'prompt corrective action' and made responsible for valuing their assets on a prudent and realistic basis, subject to review by external auditors. Capital ratio thresholds were established, on the basis of which the regulatory authorities could order banks to take remedial action. The old post-war rules no longer applied. During the high-growth period the relationship between regulator and regulated had been highly personal. The MOF had often been able to learn about potential problems before they surfaced and to devise a solution quickly enough to avert public panic. Public reports had therefore remained opaque, since full disclosure threatened to destabilize the financial markets.[10] From 1998,

---

[7]   Jennifer A. Amyx and Peter Drysdale (eds.), *Japanese Governance: Beyond Japan Inc.* (New York: RoutledgeCurzon, 2003), 3–5.

[8]   Nakaso, 'Financial Crisis', 14. For more details see Kawai, 'Reform of the Japanese Banking System'. In July 2000 the FSA absorbed the MOF's Financial Planning Bureau to form a new Financial Services Agency; this in turn took over the functions of the FRC in June 2001.

[9]   Jennifer A. Amyx, 'The Ministry of Finance and the Bank of Japan at the Crossroads', in Amyx and Drysdale (eds.), *Japanese Governance*, 55–76.

[10]   Brown, *The Ministry of Finance*, 109–13. See above pp. 102–4.

however, the bureaucratic response to self-examination by banks could, in principle, lead to closure of an institution.[11]

Within public administration, the Basic Law for Administrative Reform of 1999 altered the relationship between politicians and bureaucrats by putting policymaking firmly within the Cabinet. This transformed the vertical structure of the central bureaucracy into a horizontally integrated one that was better able to cope with cross-sector issues. More significantly, the MOF's control over budget drafting was transferred to the Cabinet to enable the priorities of policy to be more clearly established.[12]

Regulatory changes from 1997 had followed upon earlier 'Big Bang' reforms of the private banking sector, which had begun in 1996. These had been aimed at liberalizing and strengthening banking practice to increase competition, enhance transparency, and to bring the legal, accounting and supervisory systems within banking more in line with best international practice. The emphasis was on expanded user choice, quality, fairness and competition as drivers to greater efficiency. The range of activity was impressive, involving the liberalization of foreign exchange regulations, the removal of the ban on financial holding companies assisting acquisitions and mergers in the financial sector, a reduction in the constraints upon banks, insurance companies and securities firms, which prevented them from competing in each other's fields, thereby opening up greater competition, and fewer restrictions on the introduction of new financial products.[13]

Demands for greater transparency and accountability within the corporate sector during the late 1990s did bear some results. Dedicated reforms permitted the reintroduction of the holding company, providing firms with a stronger identity and greater independence. Regulations were introduced to encourage smaller and more diversified boards of directors to speed decision-making and encourage outside auditing. Steps were taken to discourage cross-shareholdings in order to weaken the corporate sector's traditional resistance to the discipline of the market. New rules were established to identify the underlying profitability of company activities by obliging them to value their securities holdings at market value rather than

---

[11]   That said, the system assumed that the banks would produce financial accounts that reflected an objective assessment of their asset positions, a procedure that was far from secure. Tamura, 'Challenges to Japanese Compliance', 39.

[12]   Molteni, 'Structural Reforms in Japan', 53–5.

[13]   For detailed discussion, see Toya, *The Political Economy of the Japanese Financial Big Bang*, 102–49.

book value prices; this made it more difficult for firms to boost their declining revenues by gaining windfall profits by selling or revaluing them.

From the 1970s to the early 1990s the ownership structure of Japanese firms, characterized by cross-shareholdings by financial institutions and others, had remained fundamentally stable. During the late 1990s, by contrast, there was a decline in the proportion of stable, institutional shareholders within keiretsu groupings. This was mirrored by a rise in foreign or domestic arms-length investors, including pension funds and investment trusts with far less homogeneous expectations. The stable shareholdings ratio[14] reported by firms and banks dropped from 45 per cent to 24 per cent and reciprocal holdings dropped from 18 per cent to 7 per cent during 1990–2003. Figure 8.1 illustrates the cross-shareholding ratios of the six principal keiretsu groups. The ratios all declined in the 1990s. While cross-shareholding between corporations decreased, ownership of corporate shares by financial institutions and banks in particular dropped significantly.[15] The dismantling of shareholding was accelerated by the rise of foreign investors. The proportion of shares held by foreigners rose (by value) from 4.7 per cent in the 1990s to 18.8 per cent in 2000; it stood at 22 per cent of all issued shares in March 2004.[16]

Despite these changes, the unwinding of cross-shareholding did not proceed uniformly. Profitable firms with easy access to capital markets proceeded to weaken their financial relationships with banks, but firms that continued to rely upon loans from their main banks sustained cross-shareholding. Managers of firms with low profitability and strong relationships with banks had little incentive to sell shares of banks whose profitability had also fallen; and banks were reluctant to sell shares of weak firms with which they were financially connected, since that risked sending negative signals to the market.[17]

In other respects, too, change was less obvious or widespread than might have been expected in the wake of financial and economic decline after

[14]   Defined as the ratio of shares held by commercial banks, insurance companies and non-financial firms to the total number of shares issued.

[15]   Hideaki Miyajima and Fumiaki Kuroki, 'The Unwinding of Cross-Shareholding in Japan: Causes, Effects, and Implications', in Aoki, Jackson and Miyajima, *Corporate Governance*, 80.

[16]   Toru Yoshikawa and Jean McGuire, 'Change and Continuity in Japanese Corporate Governance', *Asia Pacific Journal of Management* 25, no. 1 (2008): 5–24.

[17]   Miyajima and Kuroki, 'The Unwinding of Cross-Shareholding', 79–124. Defensiveness through cross shareholding re-emerged in the 2000s. See below p. 184.

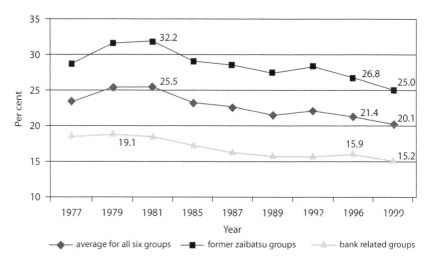

Source: Schaede, *Choose and Focus*, 91.

*Figure 8.1   Intra-group shareholding ratio, 1977–99: per cent of all group
            shares outstanding (181 member firms, not including life
            insurance companies)*

1997. It was always too much to anticipate that Japan would move wholesale from a stakeholder-based economic system to a shareholder-based one,
or that it would be rapidly transformed from a government-coordinated
economy into a liberal market one. Even its incremental moves towards
financial deregulation and administrative reforms were judged disappoint-
ing, partly because too much was expected of them.

Many in Japan believed that the 'Big Bang' shift to a market-based
financial system would create an efficient capital market that would allocate
funds to emerging growth industries and provide higher returns on private
financial assets. Such benefits, linked with a more competitive financial
services industry, would strengthen growth in a new post-industrial service-
oriented economy. Unfortunately, it was never clear what time scale officials had in mind to achieve such lofty goals. In any event, by the time the
Japanese government moved beyond announcing its regulatory reform
programme it was caught up in a full-blown banking crisis and became
more concerned with stability than with systemic change. Japan's 'Big
Bang' resulted in deregulation of the banking, securities and insurance
industries, and it introduced greater disclosure of information and reliance
upon legal rules. Nonetheless, Japan's move towards a market-centred

system of direct finance, based on a corporate bond market, was still slower than outsiders believed was needed. And it was clear in the face of continued low growth, deflation and mounting debt that it would take a far speedier and more radical programme of economic and political reform to achieve the broader societal goals expected from capital market efficiency.[18]

Japan's networked economy proved especially resilient to change. The perception of the corporation as a social institution wedded to a variety of constituencies remained vibrant; relational ties continued to dominate Japanese business practice. The era of market-oriented, transparent, short-term US style capitalism had not yet dawned.

There may have been a shift in the pattern of strategic and operational relations to align the performance of member firms within keiretsu groupings (as witnessed by less redistributive intervention during the course of the 1990s) but mutual support networks – designed to build formal and informal mechanisms of trust and reliability – were not totally or even substantially abandoned.[19] Traditional horizontal groupings may have become weaker by the late 1990s but other, more flexible, corporate arrangements emerged as keiretsu-based webs shifted from serving the macro-network to more market-oriented micro systems designed to advance the agendas of the specific firms involved.[20] Keiretsu groups continued their risk-sharing role. There is evidence that weaker firms increased their reliance upon group-provided debt and equity over the course of the 1990s.[21]

Other traditional legacies remained. Even in 1999, some 90 per cent of all companies surveyed by MITI still relied upon a main bank and two-thirds supported stable subcontracting. Renault's celebrated purchase of a controlling share of Nissan's stock in 1999 weakened key supplier ties in its wake, but Toyota tightened its own, specifically to weaken the likelihood of

---

[18]   See Bruce E. Aronson, 'A Reassessment of Japan's Big Bang Financial Regulatory Reform', Institute for Monetary and Economic Studies, Discussion Paper No. 2011-E-19, Bank of Japan, August 2011.

[19]   Andreas Moerke, 'Japanese Inter-Firm Relations: On the Way Towards a Market-Oriented Structure?', in Hunter and Storz (eds.), *Institutional and Technological Change*, 75–90.

[20]   Lincoln and Gerlach, *Japan's Network Economy*, 50, 298, 373.

[21]   Katryn L. Dewenter, 'The Risk-Sharing Role of Japanese Keiretsu Business Groups: Evidence from Restructuring in the 1990s', *Japan and the World Economy* 15, no. 3 (2003): 261–74.

foreign influence in its business affairs.[22] Although reform of the board structure occurred in a maverick company like Sony, there was less evidence of the appointment of outside directors or a reduction in the size of boards in the many other Japanese firms in need of much greater discipline.

It has been suggested that new hybrid models of corporate governance emerged during the 1990s. One type paired an insider board and traditional employment practices with market finance to replace the traditional 'J model' that had formerly paired them with main bank relational finance and long-term patterns of employment. The other, embracing much younger firms outside traditional corporate groups, retained a strong bank orientation but adopted more market-oriented employment patterns.[23] Even so, corporate governance in general was so intimately bound up with other institutional arrangements that affected employment and finance, and so affected by the differing degrees to which Japanese firms were exposed to the global export market that change proved difficult to implement swiftly or without good cause. Companies that were more globally exposed tended to be more willing to accept a shift towards greater shareholder-oriented corporate governance than were those which were more embedded in domestic institutional arrangements. At the turn of the century some dominant firms – Toyota and Canon, for example – continued to acknowledge the competitive advantages that lay in their employees' commitment to their employer firms, and they were openly sceptical of the benefits that outside directors with limited industry knowledge might bring to long-term competitiveness.[24] In other words, heterogeneity in governance practices still dominated corporate Japan at the end of the 1990s.[25]

Later in the 1990s Japan's desire to project an image of an advanced country conforming to international norms had led it to enact a raft of reformist legislation, ranging from the much-hyped 'Big Bang' to the imposition of new accounting standards; it created an independent FSA and implemented revised regulations welcoming foreign financial institutions. This all suggested that the tide had turned so far as forbearance, hesitancy and resistance to change were concerned.

The results were mixed. The hope was that arms-length rules-based regulation and greater transparency would deal a blow to the insularity

[22]   Lincoln and Gerlach, *Japan's Network Economy*, 299–341.
[23]   Gregory Jackson, 'The Japanese Firm and Its Diversity', *Economy and Society* 38, no. 4 (November 2009): 606–29.
[24]   Yoshikawa and McGuire, 'Change and Continuity', 16–18.
[25]   Ibid., 18.

characteristic of corporate Japan.[26] However, regulation and supervision continued to be highly discretionary, with underlying behaviour far removed from the ideals of international regulatory standards.[27] Many 'reforms' proved superficial and were proceeded with only if they did not fundamentally undermine the foundations of the existing system.[28]

For instance, reform within the financial sector was noticeably biased towards the securities market. The FSA displayed little zeal for bank restructuring and failed to force city banks to foreclose on insolvent enterprises.[29] Worse still, the agency encouraged banks to extend even more credit to vulnerable borrowers, permitting banks to recategorize outstanding loans to assist the process.[30] Worrying too was the fact that by the end of the 1990s around one-third of total private savings was still being channelled by the postal savings system through the Fiscal Investment and Loan Programme to fund government lending institutions that lacked transparency and effective safeguards against misallocation of resources.

Overall, the gap between strong and weak firms widened during the 1990s. The slowdown in productivity went largely unabated because of the misallocation of capital and labour resources through indiscriminate extensions of bank credit. Companies that had begun to write down debt in the early 1990s continued to do so to restore their balance sheets; this affected the pace of business investment, a trend that was in evidence down to 2005. In April 1999, the Resolution and Collection Corporation had been created to purchase distressed assets (mainly NPLs) at 'fair market value' and to reconstruct troubled companies.[31] However, only during 2001–03 was attention more deliberately focused on restructuring heavily indebted companies through the Development Bank of Japan and the Industrial Revitalization Corporation (IRC).[32]

---

[26]   Amyx and Drysdale, *Japanese Governance*, 6.

[27]   Andrew Walter, 'From Developmental to Regulatory State: Japan's New Financial Regulatory System', *Pacific Review* 19, no. 4 (2006): 405–28.

[28]   Mikuni and Murphy, *Japan's Policy Trap*, 207.

[29]   Itaru Okamoto, 'The Failure of the Japanese "Big Bang": Bureaucracy-Driven Reforms and Political Intervention', *The Japanese Economy*, 33, no. 1 (Spring 2005): 69–106.

[30]   Madsen, 'What Went Wrong', 42.

[31]   See Kenneth Kang, 'The Resolution and Collection Corporation and the Market for Distressed Debt in Japan', in Callen and Ostry (eds.), *Japan's Lost Decade*, 65–79.

[32]   See below p. 170.

Despite efforts to recapitalize the banking sector and to improve the monitoring of financial practices from 1998, the pace of change remained painfully slow. The causes were endemic. The complex interlocking array of institutions and the many social and political accommodations that had epitomized the developmental state in the high-growth period had created an inherent and powerful 'institutional logic' that hindered Japan's adjustment.[33] Since the networked institutions had well developed ways of diffusing risks and responsibilities, a substantial degree of political coordination would have been required to effect rapid or substantial alterations in established practice. In truth, there was little political will to abandon Japan's distinctive brand of political economy.[34] It was never a question of simply overcoming groups with vested interests. Revelations of corruption and ineffectiveness may have undermined the legitimacy and authority of officials within the pilot agencies over the course of the 1990s, but such events were not a major trigger for reform in a country used to less than open transactions and restricted information.

The constraints were more fundamental. The reduction in the number of Japanese ministries – from 23 to 13 – and the moves taken at the turn of the century to shift the initiative for policymaking away from bureaucrats and towards the politicians[35] did little to weaken the grip that factional vested interests had upon the LDP-led government. It seemed that the impediments to economic revitalization had merely become more political than bureaucratic, given that party organization displayed little sign of abandoning its traditional constituencies, despite their acknowledged drag on the competitive economy.[36]

Japan's particular form of capitalism reflected 'tightly bundled packages of specific national resources, institutions and legacies', which made it unlikely that any one practice or institution, even if dysfunctional, could be readily changed without requiring changes in other parts of the system.[37]

---

[33]   Mark Beeson, 'The Rise and Fall (?) of the Developmental State: The Vicissitudes and Implications of East Asian Interventionism', in Linda Low (ed.), *Developmental States: Relevancy, Redundancy or Reconfiguration?* (New York: Nova Science Publishers, 2004), 29–40.

[34]   Beeson, 'Japan's Reluctant Reformers', 25–43. For fuller discussion, see Edward J. Lincoln, *Arthritic Japan: The Slow Pace of Economic Reform* (Washington, DC: Brookings Institution Press, 2001); Richard. Katz, *Japanese Phoenix: The Long Road to Economic Revival* (Armonk, NY: M. E. Sharpe, 2003).

[35]   See above p. 136.

[36]   Amyx, 'Ministry of Finance', 9.

[37]   Berger, 'Introduction', in *National Diversity and Global Capitalism*, 22.

The existing diffusion of responsibilities and the horizontal linkages between institutions made it imperative that political leaders took bold initiatives in risky directions. They stalled.[38] In decentralized Western societies, governance was open to more dissenting criticism through constant shifts in political representation and a vibrant critical press. However, in the highly politicised economy of Japan, contrary opinion was far more stifled, which ensured only a limited degree of self-correction.[39]

Beyond the banking sector, Japan faced intractable problems. By the end of the decade the gap between what the economy produced and its productive potential was too large to be easily filled by public spending. Fiscal policy continued to be stimulatory, insofar as the automatic stabilizers of increased government outlays on unemployment benefits and social security payments continued; in themselves, though, they were insufficient to produce sustained economic growth. Japan would not countenance the disruption and unemployment that would have accompanied the scale of debt deflation being pressed upon it by the USA and the West. There remained a deep-seated reluctance to weaken the economic and social safety net that had been so laboriously constructed in the past. An unwillingness to lay off regular employees, for example, coexisted with a continued willingness to bail out suppliers and to keep funds flowing to near-bankrupt firms.[40]

Towards the end of the 1990s it was clear that Japan needed higher consumption, not greater savings, stronger industrial balance sheets, and a focus on sustainable competitive business that was aimed at greater profitability rather than increased market share. Achieving such ends would have entailed a substantial shift in strategy and mindset. Instead, following compulsively on past successes, investment continued to be poured into industries that had excess capacity globally: steel, cars and semiconductors, for example. Too many politicians and bureaucrats believed that the crisis could be solved only by whatever policies could restore previous rates of growth, by how soon debt could be purged and by how quickly a return

---

[38]   Amyx, *Japan's Financial Crisis*, 226–30.

[39]   Eric L. Jones, *The Record of Global Economic Development* (Cheltenham, UK and Northampton, MA: Edward Elgar, 2002), 123.

[40]   Taggart R. Murphy, 'The Financial Crisis and the Tectonic Shifts in the US-Japan Relationship', *Asia-Pacific Journal: Japan Focus* 32, no. 2 (October 2009).

could be made to the *status quo ante*. Few questioned whether a recovery to previous levels was even remotely likely.[41]

Other developments hampered the radicalization of economic policy. Faced with declining wages and a shift to more uncertain temporary work contracts, younger workers proved reluctant to engage in conspicuous consumption. The high-growth 'baby boomers', fearful of the value and security of their pension schemes, began to spend less in retirement. Paradoxically, deflation had helped to compensate for the slow growth of real wages; householders could wait for goods to get cheaper before buying. Although consumers therefore harboured legitimate fears about the possible effect of public debt upon their economic future, they joined others (such as those in the still-successful competitive export sectors) in arguing against any hasty or turbulent change to the existing political and economic system, as this might only make matters worse.

Seemingly obvious remedies to stalled growth were problematic. For example, selling the accumulated dollar hoards that had been laboriously built up from past trading success to help finance economic and financial reconstruction threatened to appreciate the currency to the detriment of the export sector, upon which Japan still relied. In the face of deficits likely to be made worse by the fiscal demands of an ageing population, it was always easier to apply 'the narcotic of exports'[42] than it was to restructure employment practices or to fashion policies to sustain aggregate demand, such as raising benefits for the growing number of unemployed.

As we noted earlier, only the most dirigiste definitions of the developmental state had regarded state institutions as wholly distinct from the private sector in pursuit of its declared goals. State bureaucracy had never reflected a unified, single-purpose decision maker shaping markets from afar; it was rather a set of institutions that interacted with other social groups within the market. As a consequence, different agencies and ministries entertained different bureaucratic cultures and values and served different constituency bases; it sought legitimacy and support by manipulating interest groups, creating coalitions and establishing self-serving policy preferences.

We noted above that bureaucratic autonomy had diminished to some degree from the 1970s, as interest groups gained increased access to the

---

[41]   Jones, *Global Economic Development*, 121.
[42]   Murphy, 'The Financial Crisis', (October 2009).

state apparatus.[43] During the downturn of the 1990s bureaucrats and officials lost a considerable amount of public credibility. Thereafter, economic and financial policy, far from reflecting the coherent strategy of national development in former years, became increasingly ad hoc and reactionary, as different state agencies and their sectoral alliances jostled for special attention.[44]

Although key ministries were still active in shaping the direction and substance of industrial and financial reform later in the 1990s, they worked even more fastidiously to sustain their essential power bases. The Ministry of Enterprise, Trade and Industry (METI) – as MITI was renamed in 2001 – and the MOF realised that change had to be seen to be happening. They increased industrial societal group representation on policy councils (to include potential losers as well as beneficiaries of state policy) but resisted the devolution of authority to independent regulatory agencies. They remained determined to maintain some leverage over industry and to sustain the longer-term perspective rather than short-term profit maximization.[45] As Vogel sees it, the effort to reform the distinctive institutions of Japanese capitalism 'is most accurately viewed as a social and political movement rather than a rational response to Japan's actual problems'; this could reform and strengthen the role of the Prime Minister and reduce the need for networked bargaining between ministries and the LDP, as occurred in Japan in the early 1990s, whilst still permitting strong leadership to block any liberal reform it found unpalatable.[46]

Japan found it difficult to rid itself of the developmental mindset, with its emphasis upon intervention, industrial policy and suspicion of the primacy of the free market. By the end of the 1990s government and corporations were still acting to shield agents from the full blast of international competition. Although financial deregulation, budget constraints and pressure to open trade had disabled many previous levers of control over market entry – tax incentives and subsidies, for instance – many compensatory and preferential policies were retained. These included protectionist industrial policies that did not formally violate international rules and an array of self-regulation practices across industries that enabled firms to foster either self-promotion or self-protection.

---

[43]   See above pp. 38–40.
[44]   Geoffrey R. D. Underhill and Xiaoke Zhang, 'The State-Market Condominium Approach', in Boyd and Ngo, *Asian States*, 43–51.
[45]   Vogel, *Japan Remodeled*, 61–3.
[46]   Ibid., 39.

Although total factor productivity for all industries declined during the 1990s, it decreased less in the manufacturing sector than in industry as a whole. The decline was most marked in the nonmanufacturing sectors of utilities, retail, construction, property and services, the very sectors that were still being preserved.[47] As we noted earlier,[48] the BOJ, fully aware of political acquiescence towards sectors with low levels of productivity, had justified its reluctance to embrace inflation targeting and other anti-deflationary measures because of fears that such actions might impede much-needed industrial restructuring.[49]

Restructuring entailed layoffs and possible bankruptcies, outcomes that did not fit well with contemporary political and financial priorities. As a consequence, there was no clear link between the scale of the crisis and the subsequent reform process. The Japanese government acted slowly and cautiously with banking and deflation but aggressively in the areas of accounting and public corporation reform. Under outside pressure, it was keen to act in technocratic areas such as finance, accounting and antitrust but less interested in the protected areas of labour, pensions and retail.[50] The confidence of officials in interventionist industrial policy may have waned but they did not have the capacity to invoke a more liberal model in its place. Excess capacity could have been tackled in the traditional way – that is, coordinated reductions in capacity through recession cartels – or firms could have been allowed to fail. As it was, 'the Japanese government did neither ... leaving the problem of excess capacity to fester.'[51]

There were other constraints. Because of Japan's long-standing emphasis upon job security rather than income security, Japanese workers had come to depend upon continued employment in their current firm. This had increased pressure upon the authorities to keep 'zombie' firms – with low levels of productivity – alive during economic downturns in order to preserve the social safety net for core workers, even though this frequently meant sacrificing efficiency for stability. As we shall see below, during the 1990s the majority of manufacturing firms were disinclined to dismiss core employees even in bad times and were content to use low-wage irregular

---

[47] Tatsuya Kimura and Martin Schulz, 'Industry in Japan: Structural Change, Productivity, and Chances for Growth', *The Japanese Economy* 32, no. 1 (2004): 5–44.
[48] See above pp. 130–32.
[49] Compare p. 87 above.
[50] Vogel, *Japan Remodeled*, 112.
[51] Ibid., 35.

employees in periods of economic uptake. With both management and labour fearful of creative destruction, and with seniority wages, pension regulations and the unemployment system structured to reward those who stayed with one job, growth-enhancing reform was always likely to be delayed.

Scandinavia provided a telling contrast. There, a system of 'flexicurity' developed during the 1990s; this provided displaced workers with generous unemployment compensation, health and pension plans, and assistance in finding other work when jobs were lost through necessary restructuring. There was thus less pressure – compared with the situation in Japan – to sustain inefficient firms as sources of employment and security. In return, Scandinavian workers proved more willing to cooperate with structural change since, unlike their Japanese counterparts, they felt less inclined to fall back upon the security of the firm.[52]

Japan, however, faced a more endemic problem. It lacked a vibrant political grouping pressing for fundamental change. Many of the underlying structures of the developmental state remained, the institutional legacy of the past casting a long shadow over the reform process by perpetually delivering benefits to key stakeholders.[53] Even though the post-bubble years had exposed moribund uncompetitive sectors of industry and finance, and had helped to weaken public reverence for pilot agencies clearly involved in 'pork barrel' activities, reform and liberalization remained under the purview of a government bureaucracy that was still firmly embedded in Japan's conventional political economy and resistant to reforms that might threaten its privileged position. Bureaucracies had, in the past, become virtual independent fiefdoms; factional loyalties were still entrenched and there was an inherent dislike of the devolution of regulatory power.[54] The continuing institutional legacies of the developmental state ensured a wide gap between rhetoric and reality in the reform process. Too many people had a stake in the established order.

By the end of the 1990s it was difficult for the authorities to deny that policy failures had generated overinvestment, overcapacity and a protracted

---

[52] Richard. Katz, 'A Nordic Mirror: Why Structural Reform Has Proceeded Faster in Scandinavia Than in Japan', Center on Japanese Economy and Business Working Papers, No. 265, Columbia Business School, New York, 2008, available at http://academiccommons.columbia.edu/catalog/ac:100544.

[53] Beeson, 'Japan's Reluctant Reformers', 38–41.

[54] For an illuminating review of stalled reform in the agricultural sector, see Aurelia George Mulgan, *Japan's Agricultural Policy Regime* (New York: Routledge, 2006).

banking crisis, but it was not clear to them that productive growth and stability would necessarily flow from a weakening of labour-management cooperation, more liberal hiring and firing, or a substantial withdrawal of regulation and intervention. The problem was not so much that the rules of the game needed changing slightly but that any programme of fundamental reform would require the recalibration and design of ordered regulatory intervention and a major recasting of the relationship between the regulators and the regulated.[55] As a consequence, when reform was undertaken it often amounted to strategic reinforcement of discretionary rules – a form of re-regulation rather than de-regulation. The slowness to unleash competition within telecommunications provided one example. There the government did not abandon intervention, it merely 'rearranged its particular mix of interventionist policies by reinforcing critical mechanisms of control', selectively introducing competition in specific markets whilst simultaneously ensuring that domestic firms continued to survive.[56]

Free market ideological pressure was pushing Japan towards re-examining former practices; however, the country had not devised alternative market-based reforms nor was it eager to disturb existing producer and bureaucratic interests. An enduring difficulty was that 'social-policy-oriented … economic regulation' had in the past fostered 'equity in economic outcomes', compensating in part for the absence of extensive income redistribution by an organized welfare state.[57] It was therefore never likely to be hastily abandoned, particularly when there was deep scepticism among the ruling elite over the costs and benefits of liberalization, privatization and deregulation.

The weakening of 'administrative guidance' had also created a regulatory void that trade associations eagerly and self-interestedly filled. In former years, 'strategic' industries would have been protected and supported, even at the expense of other sectors. During the high-growth years, a competitive market environment had been sustained between and within key exporting sectors open to international competition. However, by the later 1990s a

[55]　Vogel, *Japan Remodeled*, 36–8.

[56]　Steven K. Vogel, *Freer Markets, More Rules: Regulatory Reform in Advanced Industrial Countries* (Ithaca: Cornell University Press, 1996), 207.

[57]　Lonny E. Carlile and Mark C. Tilton (eds.), *Is Japan Really Changing its Ways? Regulatory Reform and the Japanese Economy* (Washington, DC: Brookings Institution Press, 1998), 6.

small number of key sectors could no longer serve the interests of increasingly independent industrial groupings whose energetic and successful members were unwilling to protect economic laggards.

Industry began to demand greater self-determination. The 'embedded mercantilism' of earlier decades slowly gave way to a form of 'permeable insulation' aimed at preserving industrial promotion or protection in a new post-developmental regime. This incorporated a less inclusive, less coherent and less binding set of arrangements but one still fashioned to enable particular industrial sectors to stave off, or at least control, the pace of enforced change.[58]

The pervasiveness of self-regulatory activity within trade associations meant that the mere removal of statutory or codified rules was not likely to guarantee freer competitive activity within the private sector. Deregulation and recession in the 1990s led Japanese trade associations to evolve important regulatory functions of their own, setting the rules of trade for their industries and reducing domestic competition for the sake of strength in overseas markets. Such self-regulation nullified any government efforts to open markets further. It also enhanced Japan's bifurcated economy by widening the gap between globally competitive and low-productivity inefficient sectors.[59]

Few industry spokesmen were willing to articulate an agenda for reform that threatened beneficial relationships with government ministers. Towards the turn of the century industry associations argued strongly in favour of protecting potential losers from the reform process. Not even the most powerful industrial federation – the Japan Business Federation, a 2002 merger of the Federation of Economic Organizations (Keidanren) and the Japan Federation of Employers' Association (Nikkeiren) – could stifle dissenting views among energy and finance interests and between large and small company members over regulatory reform. Competitive export players in autos, electronics and steel also remained ambivalent about deregulation; they were reluctant to press reform at the expense of weaker protected sectors.[60] The LDP still courted the support of the protected domestic

---

[58] Ulrike Schaede and William W. Grimes, 'Introduction: The Emergence of Permeable Insulation', *The Japanese Economy* 28, no. 4 (July–August 2000): 3–17.

[59] For fuller discussion see Ulrike Schaede and William W. Grimes (eds.), *Japan's Managed Globalization: Adapting to the Twenty-First Century* (Armonk, NY: M. E. Sharpe, 2003).

[60] Vogel, *Japan Remodeled*, 52–8.

sectors, despite electoral system changes in 1994 which gave parties greater opportunities to divide along policy lines.

Consumers also valued social stability over economic efficiency; by and large they continued to sympathise with farmers and retailers. Consumer self-sacrifice, price cartels and the absence of cheaper imported products had all been rooted in the post-war struggle for national economic strength. Though such stoicism was clearly on the wane even by the 1970s, it was more easily invoked towards the close of the century, amidst fears of what deregulation might do to the supplies of food and other necessities. The contrast often drawn between the strong manufacturing export sector and the weaker politicised domestic sector, notes Vogel, 'misjudges the policy preferences of societal actors ... and it misinterprets how these preferences are aggregated in the political arena.'[61]

Moreover, Japan remained curiously ambivalent about the potential for technological improvement. As we noted earlier, after 1950 the productivity gap between Japan and the USA narrowed; it converged to about 80 per cent of US per capita income by 1985, but progress was much slower after 1990. It was ironic that even though state-led development had helped Japan to diffuse technologies with low transaction costs during the high-growth period, the subsequent underdevelopment of the transaction service sector restricted maturing Japan from developing radical innovations and transforming its domestic market in later decades.

Expenditure on R&D had stopped growing during the early 1990s and the speed of diffusion of new technologies slowed, particularly in computers and the use of the Internet. This helped to propagate shocks and to render their effects more long lasting.[62] The past again cast a long shadow. The marginal improvements in competitiveness achieved in earlier decades – through process innovation and incremental product differentiation – had masked Japan's relative lag in basic research. Its emphasis upon firm-specific knowledge, its relative neglect until the mid-1990s of industry-science linkages designed to encourage the commercialization of scientific advance, and the low proportion of venture capital devoted to high-tech sectors, compared with the OECD average, contributed to the slowing of total factor productivity and the efficiency of R&D spending over the course of the 1990s, especially in the services sector.[63] Venture capital required a

---

[61]   Ibid., 51.

[62]   Comin, 'An Exploration of the Japanese Slowdown', 376, 379–82.

[63]   That is not to say that R&D and technological advance had been neglected in the past. During 1976–79 MITI had promoted private R&D via technological

decentralized securities market to spur indigenous innovation. Japan had excelled instead in a bank-based financial system geared to funding large firms using known technologies.

Whereas the USA benefited from a surge in IT investment after 1995, and associated improvements in productivity, such sectoral investment fell in Japan. It was argued that Japanese private businesses were more attracted by the incentives provided by government public works spending than by the risks of innovative investment.[64] New IT technology, moreover, posed special problems. It threatened disruptive change, novelty and random progress. It could disturb intimate human networks within a corporate culture that had long emphasized technological improvement through 'learning by doing' and total quality management in an integrated industrial system.[65]

Competing and contradictory forces were at work. On the one hand, the wealth-creating and technologically sophisticated industries upon which future development depended were increasingly using diffused networks of independent producers that neither required nor were responsive to old-style interventionist state-directed strategies. On the other hand, stability and success had decreased the appetite for risk, even within many high-tech companies that continued to rely on support programmes which had worked in the past.[66] After the telecommunications sector was liberalized in 1985, with the privatization of the Nippon Telegraph and Telephone Corporation,

---

research associations, the most visible being the Technology Research Association for Very Large Scale Integrated Circuits (VSLI), which involved five computer producers (Fujitsu, Hitachi, Mitsubishi Electric, NEC and Toshiba). They were charged with developing high-speed semiconductors for new domestically produced computers. Other research projects followed; however, although the VSLI initiative was generally successful, subsequent consortia were not. MITI was not always successful in choosing which technologies to support, and turf wars broke out between the private companies, MITI and other government agencies. See Callon, *Divided Sun*; Daniel Okimoto, Takuo Sugano and Franklin B. Weinstein, *Competitive Edge: The Semiconductor Industry in the U.S. and Japan* (Stanford: Stanford University Press 1984).

[64] See above pp. 110.

[65] Adams et al., *Accelerating Japan's Economic Growth*, 63–9.

[66] There were positive signs of change by the turn of the century. Existing legislation was revised to help create a supportive environment for new businesses. The Basic Law on Small and Medium-Sized Enterprises, 1999; New Business Creation Promotion Law, 1999; and the Industrial Revitalization Law, 1999 refer. In March 2001 an 'e-Japan Priority Policy Programme' was inaugurated to expand the information and communication network and to promote e-commerce.

the government allowed NTT and its group of companies to dominate the market, even though their information and communications technology lagged significantly behind the needs of an Internet-based information age.[67]

Japan was the second largest IT producer in the world in 1997. IT capital deepening is estimated to have contributed three-quarters of a percentage point a year to labour productivity growth during 1996–99, compared with a zero contribution during the previous half-decade. Nonetheless, Japan's IT usage (including Internet penetration and e-commerce) at the turn of the century lagged behind that of the UK and the USA. In Japan there was a tendency for IT investment to be targeted at improving the efficiency of existing operations and transactions, rather than seeking to transform corporate structure and activity.[68]

The slowdown in productivity growth during the 1990s encouraged a belief within government that Japan's potential growth rate had declined and could be corrected only through fundamental structural reform. Labour inputs to growth, it was argued, had fallen because of a reduction in the overall labour force and lower working hours. Declining factor productivity had reduced returns on capital, which in turn restrained corporate investment. Urgent reforms were needed, declared the 1998 *Economic Survey of Japan*, 'to effect a transition to a market-mechanism and free competition based on an economic and enterprise system with equality of opportunity, self-responsibility, information disclosure, and transparent rules.'[69]

Such developments, though welcome, were not in themselves sufficient for the task. Total factor productivity is highly procyclical. Lacklustre performance can be the *result* of stagnation rather than a fundamental cause of it. Rising unemployment and an increase in bankruptcies and insolvencies over the period from the 1990s to 2002–03 reflected inadequate factor utilization. The Japanese recession, in other words, was affected less by supply-side constraints than by insufficient aggregate demand; this is why deregulation, 'Big Bang' and administrative reforms, though welcome, failed to deliver substantive economic improvement.

---

[67]   Adams et al., *Accelerating Japan's Economic Growth*, 71–4. See above pp. 41–2.

[68]   Tim Callen and Takashi Nagaoka, 'Structural Reforms, Information Technology, and Medium-Term Growth Prospects', in Callen and Ostry, *Japan's Lost Decade*, 99–103.

[69]   FY 1998 Economic Survey of Japan, 144, cited in Yoshikawa, *Japan's Lost Decade*, 193. Hayashi and Prescott forcibly press the case that stagnation in 1990s Japan was more the result of falling total factor productivity than of low demand or a financial crisis. See above pp. 89–90.

It is notable that when Japanese productivity growth slowed, inflation did not accelerate (contrary to normal expectations). Measured by the consumer price index it averaged only 0.5 per cent during 1990–2004 and -0.5 per cent in the half-decade after 1998. The distortions of the balance sheets of firms, households and financial institutions, following the deflation of stock and land prices after 1990, had so weakened demand that even though the potential growth rate of the economy was being inhibited by problems of resource allocation, supply-side reform was itself continually hobbled by the unravelling of the bubble economy. Overall weak levels of demand perpetuated deflation and decline, and acted as a barrier to structural adjustments.[70]

By the end of the 1990s Japan had reached the limits of conventional macroeconomic policies. Lower interest rates had failed to stimulate the economy because widespread excess capacity had made private investment insensitive to interest rate changes; cutting taxes had not stimulated spending to any substantial extent because workers had become increasingly concerned about job security and future pension and medical benefits. The *expectation* of deflation had proved as debilitating as deflation itself. Even if the money base had been expanded further, it is likely that banks would have remained reluctant to increase investment loans because the proportion of nonperforming debt in their portfolios was growing as a result of prolonged economic stagnation.[71]

[70]   Kunio Okina and Shigenori Shiratsuka, 'Asset Price Fluctuations, Structural Adjustments, and Sustained Economic Growth: Lessons from Japan's Experience Since the Late 1980s', Special issue, *Monetary and Economic Studies* 22, no. 1 (2004): 143–6.
[71]   Naoyuki Yoshino and Eisuke Sakakibara, 'The Current State of the Japanese Economy and Remedies', *Asian Economic Papers* 1, no. 2 (2002): 110–26.

9. Recession, stagnation and the labour market: continuity and change in the 1990s

There was perhaps no clearer indication of the coexistence of continuity and change in Japan than that provided by shifts in labour market and employment practices over the course of the 1990s. Recession and stagnation had prompted calls from within and outside Japan for the country to reassess the value and effectiveness of core elements of its high-growth political economy. Their continued existence was deemed to be a fundamental reason for institutional sclerosis and inadequate policy response.

With low growth and lagging investment, Japan's much-vaunted 'employment system' seemed particularly ripe for change. It had long been regarded as complementary to financial and corporate governance institutions, but the weakening of main bank relationships, the partial unwinding of cross-shareholdings and the rise of foreign institutional investors seemed to pose a direct threat to stakeholder-oriented corporate governance and institutionalized employment practices.[1] Low labour mobility, seniority wages and 'lifetime' employment ran counter to the need for more flexible labour markets and cost reductions.

By 1999 established employment practices were being viewed far more critically, both within and outside of Japan, than they had been in decades past. Nissan's decision that year to reduce its workforce by 14 per cent (some 21,000 employees) was symbolic. Nippon Steel brought its six-year restructuring programme to a close in December 1999, having reduced its workforce by 45 per cent. In February 1999 the Japanese government's Economic Strategy Council recommended that employment policy should shift away from retaining workers to raising their employability in the external labour market. In the same year, the Economic White Paper cited

---

[1] Gregory Jackson, 'Employment Adjustment and Distributional Conflict in Japanese Firms', in Aoki, et al., *Corporate Governance in Japan*, 283.

employment policy as one of the 'excesses' that Japan needed to trim. And in October 1999 Nippon Keidanren (the business federation) called for employment policies that would encourage greater labour mobility. Such was the change in atmosphere that the Japan Trade Union Confederation (Rengo) called for a 'law for the protection of workers on the occasion of enterprise reorganization' to defend workers' rights upon dismissal; it also called for an overhaul of the national social welfare system to protect employees beyond firm-sponsored programmes.[2]

By the late 1990s the practice of 'lifetime employment' seemed to be an anachronistic throwback to better times and one that – in the prevailing economic climate – was strangling corporate competitiveness. Slow economic growth following the collapse of the bubble economy coincided with rising wage bills and retirement bonus payments, as workers who had joined firms during the high-growth years reached the highest levels in the wage scale and became entitled to a retirement bonus. In addition, the introduction of new accounting systems conforming to International Accounting Standards made employer commitments to retirement bonuses and pension payments liability items.[3]

Nonetheless, conventional employment practices proved highly resilient to change. Calls for Japan to abandon the long-term commitment between employers and workers (whatever its alleged benefits) had been made in decades past, but little had come of such appeals.[4] Indeed, it had been Japan's ability to respond to economic crises in earlier times without abandoning its implicit contract with workers that stiffened resistance to change during the protracted stagnation of the 1990s.[5] In the wake of the

---

[2]   Blomstrom et al., *Institutional Change*, 194–6; Susumu Watanabe, 'The Japan Model and the Future of Employment and Wage Systems', *International Labour Review* 139, no. 3 (2000): 307–33.

[3]   Watanabe, 'The Japan Model', 320.

[4]   The end of 'lifetime employment' had been announced almost every year since Abegglen referred to the practice in 1958. At the time he wrote of a 'lifetime commitment' whereby a worker would commit 'himself on entrance to the company for the remainder of his working career' and the company would agree 'not to discharge him even temporarily except in the most extreme circumstances.' See Abegglen, *The Japanese Factory*, 11.

[5]   Haruo Shimada, 'Japan's Industrial Culture and Labor-Management Relations', in Shumpei Kumon and Henry Rosovski (eds.), *The Political Economy of Japan, Vol. 3: Cultural and Social Dynamics* (Stanford: Stanford University Press, 1992), 267–91.

1970s oil shocks, for example, Japanese employers had initially renewed their commitment to employment stability, despite the decline in real GNP growth. They had reduced overtime, transferred workers within firms, inaugurated voluntary early retirement plans and cut back on fresh recruitment rather than dismiss workers. Only when matters worsened in the late 1970s did large firms downsize their regular workforce; even then it was through voluntary retirements and permanent transfers of labour.[6]

Moreover, from 1977 the government itself had acted to preserve employment stability as a key element of industrial and social harmony. It offered rebates to employers to transfer workers from declining industries to other sectors and subsidies to help them retain their existing labour force through retraining and short-term working schemes. Until 1998 employment contracts had to be either annual or of indefinite length. When the wealth effect of rising consumer demand during the bubble years prompted the expansion of productive capacity, employers hoarded labour at an aggressive rate. Even when recession struck after the bubble burst, employers resorted to conventional reductions in overtime, intra-firm labour transfers, reductions in hiring new employees and voluntary retirement schemes; they resorted to layoffs only from around 1993.[7]

With such a lingering commitment to employment stability, management during the 1990s upheld the practice of lifetime employment for their existing workforce, despite the strain that prolonged stagnation put on profits, competitiveness and viability. In the 1990s the proportion of long-tenure workers (10 years or longer) to the total number employed averaged 43 per cent in Japan, compared with 26 per cent in the USA. The 10-year job retention rates of core employees (aged 30–44, 35–39 and 40–44 with more than five years' tenure) changed little between 1977–87 and 1987–97.[8] In short, during the stagnation period of the 1990s lifetime

---

[6]   See above p. 13.

[7]   Chikako Usui and Richard A. Colignon, 'Corporate Restructuring: Converging World Pattern or Societally Specific Embeddedness?', *Sociological Quarterly* 37, no. 4 (1996): 551–78.

[8]   Moriguchi and Ono, 'Japanese Lifetime Employment'; Takao Kato, 'The End of Lifetime Employment in Japan? Evidence from National Surveys and Field Research', *Journal of the Japanese and International Economies* 15, no. 04 (2001): 489–514; Kambayashi and Kato, 'The Japanese Employment System'.

employment remained stable and robust for core employees[9] already in the system.[10]

Support for the practice did not wane significantly either. In 2002, just over half of Japanese companies were reported to be retaining both lifetime employment and seniority wages for core workers.[11] A tripartite agreement set up in December 2002 – between representatives of the government, employers and employees – stressed the need for greater labour mobility but noted that 'employers will make even greater efforts than before to maintain and secure employment. Labour will be flexible concerning working conditions when maintaining employment is at stake. The government will ... offer more support to enterprises' efforts to ensure job security.'[12] A METI survey of corporate employment systems in 2003 found continued support for lifetime employment in over 80 per cent of firms.[13] Likewise, surveys of Japanese managers and executives between 2001 and 2005 revealed their continued commitment to the job security of their core employees, despite

---

[9]   The problem of charting the resilience of lifetime employment lies partly in the absence of an agreed empirical definition of the term. See above p. 16. In our context, the core workforce refers to male regular employees in firms employing more than 500, together with male regular employees in the government sector, excluding part-time and temporary workers, executives, the self-employed and contract workers.

[10]   Ono, 'Japanese Lifetime Employment', 491–8; Kato, 'The End of Lifetime Employment'; Marcus E. Rebick, *The Japanese Employment System: Adapting to a New Economic Environment* (Oxford: Oxford University Press, 2005), 38–41. For case study evidence in the automobile, electronics, retail and construction sectors over the 1990s and during the early years of the new century, see Arjan B. Keizer, *Changes in Japanese Employment Practices: Beyond the Japanese Model* (New York: Routledge, 2010), 58–142. It should be noted, however, that although the tenure of existing full-time core employees did not shrink noticeably during the period of stagnation in the 1990s, the length of tenure varied according to the attributes of workers and firms. Much depended on how much tenure a worker had in the first place. For a group of workers, the higher the pre-existing level of tenure, the greater was the average increase in tenure. So far as women were concerned, the ratio of the 10-year retention rate of female regular employees aged 30–35 with up to five years of tenure, for example, fell from 68 per cent in 1982–92 to 43 per cent during 1992–2002. Among younger employees (20–24 and 25–29) and middle-aged employees with short tenure, the job retention rates fell noticeably over the bubble and post-bubble periods. Satoshi Shimizutani and Izumi Yokoyama, 'Has Japan's Long-Term Employment Practice Survived? Developments Since the 1990s', *Industrial and Labor Relations Review* 62, no. 3 (2009): 313–26.

[11]   Cargill and Sakamoto, *Japan Since 1980*, 239.

[12]   Keizer, *Japanese Employment Practices*, 20.

[13]   Jackson, 'Employment Adjustment', 285.

signs of greater shareholder orientation within Japanese corporations.[14]
Nippon Keidanren reinforced its commitment to lifetime employment
during the early years of the new century. As late as 2007, it declared that
'the Japanese employment system, characterized by long-term employment
and in-house labour-management relations, generally works well.'[15] Workers (both young and old) and personnel managers surveyed in 2004 demonstrated a continuing and strong commitment to employment security.
Allegations of the demise of lifetime employment were somewhat prema-
ture.[16]

The continuing and explicit commitment to lifetime employment is not
difficult to explain. Employment security had become so embedded in
Japanese society that its continuation, even in straightened times, was
judged less in terms of its direct economic returns (in firm-level efficiency,
for example) and more in terms of its social benefits.[17] The development of
Japan's post-war employment system had been an holistic one, with interlocking and mutually reinforcing elements. By the end of the high-growth
period the traditional employment system had evolved into 'a coherent
cluster of complementary employment practices', which were always more
likely – than hasty ill-conceived reforms were – to produce deliberate and
prudent responses to outside shocks.[18]

The firm as a community of managers and workers with mutual expectations had survived the recessions that occurred before the 1990s, such as

---

[14]   Katsuhito Iwai, 'What Will Become of the Japanese Corporation?', in
Hamada et al., *Miraculous Growth*, 56–7.
[15]   Keizer, *Japanese Employment Practices*, 20–21.
[16]   This may not have been without long-term cost, though. The persistence of a
rigid employment system, with its inbuilt set of obligations and commitments, has
been linked with the rise in the age people marry and the decline in the birth rate;
this is because men have become fearful that marriage, children and home duties
could conflict with job security and promotion. Keizer, *Japanese Employment
Practices*, 24–5. A survey by the Japan Institute for Labour Policy and Training in
2003 found that just over 36 per cent of firms supported the continuation of lifetime
employment, with only a minority (15 per cent) urging a fundamental review. Arjan
B. Keizer, 'Non-Regular Employment in Japan: Continued and Renewed Dualities', *Work, Employment and Society* 22, no. 3 (2008): 409.
[17]   Moriguchi and Ono, 'Japanese Lifetime Employment', 170.
[18]   Kambayashi and Kato, 'The Japanese Employment System', 25–6; Kimura
and Schulz, 'Industry in Japan', 10–16, 32–3; Yoshio Higuchi, 'Trends in Japanese
Labour Markets', in Mari Sako and Hiroki Sato (eds.), *Japanese Labour and
Management in Transition: Diversity, Flexibility and Participation* (New York:
Routledge, 1997), 27–52.

those occasioned by the two oil crises in the 1970s and the appreciation of the yen in 1985. Moreover, from the 1970s trade unions had increasingly put the goal of employment protection ahead of wage gains.[19] In addition, the decline of Shunto as a wage determining system, in favour of more local decision making, reinforced influence at the enterprise level, where guarantees of job security for prime-age men were more readily sustained. So long as strong internal linkages persisted between managers, employees and business strategy, incorporating a relatively egalitarian distribution of rewards and the possibility of internal advancement to board level, for example, the commitment to lifetime employment was strengthened and perpetuated.[20]

Such resilience came at a cost, though. Restrictions on new permanent hires and continuing economic stagnation during the 1990s raised unemployment rates among those seeking full-time employment to levels hitherto unknown. Historically, unemployment had remained low in Japan, relative to other industrialized nations, because downturns in market conditions were usually met by cutting back on overtime, absorbing labour in-house through reassignments within the firm, increasing wage flexibility (especially in the payment of bonuses) or by people (mainly women) dropping out of the labour force as they ceased looking for work.[21] Such practices, however, were insufficient to cope with the changed economic climate of the 1990s. Japan's overall unemployment rate rose more than two-and-a-half times between 1990 (2.1 per cent) and 2002 (5.4 per cent). Unemployment was particularly pronounced among females, the young and the old (60–64). Youth unemployment (in the 15–24 age group) more than doubled – from 4.3 per cent to 9.6 per cent – between 1990 and 2001, bringing it close to the weighted average for OECD countries.

The continuing commitment of large firms to regular employees during the 1990s disguised significant changes in the composition of the labour market. During periods of cyclical downturn in earlier years employers had customarily reduced part-time and temporary jobs (especially among low-wage female workers in the textile and consumer electronics industries) in order to accommodate the costs of supporting the lifetime employment system for male breadwinners.[22] With employers in the 1990s refusing to

---

[19]   See above pp. 14–15.
[20]   Jackson, 'Employment Adjustment', 306–7.
[21]   Yoshikawa, *Japan's Lost Decade*, 135–41.
[22]   Heidi Gottfried, 'Pathways to Economic Security: Gender and Nonstandard Employment in Contemporary Japan', Social Indicator Research 88, no. 1 (2008): 179–96; Hiroyuki Odagiri, *Growth Through Competition, Competition Through*

renege on existing implicit long-term employment contracts with core male workers, even during periods of prolonged stagnation, there was a marked shift towards part-time, temporary and nonregular[23] employment. As a consequence, the burden of labour market adjustment fell disproportionately upon particular groups, especially middle-aged female employees with short tenure and young workers, who constituted a convenient 'shock absorber' as recession deepened.

The number of young people (predominantly high-school graduates, females and job seekers in their early 20s) employed in non-permanent jobs because of a lack of regular employment increased dramatically over the decade, and at an increasing rate from 1994.[24] The overall share of part-time to total employment between 1975 and 2000 rose from 2.7 per cent to 10.5 per cent in manufacturing, from 5.6 per cent to 25.5 per cent in wholesale and retail, and from 2.9 per cent to 12.4 per cent in services.[25] Although, to put it another way, the turnover of core employment was much lower than the turnover of non-core employment during the 1990s, the decade saw an overall decline in the share of regular full-time work. Even though the core employment system remained largely intact, it shrank. Whereas in 1991 some 82 per cent of Japanese workers were in regular full-time employment under contracts of unspecified duration, the figure peaked in 1994 and stood at only 67 per cent in 2007.[26]

These shifts were partly rooted in the institutional architecture of the traditional Japanese employment system and proved relatively easy to countenance. A rise in part-time employment had been evident in Japan well before the recession, and would probably have continued even without deepening stagnation. However, the practice became more prominent and strategic during the 1990s, compared with what it had been in earlier

---

Growth: Strategic Management and the Economy in Japan (New York: Oxford University Press, 1992), 56; Usui and Colignon, 'Corporate Restructuring'. Differences in the elasticity of output by male employees and female employees were large and often statistically significant during the 1970s and 1980s. See Susan N. Houseman and Katharine G. Abraham, 'Female Workers as a Buffer in the Japanese Economy', *American Economic Review* 83, no. 2 (1993): 45–51.

[23]   This is distinct from the 'standard' employment of school-leavers and graduates for the duration of their career; that is, until mandatory retirement age.

[24]   Yanfei Zhou, 'The Trend Toward Nonregular Employment Among Young Workers, 1994–2003', *Japanese Economy* 36, no. 4 (2009): 105–6.

[25]   Gottfried, 'Pathways to Economic Security', 184.

[26]   Kenn Ariga and Ryosuke Okazawa, 'Labor Immobility in Japan: Its Causes and Consequences,' in Hamada et al., *Japan's Bubble*, 263–308.

decades. Firms grew increasingly reluctant to train additional personnel (even university graduates) to sustain the industrial base.[27] As a result, the proportion of employees fully incorporated into the traditional employment model declined over the decade.[28] Making greater use of a more contingent workforce proved to be a more viable option.

Rather than reduce the numbers of part-time, female and temporary workers in the face of weak demand (the 'buffer' of earlier decades), firms began to increase their number in the late 1990s in order to reduce costs. In some respects, therefore, the period witnessed not so much the abandonment of the permanent employment system as an intensification of Japan's long-standing use of a two-tier (core/peripheral) labour force designed to serve the needs of business.[29] This shift in employment practice varied across industries. In the automobile sector many firms remained strongly dependent upon regular employees to help sustain flexible working practices and job rotation. The shift towards non-standard employment spread more easily in the retail sector and even in the electronics industry, where standardization and modularization had widened the possibility of hiring nonregular workers.

Overall, therefore, there was little change in the internal labour market for regular employees during the stagnant 1990s but there was a strengthening of the duality between regular and nonregular employment, as Figure 9.1 (a and b) shows.[30]

The likelihood of job separations for core workers remained fairly stable over the decade, while the total population of workers covered by lifetime employment diminished as employers prioritized core workers at the

---

[27] Masanori Hashimoto and Yoshio Higuchi, 'Issues Facing the Japanese Labor Market', in Ito et al., *Reviving Japan's Economy*, 344.

[28] Zhou, 'The Trend Toward Nonregular Employment', 106; Moriguchi and Ono, 'Japanese Lifetime Employment', 166; Kenn Ariga, Giorgio Brunello and Yasushi Ohkusa, *Internal Labor Markets in Japan* (Cambridge: Cambridge University Press, 2000), 189–206.There were also severe legal constraints on the abuse by employers of the right to dismiss.

[29] Leon Wolff, 'The Death of Lifetime Employment in Japan?', in Nottage et al., *Corporate Governance*, 53–80.

[30] For discussion of labour market trends over the 1990s as a whole, see Rebick, *The Japanese Employment System*; and Yuji Genda and Marcus E. Rebick, 'Japanese Labour in the 1990s: Stability and Stagnation', *Oxford Review of Economic Policy* 16, no. 2 (2000): 85–102.

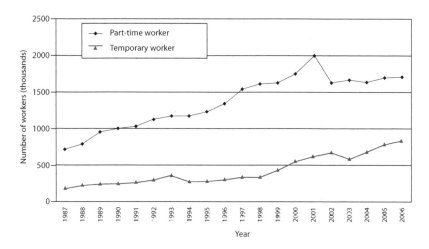

Figure 9.1a Changes in the number of regular and nonregular workers (male)

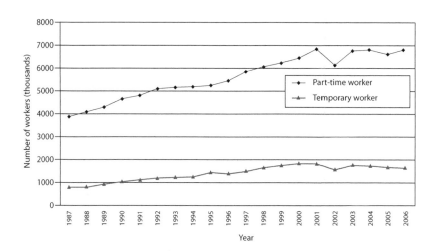

Source: Adapted from Suzuki, 'Employment Relations in Japan', 398.

Figure 9.1b Changes in the number of regular and nonregular workers (female)

expense of new hires.[31] The ratio of job offers to job applicants, regarded as a more sensitive measure of cyclical change than the unemployment rate, fell to an historic low of 0.47 in 1998.[32]

The extraordinary business climate from the early 1990s had obliged many firms to undertake drastic restructuring measures, including wage cuts, downsizing of the labour force, boosting early retirement and freezing or reducing annual wage increments. But such measures were essentially emergency reactions that would allow them to cope with two especially large age groups of employees against the background of economic recession: the near-retirement groups recruited during the high-growth years, and those who had joined firms during the bubble economy and who were now in their 30s.[33]

On the whole, firms remained reluctant to depart from traditional methods of employment adjustment. Even as late as 2002, the strategies adopted by industry to adjust personnel revealed a distinct preference for natural attrition, restrictions on hiring and voluntary retirement incentives rather than dismissals, as Table 9.1 indicates.

The 2003 METI survey referred to earlier[34] revealed that few firms resorted to outright layoffs of regular employees. Their aim of preserving their core workforce was achieved largely by reducing intake, offering incentives for older workers to leave and by shifting employment to related firms.[35]

These changes produced mixed blessings. The growing use of a contingent labour force introduced increased flexibility in the workplace without altering employment stability for regular workers and it supported cost cutting. However, it also undermined Japan's traditional strength of having a well-trained and devoted workforce committed to sustaining corporate objectives, however much outsiders regarded that as an affront to the dignity and freedom of the labour force. At the same time, the retention of traditional mid-career core workers who were subject to in-house training

---

[31]   Consider an analogy between the labour force and a bath. Water flowing into the bath represents the movement of workers into the core, while water flowing out represents workers moving out of the core. The water level is the stock of core workers. That level remains the same or decreases because little water is flowing out, and the flow of water into the bath is being choked off. Ono, 'Lifetime Employment', 23.

[32]   Yoshikawa, *Japan's Lost Decade*, 135.

[33]   Watanabe, 'The Japan Model', 328.

[34]   See above pp. 157–8.

[35]   Jackson, 'Employment Adjustment', 289–90.

Table 9.1   Strategies for personnel adjustment by industry (January–February 2002)

Percentages of firms; multiple answers

	Total	Construction	Consumer manufacturing	Machinery manufacturing	Wholesale, trade, food	Finance, insurance
Natural attrition[1]	81.6	81.0	81.5	85.0	81.3	89.9
Employment restraint[2]	76.9	82.8	78.5	81.3	77.8	77.2
Voluntary retirement invitation and early retirement preference[3]	34.2	48.3	36.9	44.9	19.6	25.3
No contract renewal for contract and part-time employees	29.7	22.4	35.4	42.1	27.1	11.4
Expansion of *shukkō* and *tenseki*[4]	26.0	46.6	18.5	30.8	29.2	24.1
Dismissal	6.9	1.7	10.8	5.6	7.6	2.5
Others	1.3	0.0	0.0	2.8	2.1	2.5

Notes:
1   Including employees reaching the age limit and leaving at personal convenience through existing systems for early retirement, *shukkō* and *tenseki*.
2   Including new graduates, mid-career hiring and short-term, seasonal and part-time employees.
3   The creation or expansion of.
4   The percentages of employees on *shukkō* were limited. In 2000, the percentages for the different age groups were as follows: 20–24: 0.23%; 25–29: 0.18%; 30–34: 0.23%; 35–44: 0.26%; 45–54: 0.35%; 55–59: 0.41%. Moreover, the percentages have been rather stable since the height of the bubble in the late 1980s.

Source: Keizer, *Changes in Japanese Employment Practices*, 45.

and bound to the firm reduced Japan's overall ability to reallocate employees with specialist skills more freely within the economy. This constraint reflected the legacy of past practice, one that had become both an output (the dominance of lifetime employment being the direct outcome of agreed norms) and an input (the consequent lack of an active labour market predisposing employers to opt for established practices that 'locked' workers and employers together in a set of mutual obligations).[36] In other words, the Japanese labour market had matured without having developed an adequate infrastructure to facilitate the efficient reallocation of workers across the corporate divide, in response to shifting demand.[37]

With fewer workers entering core full-time positions, there was more competition for the limited supply of jobs in non-core sectors. During the first half of the 1990s, Japan had been under pressure to cut costs and improve productivity, owing to the competitive strain imposed by the high real exchange rate of the yen. Lower consumption of domestically produced manufactured goods combined with increased offshore production[38] had reduced demand for workers, even in high-productivity growth sectors. It was the difficulty that non-core sectors faced in absorbing workers no longer entering lifetime employment that helped to increase unemployment and part-time/temporary employment during the lost decade.[39] This was a serious development because of the difficulty workers faced in embarking upon a regular employee track once they became trapped into atypical employment.[40]

---

[36]   Keizer, *Japanese Employment Practices*, 41.

[37]   Moriguchi and Ono, 'Japanese Lifetime Employment', 168; Kimura and Schulz, 'Industry in Japan', 33.

[38]   See above pp. 96–7.

[39]   Ariga and Okazawa, 'Labor Immobility', 264–8, 287–8.

[40]   Keizer, 'Non-Regular Employment', 413–20. The consequences were not always favourable, even to the retained labour force. A survey of human resource managers and middle managers in eight medium-sized Japanese organizations in 2003 showed that while middle managers felt relatively secure in their jobs, the nature of their work had altered; they were now faced with a greater range of tasks, longer hours, more accountability and stress, and a worsening work-life balance. Tetsuya Iida and Jonathan Morris, 'Farewell to the Salaryman? The Changing Roles and Work of Middle Managers in Japan', *International Journal of Human Resource Management* 19, no. 6 (2008): 1072–87. See also John Hassard, Jonathan Morris and Leo McCann, 'Hard Times for the Salaryman: Corporate Restructuring and Middle Managers' Working Lives', in Peter C. D. Matanle and Wim Lunsing (eds.), *Perspectives on Work, Employment and Society in Japan* (Basingstoke: Palgrave, 2006), 98–117.

Although there were more noticeable shifts in conventional practice within wage policies, reform was still muted. After 1997 Japanese firms displayed an increasing tendency to depart from the seniority wage system, a prominent characteristic of the high-growth social contract with workers, and to move towards merit and performance payments.[41] The proportion of firms that had abolished automatic annual pay rises during the previous three years had risen from under 4 per cent in 1996 to over 10 per cent in 1999, while the proportion that linked their pay systems to performance increased from 12 per cent in 1996 to 23 per cent in 2007.[42] During the post-bubble period, there had also been a noticeable rise in the number of Japanese firms using work-based wage systems in preference to age-based living-wage agreements. One trend was towards systems that provided a stable income that was based on more equal annually increasing monthly wages, with competitive incentives offered through varied biannual bonuses.

Such changes, however, represented more of a 'calibration' of the internal labour market system than the beginnings of fundamental reform. The trend towards work-based wage systems, for example, was focused more upon the managerial class in large firms, with personal factors such as age and length of service remaining almost as important as ever in the case of production and other ordinary workers.[43] Moreover, the increase in performance-related pay enabled many firms to reduce labour costs while upholding the policy of no dismissals. Likewise, when a gradual dismantling of the seniority wage system did occur, it was often regarded as the sacrifice needed to maintain job security.[44]

The accepted legitimacy of lifetime employment served to constrain change by persuading firms to change the rules of the internal labour market system rather than to challenge its existence. If anything, the intensified internationalized and competitive environment of the post-1990s put a premium upon peaceful and cooperative industrial relations and upon the

---

[41]   Jackson, 'Employment Adjustment', 285.

[42]   Kambayashi and Kato, 'The Japanese Employment System', 18–19; Marcus E. Rebick, 'Japanese Labor Markets: Can We Expect Significant Change?', in Blomstrom et al., *Japan's New Economy*, 133–6. The proportion of firms that abolished seniority wages fell to 7 per cent in 2007 but this was still higher than it had been in 1996.

[43]   Watanabe, 'The Japan Model', 324–8, 330.

[44]   Canon, for example, introduced merit payments as a way of reducing costs in order to protect lifetime employment for core workers. Cargill and Sakamoto, *Japan Since 1980*, 240.

security of employees' livelihoods. This made it less likely – rather than more likely – that Japanese firms would renounce what they regarded as important sources of their competitive strength.[45] In other words, the renewed role of nonregular employment and altered wage systems had not replaced existing practices; they were merely layered upon them.[46]

[45]   Watanabe, 'The Japan Model', 329.
[46]   Jackson, 'Employment Adjustment', 298.

10. 'Lost decades?' Japan's political economy in the new millennium

It is not our purpose here to provide a detailed macroeconomic or micro-economic analysis of Japan's economic fortunes since the turn of the century. We identify instead some of the broader changes that occurred within Japan before the dramatic turnaround in the international financial and economic climate from 2007–08 onwards to indicate the extent to which the experience of recession and stagnation during the 1990s subsequently affected the content and purpose of the country's distinctive political economy during the early years of the new millennium.

Emerging from the 'Lost Decade'

The aberration in Japan's 1990s recession had not been the behaviour of growth – the country had witnessed a series of recoveries aborted by policy errors – but rather the persistence of deflation and low aggregate demand. Japan had not been obliged during its 'lost decade' to reallocate productive resources across export sectors because prospects there had not fundamentally deteriorated.[1] The economy had not collapsed. What proved decisive was the worsening domestic economic situation from 1997, in the midst of a banking crisis, a credit crunch, a widening in the gap between actual and potential output, a curb on the effectiveness of fiscal stimulus and falling confidence.

It is arguable that by the turn of the century it was too soon to know just how long a shadow the experiences of the previous decade had cast. Nor was it clear whether the lessons of recession and stagnation would usher in fundamental reform rather than a recalibration of the country's administrative, economic and corporate activities.

Initially the signs were mixed. High real interest rates and the expectation of future deflation continued to discourage investment and consumption;

---

[1]   Posen, 'The Realities and Relevance of Japan's Great Recession', 2.

this widened the GDP gap and drove prices even lower.[2] It was as clear in the early years of the new millennium, as it had been during the unfolding of Japan's recession and stagnation in the 1990s, that even though monetary policy alone could not solve Japan's economic problems in the absence of financial and nonfinancial restructuring and altered policy priorities, monetary reflation – which was aimed at restoring balance sheets and aggregate demand – remained a crucial step towards closing the gap between the country's actual growth and its potential growth. That was even more critical because the capital position of Japanese banks remained weak during the early years of the new century, despite huge write-offs of NPLs.[3]

In 2001 the Japanese economy was still suffering from meagre real GDP growth, a record level of registered unemployment (5 per cent), protracted stagnation and continued deflation. The value of NPLs held by Japanese financial institutions in 2001 was estimated to be US$600 billion greater than had been recorded in 1998. At their peak in March 2002, NPLs of major banks (city banks, trust banks and long-term credit banks) accounted for 9.6 per cent of all outstanding loans.[4]

The economy had strengthened in early 2000, on the back of a buoyant world economy and an expanding global electronics market; however, the surge was short lived. Although a rising number of companies engaged in major restructuring plans, these frequently involved reducing the workforce through orderly retirement or restrictions on hiring, as we have already noted.[5] The fall in debt-to-equity ratios that had begun in the latter half of the 1990s continued but the ratio was still high at the turn of the century.[6] Faced with deteriorating confidence in the economy and the financial system, in mid-2001 the government called on major banks to eliminate two

---

[2]   Ito and Mishkin, 'Monetary Policy in Japan', 110–12.

[3]   Takeo Hoshi and Anil K. Kashyap, 'Solutions to Japan's Banking Problems: What Might Work and What Will Definitely Fail', in Takatoshi Ito, Hugh Patrick and David E. Weinstein (eds.), *Reviving Japan's Economy* (Cambridge, MA: MIT Press, 2005), 147–95.

[4]   Jackson, and Miyajima, 'Diversity and Change', 13.

[5]   See above pp. 163–5.

[6]   As usual, there were important sectoral differences. While the debt-to-equity ratio for the whole industrial sector was above 290 per cent in fiscal 2000, it was better in export-oriented industries – below 95 per cent in Sony and 135 per cent in Toyota – but worse in lagging nonmanufacturing sectors, especially the construction sector (over 1,200 per cent for general contractor Kajima Corporation). International Monetary Fund, Japan: Selected Issues: IMF Country Report No. 04/247 (Washington, DC: International Monetary Fund, 2004), 85.

categories of NPLs – loans to bankrupt companies and loans to near-bankrupt companies – over a two-year period.

During 2001 the FSA had obliged banks to reclassify loans to indicate more clearly where bad debts lay. The banks themselves were subjected to stringent inspection, especially over the quality of their lending practices. The aim was to remove half of their NPLs within one year and to halve the ratio of all NPLs held by the major banks by March 2005. The recapitalization and restructuring of the Resona Bank in 2003 also seemed to signal a determination to resolve the problems of bad debt and to forestall a deeper banking crisis.[7] In April 2003 the government established the Industrial Revitalization Corporation of Japan (IRCJ) to promote the restructuring of troubled but viable firms by purchasing their loans from secondary banks.[8]

Reorganization of the banking system proceeded. Most of the banks that had failed and been nationalized since 1998 were reprivatized. In March 2000 the Long-Term Credit Bank was sold to a consortium of foreign investors, and, in September 2000, ownership of the Nippon Credit Bank was transferred to a domestic consortium. Both banks received injections of public capital and were cleared of most of their bad debts. Following the example of Mizuho, a bank holding company that united three of Japan's largest banks (the Industrial Bank of Japan, the Dai-Ichi Kango Bank and the Fuji Bank) in October 2000, two other organizations (UFJ and Mitsubishi Tokyo) opted for a holding structure; meanwhile the Sumitomo and Sakura banks engaged in a full-scale merger.[9] In June 2001, an ambitious blueprint for reform – Structural Reform of the Japanese Economy: Basic Policies for Macroeconomic Management – was approved in cabinet. This promised a resolution of the NPLs problem, extended privatization of public and semi-public institutions, extra support for business start-ups, efforts to encourage greater investment in capital markets rather than in savings in banks, fiscal reform, and a strengthening of welfare and insurance.

Reassuring though these various developments were, the faltering policies of the BOJ continued to cause concern. Believing the economic

---

[7]   Resona, Japan's fifth largest bank at the time, had a capital adequacy ratio (its capital divided by its assets, weighted by risk) of only 2.07. This was half of that required for a domestically operating bank and a quarter of the 8 per cent required by banks operating internationally. The government organized a bailout of 2 trillion yen, ending up owning more than half of the bank's equity.

[8]   Fuji and Kawai, 'Lessons from Japan's Banking Crisis', 7.

[9]   Ibid., 77.

recovery of 2000 was stronger and more sustained than it turned out to be and that deflationary concerns had abated, the BOJ, to the consternation of outside observers, abandoned the zero interest rate policy it had adopted in February–March 1999.[10] In August 2000 it promptly raised rates in the midst of ongoing deflation. Japan promptly fell into recession. Real GDP grew by only 0.16 per cent in 2001 and by 0.26 per cent in 2002; in each year the rate of core consumer price *deflation* was almost 1 per cent.[11] In the USA per capita GDP had risen by 22 per cent over the period from 1991 to 2002, but by only 7 per cent in Japan during the same period. As a consequence, the per capita income gap between Japan and the USA in 2002 was larger than it had been in 1980.[12]

Faced with a sluggish economy, triggered in part by the burst of the global IT bubble, the BOJ was forced to reverse policy in March 2001 and once again lowered the interest rate to zero. Although the BOJ now claimed that it would not reverse the zero interest rate policy until deflation was over and unlikely to return, it still refused to nominate a specific price-level target. Its management of expectations fell far short of what the nervous economic climate required. The BOJ remained convinced, as it had been in the 1990s, that deflation was beneficial because it was driven by deregulation, imports and technology, and it remained sceptical of any efforts to raise inflationary expectations. Its rhetoric convinced the markets that policy would swiftly be reversed, as it had been in the past, should the BOJ judge it to be necessary.

From September 2002 the BOJ engaged in an unprecedented bailout of the banking system. It bought up the corporate shares of banks; this immediately increased the money base, as bank current accounts with the BOJ rose. However, it still refused to commit to any aggressive printing of yen or to buying yen-denominated assets.[13] Moreover, much of the expanded money supply stayed within the banking system. Banks were still

---

[10] Governor Hayami had considered the zero rate policy to be an emergency measure only; its aim was to help banks and corporations pay off bubble-inflated loans.

[11] Obstfeld, 'Time of Troubles', 60.

[12] Hamada et al., *Japan's Bubble*, 1.

[13] Adam S. Posen, 'Deflation and the Bank of Japan', *The Japan Times*, 23 September 2002.

unwilling to lend and firms unwilling to borrow. Quantitative easing had not diminished expectations that deflation was likely to persist.[14]

Matters improved somewhat from 2003. The replacement of Hayami with Governor Fukui in March 2003 coincided with a more explicit indication that zero interest rates would continue until inflation was clearly above zero; once again, though, there was no commitment to precise numbers. The BOJ engaged in much greater – and unconventional – monetary expansion, and it continued to do so down to 2005–06. It did this by raising, in stages, the current account (reserves) of commercial banks at the BOJ and purchasing long-term government bonds. Although this quantitative easing helped to reduce uncertainty and instability within financial markets, the subsequent growth in bank liquidity came at a time when banks were already harbouring excess reserves; what was needed was a turnaround in corporate and consumer confidence.

The additional liquidity did little to encourage troubled banks to extend additional credit.[15] Moreover, engaging in monetary easing by increasing the reserves that banks held at the BOJ did not increase the amount of money held by the public. The money supply multiplier declined because the public continued to exercise a preference for cash. With financial institutions holding more in reserve, relative to their lending, the BOJ was effectively 'steering the economy with a remote control from a distance.'[16]

The institutional changes adopted by the Koizumi administration from April 2001 are customarily judged to have signalled the turning point in Japan's economic fortunes. It had been Prime Minister Koizumi who had pressured the BOJ, despite its nominal independence, to adopt a more aggressive monetary policy to fight deflation. Under the premier's prompting, from 2002 the newly appointed head of the FSA, Heizo Takenaka, pressed banks to tackle the problem of NPLs with more vigour and to accept mergers and foreign acquisitions within their own ranks. A limit on the amount of bank deposits subject to government guarantee was formally instituted in 2005; this was 10 years after the idea was mooted.

With Japan having failed to transform telecommunications from a switched network system to the Internet access system in the 1990s,

---

[14]   Kunio Okina and Shigenori Shiratsuka, 'Policy Commitment and Expectation Formation: Japan's Experience Under Zero Interest Rates', *North American Journal of Economics and Finance*, no. 1 (2004): 75–100.

[15]   Obstfeld, 'Time of Troubles', 60.

[16]   Koichi Hamada, 'Policy Making in Deflationary Japan', *Japanese Economic Review* 55, no. 3 (2004): 235.

strategic measures were introduced to promote investment in information technology to help transform Japan into a 'knowledge-emergent society'.[17] Privatization of the postal savings system and other government financial institutions, though initiated as a policy objective under the previous Hashimoto government, finally passed into law in 2005. This effort to direct greater funds into the private economy and to break the traditional and often politically motivated influence of government in the intermediation of financial resources seemed, above all else, to signal a determined break with the past. And it was Koizumi who had worked assiduously to weaken factional power-broking within the LDP, increasing his personal influence in policymaking. He was committed to structural change and fiscal consolidation, especially public works spending, even at the expense of the LDP's vested interests. Koizumi's push for economic modernization through market-oriented reform, free of the worst excesses of political patronage and obfuscation, attracted the voting public, who delivered electoral victory to the LDP and its coalition partner in September 2005 after the Prime Minister called a snap election to outdo those parliamentarians opposed to his plans for post office privatization.

Until 2003 the Japanese economy had performed disappointingly after the growth spurt at the turn of the century. For years Japan had shouldered the cost of below-potential growth bequeathed by continued deflation, uncertainty and inadequate aggregate demand. Real as distinct from nominal interest rates remained high because of falling prices. At the end of 2003 the consumer price index was around 4 per cent lower than its peak in 1997. Measured by nominal GDP, the Japanese economy was estimated to be about 4 per cent smaller in 2003 than it was in 1997. Unemployment continued to rise to levels hitherto unknown; meanwhile, by 2003 the percentage growth rate of GDP had barely reached the level achieved in 1995. As the economy shrank, so did tax revenues. Deflation moreover had increased the real burden of nominally contracted debt held by government and by corporations.

Nevertheless, Japan's economic situation improved noticeably towards the middle of the decade, as Table 10.1 below indicates. A low real exchange rate aided a strong expansion in exports from 2003, especially to the USA and China (which increasingly demanded import components from Japan: the demand shock that Japan so badly needed). From 2003 to 2006 the average annual growth rate of real GDP in Japan (2.3 per cent) matched that achieved by the European Union during the same period and

---

[17] Adams et al., *Accelerating Japan's Economic Growth*, 74–82.

surpassed Japan's cyclical expansions of the late 1960s.[18] The number of new defaulting companies declined. A major write-off of bad loans by banks and the repayment of loans by borrowing firms resulted in a significant reduction in the corporate sector's debt.[19] By the end of September 2005 the ratio of NPLs at major banks had fallen from a peak of 8.5 per cent in 2002 to below 2.5 per cent. In 2005 the ratio of company profits to sales reached the peak levels seen in the late 1980s, while capacity utilization rates returned to their 1980–89 average range. Mergers across keiretsu boundaries were more commonplace than in the 1990s.[20] Joint ventures between Japanese companies and foreign firms – and even foreign ownership of formerly Japanese firms – were also more evident. Foreign ownership of company shares accounted for almost a quarter (23.7 per cent) of all stocks in Japan in 2004. Corporations at last began to reverse their preference for paying down debt and began to borrow again from 2005, spurred by the prospect of rising exports to China and southeast Asia.[21]

Weary critics of Japan's penchant for muddling through could not deny that the incremental reforms in financial regulation, corporate law and banking policy that had followed in the wake of the banking crisis and stagnation in the late 1990s had set new standards of behaviour and practice. Schaede in particular is in little doubt that the crisis of the late 1990s had a searing effect upon the corporate sector. Schaede argues that large firms underwent a dramatic and irreversible period of change and renewal from 2002. Business strategy shifted from the mass production of high-quality standardized goods (perfectly rational in 'Old Japan' where the traditional focus had been upon sales growth) towards new differentiated products in core areas; these were produced in a leaner, more competitive and more profit-oriented environment.

The tipping point of the late 1990s, it is further argued, demonstrated that 'an industrial structure geared to stability and security no longer matched reality.'[22] Large (predominantly exporting) manufacturing firms were starting to embrace competition in the market place. They had rejected the

---

[18]   Yoshikawa, *Japan's Lost Decade*, 220.

[19]   Fukao, 'Financial Crisis', 274.

[20]   Daniel Citrin and Alexander Wolfson, 'Japan's BACK! After Its Lost Decade, Japan's Economy is Set On a Recovery Path', *Finance and Development* 43, no. 2 (2006): 24–7.

[21]   Koo, *The Holy Grail*, 39.

[22]   Ulrike Schaede, *Choose and Focus: Japanese Business Strategies for the 21st Century* (Ithaca: Cornell University Press, 2008), 18, 254.

Table 10.1   The Japanese economy emerging from the lost decade

	1992	1993	1994	1995	1996	1997	1998	1999	2000	2001	2002	2003	2004	2005
GDP growth rate (% p.a.)	1.0	0.2	1.5	1.9	2.6	1.4	-1.9	-0.1	2.9	0.4	0.1	1.8	2.3	2.6
Unemployment rate (% of labour force)	2.2	2.5	2.9	3.1	3.4	3.4	4.1	4.7	4.7	5.0	5.4	5.3	4.7	4.4
Consumer price index (% change p.a.)	1.7	1.3	0.7	-0.1	0.1	1.7	0.7	-0.3	-0.7	-0.7	-0.9	-0.3	0.0	-0.3
Earnings (% change p.a.)	2.2	1.9	2.3	2.1	1.9	1.5	-0.2	0.2	0.3	-0.6	-1.7	0.0	-0.1	0.7
Deficit (% of GDP)	-1.7	-4.6	-5.7	-6.6	-6.8	-5.6	-6.9	-8.3	-8.0	-6.2	-7.7	-7.4	-6.2	-6.1
Current account (US$ billion)	112.5	131.9	130.4	110.0	64.7	97.4	119.0	115.2	119.3	88.6	112.0	136.6	171.2	167.5
Investment to GDP ratio (%)	28.9	28.0	27.5	27.2	27.8	27.1	25.7	25.7	25.2	24.9	23.6	23.3	23.0	23.3
IT investment to GDP ratio (%)	2.3	2.2	2.3	2.7	3.2	3.2	3.2	3.4	3.7	4.0	3.9	3.9	4.0	4.1

Source: Adams et al., *Accelerating Growth*, 10.

post-war tradition of socializing risk and had embarked upon more market-oriented relationships with suppliers, banks and employees in order to become focused, innovative competitors. Since deregulation had long since reduced the role of the main banks as the principal source of corporate finance, firms were now able to choose the bank with which to conduct financial business. They were also able to alter their employment contracts in the pursuit of flexibility and to shed non-core secondary or unprofitable businesses; and they could at times create, through restructuring, new, large entities that cut across existing keiretsu boundaries.

According to Schaede, it was the shift from informal regulation to legal, rules-based procedures, the pressure for greater transparency and account-ability, and the need to sustain cost competitiveness following upon the late 1990s economic stagnation that underpinned such transformative activities between 2002 and 2006. For example, a revision in the Labour Standards Law in 2004 fixed the maximum duration of an employee's part-time contract to three years. This 'reduced the fear of hiring' and strengthened the move within firms towards greater employment flexibility, which 'increased employment options for job seekers.'[23] Schaede suggests that, after the 1990s, the 'Japanese model' turned out to be more selective and differentiated, subject to continuous redefinition. Companies proved more discriminating in the nature and extent of their relationships with workers, banks and other firms.[24]

So far as corporate governance is concerned, however, the evidence points to a far more gradual transformation than the above might suggest.[25] Innovations in corporate governance were not linear or straightforward. Diverse systems emerged in the aftermath of the long recession. Even though the spread of foreign institutional investors, from the USA and the UK in particular, had strengthened the prospect of change in institutional outlook,[26] many Japanese firms retained traditional corporate practices.

---

[23]   Ibid., 190, 198.

[24]   Vogel, *Japan Remodeled*, 220.

[25]   Anderson, 'Introduction: Japan's Gradual Transformation in Corporate Gov-ernance', in Nottage, et al., *Corporate Governance*, 1–20.

[26]   Foreign ownership as a percentage of total market capitalization at the Tokyo Stock Exchange increased from 5.3 per cent in March 1987 to 28 per cent in March 2007. Schaede, *Choose and Focus*, 110–11. Foreign investors acquired dominant holdings in Nissan and Mitsubishi Motors as well as in the bankrupt Long-Term Credit Bank of Japan.

Toyota and Canon, for example, stressed the continuing importance of firms as communities of employees rather than shareholders and the value of 'insider-dominated' board structures as sources of competitive strength.[27]

Despite changes in company law that permitted, for example, the use of more outside directors, corporate board structures based on an executive committee, and greater ease in facilitating mergers and acquisitions, including hostile takeovers, the direct effects of such legal changes upon corporate behaviour proved to be less far-reaching than was anticipated. Japan's stakeholder-based corporate governance practices remained more prominent than did any shift towards shareholder value maximization. Hostile takeovers remained an anathema; corporations tended to adopt only those changes that fitted with existing incentives and institutions.[28]

Caucus politicians within government, aware that further substantial industrial restructuring threatened to stretch the already inadequate social welfare system at a time when unemployment had already risen to unprecedented levels, continued to modify the pace of reform. By curbing public investment, the Koizumi administration certainly put an end to expansionary fiscal policy from 2001. Nonetheless, during 2002–04 annual deficits were the second largest in history. Public investment may have been cut, but more than 50 trillion yen worth of taxpayers' money was used to tackle bad loans in banking, arguably a change in the role of public finance rather than an outright rejection of its utility.[29] The neoliberal flurries of the Koizumi administration had resulted in a realignment rather than an overthrow of Japanese developmental capitalism, a reinforcement of the goal of economic nationalism through strategic planning and cooperation among the principal economic agents but often incorporating a hefty dose of discretion when it came to the speed and content of altered practice.[30]

---

[27] Toru Yoshikawa, Lai Si Tsui-Auch and Jean McGuire, 'Corporate Governance Reform as Institutional Innovation: The Case of Japan,' *Organization Science* 18, no. 6 (2007): 973–88.

[28] For evidence, see Hugh D. Whittaker and Simon Deakin (eds.), *Corporate Governance and Managerial Reform in Japan* (New York: Oxford University Press, 2009).

[29] Yoshikawa, 'What Have We Learned'.

[30] Ulrike Schaede and William W. Grimes (eds.), 'Permeable Insulation and Japan's Managed Globalization', in Ulrike Schaede and William W. Grimes, (eds.), *Japan's Managed Globalization: Adapting to the Twenty-First Century*, (Armonk, NY: M. E. Sharpe, 2003), 243–54;.Vogel, *Japan Remodeled*, 205–7.

The Legacy of Export-led Development

It was fortunate for Japan that, from the turn of the new millennium, it possessed companies still able to compete successfully in international markets, especially in motor vehicles, semiconductors, plastics, organic chemicals, and scientific, optical and electrical apparatuses. Total trade volumes in US dollars had grown continuously over the 20 years since 1986, though the growth of both exports and imports slowed during the second half of the 1990s, at the time of the East Asian financial crisis. Nonetheless, Japanese export competitiveness had remained sufficient to keep the current account balance steadily in surplus throughout those two decades.[31]

The international economy presumed that market forces alone would push Japan towards a greater expansion of its domestic economy with less reliance upon exports. However, geopolitics had always been a dominant influence upon the context and direction of Japanese economic policy throughout the post-war period. With the collapse of the Soviet Union in 1991, the Cold War logic that had cemented Japanese/US military-economic relationships had fractured. Thereafter, though, neither the USA nor Japan was prepared to sever the political-economic ties of the Cold War era. Japan continued to benefit from privileged access to the US market and to deploy protectionist mercantilism at home because it remained an important political and military satellite of the USA in East Asia.[32] It remained as willing as ever to support US financial hegemony. Japanese power holders 'continued to display ambivalence about the transforming power of capitalist relations; they remained unwilling to turn over decisions about the direction of the economy to markets they could not control and did not trust.'[33]

Japan's economic recovery between 2004 and 2007 had been underpinned by growth in exports, aided by a significant fall in the real value of the yen. For decades, though, Japan had neglected to address the fundamental problems of flagging demand and low productivity, especially in services and manufacturing for domestic consumption. Even when Japan's successful exporters had been earning substantial profits in the immediate past,

---

[31]   Adams et al., *Accelerating Growth*, 13.

[32]   Chalmers A. Johnson, 'Economic Crisis in East Asia: The Clash of Capitalism,' *Cambridge Journal of Economics* 22, no. 6 (1998): 653–61; Johnson, 'Japanese "Capitalism" Revisited', 64–66.

[33]   R. Taggart Murphy, 'A Loyal Retainer?', 15.

increasing capital investment in cars, machine tools and electronics in particular, they had proved reluctant to expand wages. For many years, consumption had been supported by households running down their savings. The shrinking working-age population, the increasing reliance by corporations upon lower-paid contract workers, and the growing uncertainty among the ageing population about the future of public finances served thereafter to curb domestic demand and, with it, potential growth. Anaemic domestic consumption, however, meant that even moderate recovery remained heavily dependent upon export growth.

Japan's exposure to the substantial decline in export demand, following the international financial crisis in 2007–08, revealed how dependent the country was upon external developments over which it had little control. As the world financial crisis intensified, so did recourse to the yen as a 'safe' currency; this exposed the country to an asset-market driven currency appreciation, which threw Japan's growth into reverse. Because Japanese interest rates had been considerably lower than those in the USA and elsewhere between 2002 and 2007, the yen remained weak as investors converted the currency into dollars. The weak exchange rate helped drive Japanese economic growth but the export price advantage was lost after 2007, once USA interest rates began to fall and the yen started to appreciate.[34] Such appreciation undercut the price competitiveness of Japanese exports and eroded the yen value of profits made overseas.

Policy Paralysis and the 'Japanese Model'

For all the enforced changes wrought upon Japan's economy in the wake of the 'lost decade', deflation, over-capacity, depressed domestic demand, rising public debt and an all-too-common stalemate in domestic politics were patently evident towards the end of the first decade of the millennium.[35] Although 95 per cent of Japan's public debt was domestically held and financed by bonds that attracted low interest rates, suggesting that the

---

[34]   Murphy, 'Financial Crisis', October 2009.

[35]   The Democratic Party of Japan gained power in 2009 but faced an opposing LDP in the Upper House from July 2010; the penchant for changing Prime Ministers (14 in the post since the bubble burst, with yet another departure following upon the 2011 earthquake/tsunami disaster) was seemingly unabated.

problem was less severe than outside observers might think, its level (close to 200 per cent of GDP in 2010 and rising) was unsustainable in the long term.[36]

Japan faced a particularly difficult fiscal dilemma. Any efforts to stabilize public debt over the medium term – by cutting public investment and benefits or by raising taxes, for example – constantly threatened economic growth. Despite life-cycle hypotheses which suggest that savings rates tend to decline as the share of an elderly population increases, any reform of social security benefits in Japan always threatened to increase the level of saving and reduce demand as older people anticipated having to finance privately more of their consumption in retirement.[37]

The average annual percentage change of GDP in Japan over 2000–06 stood at 1.0 compared with 3.6 in the USA. The comparative figures for business investment were -0.5 and 9.0 respectively.[38] Despite the creation of new firms in specific high-tech sectors, such as (but not only) biotechnology,[39] Japan continued in general to lag behind the USA and Europe in venture capital activity. The fact that the potential pool of young, educated and flexible talent needed for innovative technological progress in the immediate term was itself under threat because of the decline in the cohort of those aged 20–24 within the total population hardly bode well for the future.

In 2009 Japan's per capita GDP stood at 4.1 million yen, which was 14 per cent higher than it had been in 1990 (measured in 2000 prices). Had the country's growth rate been even 2.0 per cent over that time, instead of the registered 1.1 per cent, per capita GDP in 2009 would have been 46 per cent higher in inflation-adjusted terms than in 1990. Japanese real per capita GDP did rise between 1997 and 2008, but average household income levels fell more than prices did, making people worse off.[40] There was no

---

[36]   Christian Broda and David E. Weinstein, 'Happy News from the Dismal Science: Reassessing Japanese Fiscal Policy and Sustainability', in Ito et al., *Reviving Japan's Economy*, 39–78.

[37]   International Monetary Fund. Japan: 2007 Article IV Consultation-Staff Report; and Public Information Notice on the Executive Board Discussion: IMF Country Report No. 07/280 (Washington, DC: International Monetary Fund, 2007).

[38]   Adams et al., *Accelerating Growth*, 19.

[39]   For a fuller discussion, see Kathryn Ibata-Arens, *Innovation and Entrepreneurship in Japan: Politics, Organization, and High Technology* (New York: Cambridge University Press, 2005).

[40]   Edward J. Lincoln, 'The Heisei Economy: Puzzles, Problems, Prospects,' *Journal of Japanese Studies* 37, no. 2 (2011): 358.

gainsaying that the legacies of the 1990s had bequeathed a fundamental measure of economic underperformance.

Without a commitment to accommodating monetary policy to offset fiscal tightening or systematic efforts to raise general levels of disposable income, the tendencies towards low potential growth and damaged confidence were intensified. Considerable effort was devoted towards stemming the higher nominal value of the yen after 2007. However, decades of deflation had lowered the yen-based costs of exporters, thus lowering the real, price-adjusted value of the yen and nullifying much of the effect of the government's exchange rate policy.

What was needed more than currency intervention was a pro-growth, pro-competitiveness agenda.[41] However, shifting employment patterns during the 1990s had embedded low wage growth in a two-tier labour market. Uncertainty had continued to stymie domestic demand during the 2000s, just as low tax revenue from poor growth strained the ever-rising national debt. That remained Japan's dilemma. The shrinking labour force, combined with the fiscal burden of an ageing population, reduced Japan's trend growth rate to only 1–1.5 per cent. Given such projections of modest growth, direct action to lower public debt remained critical. Tax hikes, however, remained unpopular and, as was demonstrated in 1997, were likely to prompt further decline at a time when domestic demand was already weak.

Rengo (the Japan Trade Union Confederation) had bemoaned the cumulative impact of changed employment practices. In a strategy white paper in 2003, it noted that:

> employers have intensified their efforts to secure short-term profits by cutting personnel expenditures, by suppressing wage increases and making employment adjustments [i.e. dismissing employees]. This business behaviour has generated a vicious macro spiral: workers' anxiety about jobs and living suppresses private consumption, which reduces demand and makes the market sluggish, in turn undermining corporate performance.[42]

The orientation of public policy along more competitive neoliberal lines was further weakened by evidence of growing income inequality. In the 1970s Japan had the most equal distribution of income of all OECD

---

[41]   See Richard Katz, 'Tokyo's Intervention That Can't', *The Wall Street Journal*, 1 November 2011.

[42]   Carlile, 'The Japanese Labor Movement', 197.

countries. The growing proportion of older people in the population there-after pushed the country towards greater inequality; even among the working-age population, though, there was greater inequality from the 1980s. It increased further during the 1990s as corporations came increas-ingly to rely upon nonregular and relatively low paid (temporary or part-time) workers.[43] By 2000 measured inequality exceeded the OECD average. Japan's Comprehensive Survey of Living Conditions, conducted by the Ministry of Health, Labour and Welfare, examined trends in both the market and disposable income (after taxes and transfer payments) over the period from 1985 to 2000. Each tends to reduce income disparities. Inequal-ity had increased for both working-age and elderly people.[44] Such develop-ments put a strain on the already parlous social security system and acted as a break on speedy, market-oriented reforms, which many feared would only worsen their predicament.

The revision of the law in 2004, which allowed employment contracts to be counted as temporary for up to three years, may have been regarded within the corporate sector as a positive move towards making the employ-ment system 'more flexible, transparent, and efficient'[45] but it did not appear so to those most affected. The percentage of nonregular workers to total workers increased from 20.2 per cent in 1994 to 31.5 per cent in 2004. Demand for nonregular workers still exceeded that for regular workers in 2006, despite the fact that economic recovery had increased the demand for labour overall. Only in 2007 did the unemployment rate fall below 4 per cent.

With low domestic demand, falling wages, insecure employment and the continuing threat of fiscal unsustainability, the prospects for a stable recovery towards the end of the first decade of the millennium were always in doubt, even before the downturn in exports in the wake of the inter-national financial crisis of 2007–08. Caution reigned. It was noteworthy that, in the mid-2000s, the legal shifts to moderate rigid rules on layoffs did not establish precise rules for dismissal. Nor was it altogether surprising that when Japan fell into recession again – from mid-2008 until spring

---

[43]   Arthur J. Alexander, *The Arc of Japan's Economic Development* (London: Routledge, 2008), 203–4.

[44]   International Monetary Fund. Japan: 2007 Article IV Consultation-Staff Report; and Public Information Notice on the Executive Board Discussion: IMF Country Report No. 07/280 (Washington, DC: International Monetary Fund, 2007), 25.

[45]   Schaede, *Choose and Focus*, 198.

2009 – the adjustment in the labour market proved far less severe than might have occurred had employers used the relative freedom they had obtained to dismiss part-time and temporary workers.

Despite the intensification of deregulation and privatization that had occurred in Japan since the 1980s[46] and which continued during the first few years of the new century, it was by no means clear by the late 2000s that the country was prepared to embrace greater market-oriented policies. Japan found itself under pressure to abandon a supposedly outmoded model of political economy long before it had seriously contemplated adopting a Western liberal market model as a viable or speedy option. Bureaucrats, though anxious to raise their profile among politicians and the wider public, still lacked any real conviction for free market economics and engaged in incremental rather than substantive reform.[47] The country had deregulated and reregulated; for years it had sustained a heady mix of inertia and reactive change, saddled as it was with a complex, inter-related institutional structure that often defied the rational presumptions of neoclassical economics. Discussions of convergence or of 'unleashing the market' implied that Japan knew (or should have known) what practices and policy priorities needed changing, in what timeframe and in whose interests.

To some, the reinvigoration of Nissan from 2002 became a powerful symbol of the broader changes that could occur if Japan embraced greater liberalization and more flexible labour markets. But the prospect of creeping foreign control and the corporate expectations that could follow in its wake projected a scenario so much at odds with Japanese patterns of behaviour that conversion to the unseen hand of the market as a policy priority remained as elusive as ever. In December 2006 it was Bunmei Ibuki, the Minister of Education in Shinzo Abe's administration, who called for 'corrective measures' to counteract 'the principle of free competition and its corollary, the supremacy of the market economy', which were undermining Japan's 'collective consciousness.'[48]

Inward foreign direct investment to Japan had reached a record level in March 2005, exceeding the country's outward investment for the first time in its post-war history. A noticeable increase in mergers and acquisitions within pharmaceuticals and retailing, and the attempt by Livedoor (the

---

[46]   During the 1960s and 1970s deregulation programmes had been applied to the steel and textile industries. In the 1980s they applied to the automobile sector as well as to interest rates and international capital flows.

[47]   Vogel, *Japan Remodeled*, 35.

[48]   *The Japan Times*, 13 December 2006.

Internet company) to buy out Nippon Broadcasting System during 2005
reflected the changing environment within which corporations were operating.[49] In defence, elements of traditional financial and corporate activity
resurfaced. High-trust partnerships and the retention by businesses of a
stable, trained and motivated workforce committed to the firm were openly
regarded as the means of retaining, not destroying, competitive advantage.[50]

The ratio of cross-shareholdings among listed companies in Japan rose in
2007, for the first time since the beginning of the 1990s, as Japanese
companies moved to fend off takeover bids from foreign capital and
investment funds.[51] The renewed interest in cross-shareholding was most
evident in the steel, paper and energy sectors, though revived webs of
interlocking shareholdings were particularly noticeable within automobiles
and electronics in 2007; this involved Toyota, Honda and Nissan on the one
hand, and Toshiba, Sharp, Pioneer, and Panasonic on the other.[52] As late as
2009, moreover, it was evident that corporations (for loans) and households
(for savings) continued to favour banks rather than stocks and bonds.[53]

With the BOJ still convinced, in the mid-2000s, that deflation was the
result of structural impediments rather than monetary policy, and with the
MOF haunted by its earlier attempt to raise taxes before recovery was
underway in 1997, there was little discussion of deploying a unified
monetary and fiscal policy to encourage sustainable growth. The sheer
persistence of deflation had its own debilitating effect. Confidence had been
severely shaken during the 1990s but, with nominal interest rates so low,
deflation had delivered investors a risk-adjusted return. The significant rally
in 10-year government bonds in 2005 – from their trough in 1990 – reflected
how risk-averse the Japanese saver continued to be. Moreover, during the
high-growth period, the 'losers' in society had been compensated through

---

[49]   Ozawa, 'Institutionally Driven Growth', 127–9.
[50]   Lincoln and Gerlach, *Japan's Network Economy*, 376.
[51]   *The Japan Times*, 2 September 2007. Schaede sees this not as a return to
old-style defensive activity so much as a move to strategic-oriented relations based
upon market considerations rather than mere business group membership or long-
term trade relations. Schaede, *Choose and Focus*, 55. See also Mitsuhiro Kamiya
and Tokutaka Ito, 'Corporate Governance at the Coalface: Comparing Japan's
Complex Case Law on Hostile Takeovers and Defensive Measures', in Nottage et
al., *Corporate Governance*, 178–96.
[52]   'Criss-Crossed Capitalism: Japanese Firms' Tradition of Cross-Shareholdings is Causing Problems', *The Economist*, 6 November 2008, available at
http://www.economist.com/node/12564050.
[53]   Lincoln, 'The Heisei Economy', 366–7, 369.

public works and other forms of subsidized lending financed from growth revenues. Two decades of slow growth made it more difficult to sustain previous levels of compensation. Workers, consumers and households, aware of the dramatic shift in circumstance, remained suspicious of any further radicalization of policy, which might weaken the underlying prem- ises of the post-war social contract. The LDP's devastating defeat in the 2007 upper house elections was commonly regarded as a reaction to the economic disparities that liberal market reforms had delivered since 2001.[54]

The difficulties Japan faced 10 years and more after emerging from the 'lost decade' were the more intractable because they transcended the obvious (and not uniquely Japanese) need to balance the pursuit of effi- ciency and competitiveness with fiscal, social and political stability. What- ever the actual or perceived shortcomings of Japan's post-war political economy, many observers conceded that, in principle, Japanese authorities probably still possessed greater opportunities than those elsewhere to deploy public tolerance, discipline, cooperation and a nationalistic drive for economic success to the nation's advantage. What Japan needed, as Katz puts it, was 'to pick and choose the combination of global "best practices" – including Japan's own best practices – that work best for Japan'. Japan did not need 'to remould itself into … the American model… . It need[ed] to forge a revitalized Japanese model.'[55]

That remains a formidable task. During the high-growth period, the trade-off between greater risk-taking, efficiency and stability had been relatively easier to accomplish because the risks were shared and their magnitude was lower than they subsequently became. Sluggish growth, low domestic demand and fiscal indebtedness remain immutable traits of post- 1990s Japan. If the authorities had wished to challenge the idea that Japan inevitably faced permanently lower growth rates, fiscal denouement and the eclipse of a younger generation's aspirations, they would have to have domesticated their political and economic systems with what Jones has termed 'open, non-destructive conflict' incorporating behavioural, institu- tional and political changes 'extensive enough to constitute a second miracle.'[56]

Whether such transformative changes are likely to occur, even in the medium term, remains a highly debateable question. Japan will continue to face the fiscal burden of a rising ratio of net government debt to GDP as

---

[54] Cargill and Sakamoto, *Japan Since 1980*, 22.
[55] Katz, 'A Nordic Mirror', 46.
[56] Jones, *Global Economic Development*, 130–31.

social security related pension, health and long-term care expenditures for a rapidly ageing population rise. It has been estimated that a new Japanese growth miracle – a productivity growth rate faster than 4 per cent a year down to 2021 – would be needed for Japan to eliminate debt at 2011 levels.[57] Such an unrealistic scenario points instead to the continuance of gruelling political battles pitched between the need for reduced government expenditures and tax rises (including perhaps lower or targeted social security entitlements) and the urgent need to engender and sustain impulses to growth, even at the cost of short-term fiscal consolidation.

During the catch-up period it had been relatively easy for Japan to adapt foreign technology for domestic use, using a limited cadre of scientists and engineers and workers with middle-level education. However, the growing need for higher levels of human capital and for demand-creating innovation have made it imperative for Japan to foster creative, highly trained specialists and to open itself up to international and unconventional corporate, employment and remuneration practices, knowing that its shrinking working-age population will render labour and technological adaptation increasingly difficult within the coming decades.[58]

The maintenance of export competitiveness will remain an enduring concern of the Japanese authorities, even if they concede the need to strike a better balance between external and domestic demand. The essential difficulty is that it is always easier to list the opportunities available for stimulating growth in Japan than to know if and when they will be implemented. There is a continued need, for example, to rectify the previous neglect of demand and deflation, to overcome the legacies of opaqueness, forbearance, procrastination and bureaucratic defensiveness imparted from the 1990s, to foster greater labour productivity, to increase the participation of women in the labour force, to use older workers more imaginatively, to tap into new types of goods to unleash the pent-up demand of the aged but wealthy population (greater deregulation of healthcare, tourism, nursing and leisure provide parallel openings), to accelerate public and private investment in the development of new IT technologies and high-tech clusters, to promote greater use of IT in finance, retail and wholesale distribution, to encourage greater foreign direct investment and the marketing of Japanese government bonds to foreigners, to foster greater

[57]   Selahattin Iu and Nao Sudo, 'Will a Growth Miracle Reduce Debt in Japan?', Institute of Monetary and Economic Studies, Discussion Paper Series 2011-E-1, Bank of Japan, January 2011.

[58]   Hayami and Godo, 'The Role of Education in the Economic Catch-Up', 131.

integration in Asian markets (including a possible transpacific free trade area), and to re-examine existing policies towards immigration.[59]

Factional politics favouring vested interests and a proclivity towards conservatism and compromise could smother any such developing agenda. It remains to be seen whether Japan's leaders have the capacity and determination to make painful choices against past practice, knowing that the sacrifices required from both the public sector and the private sector will be neither equal nor short lived. To continue shirking the task would be to squander the legacy of Japan's past success and to remain relentlessly subjugated by the stagnation of recent decades. The Japanese people deserve better.

---

[59] For further discussion, see Adams et al., *Accelerating Growth*, Chapters 13 and 14.

Bibliography

Abe, Etsuo. 'The State as the "Third Hand": MITI and Japanese Industrial Development after 1945', in Etsuo Abe, and Terence R. Gourvish, eds. *Japanese Success? British Failure? Comparisons in Business Performance Since 1945.* Oxford: Oxford University Press, 1997, 17–44.

Abe, Masahiro, and Takeo Hoshi. 'Corporate Finance and Human Resource Management in Japan.' In Aoki et al., *Corporate Governance in Japan*, 257–81.

Abegglen, James C. *The Japanese Factory: Aspects of Its Social Organization.* Glencoe, IL: Free Press, 1958.

Abramovitz, Moses. 'Catch Up and Convergence in the Post-War Boom and After.' In William J. Baumol, Richard R. Nelson, and Edward N. Wolff, eds, *Convergence of Productivity: Cross-National Studies and Historical Evidence*, 86–125.

Abramovitz, Moses. 'Catching Up, Forging Ahead, and Falling Behind.' *Journal of Economic History* 46, no. 2 (1986): 385–406.

Adams, Gerard F., Lawrence R. Klein, Yuzo Kumasak, and Akihiko Shinozaki. *Accelerating Japan's Economic Growth: Resolving Japan's Growth Controversy.* New York: Routledge, 2008.

Ahearne, Alan G., and Naoki Shinada. 'Zombie Firms and Economic Stagnation in Japan.' *International Economics and Economic Policy* 2, no. 4 (2005): 363–81.

Alexander, Arthur J. *The Arc of Japan's Economic Development.* London: Routledge, 2008.

Allen, Franklin, and Hiroko Oura. 'Sustained Economic Growth and the Financial System.' Discussion Paper No. 2004-E-17, Institute for Monetary and Economic Studies, Bank of Japan, August 2004.

Amyx, Jennifer A. *Japan's Financial Crisis: Institutional Rigidity and Reluctant Change.* Princeton, NJ: Princeton University Press, 2004.

Amyx, Jennifer A. 'The Ministry of Finance and the Bank of Japan at the Crossroads.' In Jennifer A. Amyx, and Peter Drysdale, eds, *Japanese Governance: Beyond Japan Inc.*, 55–76.

Amyx, Jennifer A., and Peter Drysdale, eds. *Japanese Governance: Beyond Japan Inc*. New York: RoutledgeCurzon, 2003.

Anchordoguy, Marie. *Reprogramming Japan: The High Tech Crisis Under Communitarian Capitalism*. Ithaca: Cornell University Press, 2005.

Aoki, Masahiko, Gregory Jackson, and Hideaki Miyajima, eds. *Corporate Governance in Japan: Institutional Change and Organizational Diversity*. New York: Oxford University Press, 2007.

Aoki, Masahiko, ed. *Economic Analysis of the Japanese Firm*. New York: North Holland, 1984.

Aoki, Masahiko. *Information, Corporate Governance, and Institutional Diversity*. Oxford: Oxford University Press, 2000.

Aoki, Masahiko, Hyung-Ki Kim, and Masahiro Okuno-Fujiwara, eds. *The Role of Government in East Asian Economic Development: Comparative Institutional Analysis*. New York: Oxford University Press, 1997.

Aoki, Masahiko, and Hugh Patrick, eds. *The Japanese Main Bank System: Its Relevance for Developing and Transforming Economies*. Oxford: Oxford University Press, 1994.

Aoki, Masahiko, Hugh Patrick and Paul Sheard. 'The Japanese Main Bank System: An Introductory Overview.' In Aoki and Patrick, eds, *The Japanese Main Bank System*, 3–50.

Arai, Yoichi, and Takeo Hoshi. 'Monetary Policy in the Great Stagnation.' In Hutchison and Westermann, eds, *Japan's Great Stagnation*, 157–81.

Ariga, Kenn, Giorgio Brunello, and Yasushi Ohkusa. *Internal Labor Markets in Japan*. Cambridge: Cambridge University Press, 2000.

Ariga, Kenn, and Ryosuke Okazawa. 'Labor Immobility in Japan: Its Causes and Consequences.' In Hamada et al., *Japan's Bubble*, 263–308.

Arikawa, Yasuhiro. 'Financial Systems and Economic Development: The Case in Japan.' In Koichi Hamada, Keijiro Otsuka, Gustav Ranis, and Ken Togo, eds, *Miraculous Growth and Stagnation in Post-War Japan*, 40–53.

Arikawa, Yasuhiro, and Hideaki Miyajima. 'Relationship Banking and Debt Choice: Evidence from Japan.' *Corporate Governance: An International Review* 13, no. 3 (2005): 408–18.

Arikawa, Yasuhiro, and Hideaki Miyajima. 'Relationship Banking in Post-Bubble Japan: Coexistence of Soft- and Hard-Budget Constraints.' In Masahiko Aoki, Gregory Jackson, and Hideaki Miyajima, eds, *Corporate Governance in Japan: Institutional Change and Organizational Diversity*, 51–78.

Armstrong, Shiro. 'What Japan Can Do About Its Malaise.' *East Asian Forum*, 16 August 2010. Available at http://www.eastasiaforum.org/2010/08/16/what-japan-can-do-about-its-malaise-weekly-editorial.

Aronson, Bruce E. 'A Reassessment of Japan's Big Bang Financial Regulatory Reform.' Institute for Monetary and Economic Studies, Discussion Paper No. 2011-E-19. Bank of Japan, August 2011.

Asako, Kazumi, Takatoshi Ito, and Kazunori Sakamoto. 'The Rise and Fall of Deficit in Japan, 1965–1990.' *Journal of the Japanese and International Economies* 5, no. 4 (1991): 451–72.

Austin, Ian P. *Common Foundations of American and East Asian Modernisation: From Alexander Hamilton to Junichero Koizumi*. Singapore: Select Publishing, 2009.

Baba, Naohiko, Shinichi Nishioka, Noboyuki Oda, Masaaki Shirakawa, Kazuo Ueda, and Hiroshi Ugai. 'Japan's Deflation, Problems in the Financial System, and Monetary Policy.' *Monetary and Economic Studies* 23, no. 1 (2005) 47–111.

Bailey, David, Dan Coffey, and Phil Tomlinson, eds. *Crisis or Recovery in Japan: State and Industrial Economy*. Cheltenham, UK and Northampton, MA: Edward Elgar, 2007.

Bank of Japan. *On Price Stability*. Tokyo: Bank of Japan, 2000.

Barrel, Ray, and Phillip E. Davis. 'The Evolution of the Financial Crisis of 2007–8.' *National Institute Economic Review* 206, no. 1 (2008): 5–14.

Barsky, Robert. 'The Japanese Asset Price Bubble: A Heterogeneous Approach.' In Hamada et al., *Japan's Bubble*, 17–49.

Baumol, William J., Richard R. Nelson and Edward N. Wolff. *Convergence of Productivity: Cross-National Studies and Historical Evidence*. New York: Oxford University Press, 1994.

Bayoumi, Tamim A. 'The Morning After: Explaining the Slowdown in Japanese Growth in the 1990s.' *Journal of International Economics* 53, no. 2 (2001): 241–59.

Bayoumi, Tamim A., Charles Collyns, eds. *Post-Bubble Blues: How Japan Responded to Asset Price Collapse*. Washington, DC: International Monetary Fund, 2000.

Beason, Dick, and Dennis Patterson. *The Japan That Never Was: Explaining the Rise and Decline of a Misunderstood Country*. Albany: State University of New York Press, 2004.

Beason, Richard, and David E. Weinstein. 'Growth, Economies of Scale, and Targeting in Japan (1955–1990).' *Review of Economics and Statistics* 78, no. 2 (1996): 286–95.

Beeson, Mark. 'Japan's Reluctant Reformers and the Legacy of the Developmental State.' In Anthony B. L. Cheung and Ian Scott, eds, *Governance and Public Sector Reform in Asia: Paradigm Shifts or Business as Usual?* 25–43. London: RoutledgeCurzon, 2003.

Beeson, Mark, ed. *Reconfiguring East Asia: Regional Institutions and Organizations After the Crisis*. London: RoutledgeCurzon, 2002.

Beeson, Mark. *Regionalism and Globalization in East Asia: Politics, Security and Economic Development*. Basingstoke: Palgrave Macmillan, 2007.

Beeson, Mark. 'The Rise and Fall (?) of the Developmental State: The Vicissitudes and Implications of East Asian Interventionism.' In Linda Low, ed., *Developmental States: Relevancy, Redundancy or Reconfiguration?* 29–40. New York: Nova Science Publishers, 2004.

Berger, Suzanne, and Ronald P. Dore. *National Diversity and Global Capitalism*. Ithaca: Cornell University Press, 1996.

Berger, Suzanne. 'Introduction.' In Berger, and Dore, eds, *National Diversity and Global Capitalism*, 1–29.

Bernanke, Ben S. 'Japanese Monetary Policy: A Case of Self-Induced Paralysis?' In Ryoichi Mikitani, and Adam S. Posen, eds, *Japan's Financial Crisis and its Parallels to U.S. Experience*, 149–66. Washington, DC: Institute for International Economics, 2000.

Block, Fred L. 'Disorderly Coordination: The Limited Capacities of States and Markets.' In Leonardo Burlamaqui, Ana Célia Castro, and Ha-Joon Chang, eds, *Institutions and the Role of the State*, 53–72. Cheltenham, UK and Northampton, MA: Edward Elgar, 2000.

Block, Fred L. *The Origins of International Economic Disorder*. Berkeley, CA: University of California Press, 1977.

Blomstrom, Magnus, and Sumner J. La Croix, eds. *Institutional Change in Japan*. London: Routledge, 2006.

Blomstrom Magnus, Byron Gangnes, and Sumner J. La Croix, eds. *Japan's New Economy: Continuity and Change in the Twenty-First Century*. New York: Oxford University Press, 2001.

Boltho, Andrea, and Jenny M. Corbett. 'The Assessment: Japan's Stagnation – Can Policy Revive the Economy?' *Oxford Review of Economic Policy* 16, no. 2 (2000): 1–17.

Boroi, Claudio. 'Comment on "Financial Crisis and Lost Decade".' *Asian Economic Policy Review* 2, no. 2 (2007): 301–2.

Boyd, Richard, and Tak-Wing Ngo, eds. *Asian States: Beyond the Developmental Perspective*. London: RoutledgeCurzon, 2005.

Boyd, Richard, and Tak-Wing Ngo. 'Emancipating the Political Economy of Asia from the Growth Paradigm.' In Boyd, and Ngo, eds, *Asian States*, 1–18.

Brenner, Robert. 'The Capitalist Economy, 1945–2000.' In David Coates, ed., *Varieties of Capitalism, Varieties of Approaches*, 211–41. New York: Palgrave Macmillan, 2005.

Broda, Christian, and David E. Weinstein. 'Happy News from the Dismal Science: Reassessing Japanese Fiscal Policy and Sustainability.' In Takatoshi Ito, Hugh Patrick, and David E. Weinstein, eds, *Reviving Japan's Economy*, 39–78. Cambridge, MA: MIT Press, 2005.

Brown, Robert J. *The Ministry of Finance: Bureaucratic Practices and the Transformation of the Japanese Economy*. Westport, CN: Quorum Books, 1999.

Burlamaqui, Leonardo, Ana C. Castro, Ha-Joon Chang, eds. *Institutions and the Role of the State*. Cheltenham, UK and Northampton, MA: Edward Elgar, 2000.

Caballero, Ricardo J., Takeo Hoshi, and Anil K. Kashyap. 'Zombie Lending and Depressed Restructuring in Japan.' *American Economic Review* 98, no. 5 (2008): 1943–77.

Calder, Kent E. *Crisis and Compensation: Public Policy and Political Stability in Japan, 1949–86*. Princeton, NJ: Princeton University Press, 1988.

Calder, Kent E. *Strategic Capitalism: Private Business and Public Purpose in Japanese Industrial Finance*. Princeton, NJ: Princeton University Press, 1993.

Callen, Tim, and Jonathan D. Ostry, eds. *Japan's Lost Decade: Policies for Economic Revival*. Washington, DC: International Monetary Fund, 2003.

Callen, Tim, and Takashi Nagaoka. 'Structural Reforms, Information Technology, and Medium-Term Growth Prospects.' In Callen, and Ostry, eds, *Japan's Lost Decade*, 80–109.

Callon, Scott. *Divided Sun: MITI and the Breakdown of Japanese High-Tech Industrial Policy, 1975–1993*. Stanford: Stanford University Press, 1993.

Campbell, John C., and Ethan Scheiner. 'Fragmentation and Power: Reconceptualizing Policy Making Under Japan's 1955 System.' *Japanese Journal of Political Science* 9, no. 1 (2008): 89–113.

Cargill, Thomas F. 'Central Banking, Financial, and Regulatory Change in Japan.' In Magnus Blomstrom, Byron Gangnes, Sumner J. La Croix, eds, *Japan's New Economy*, 145–61. New York: Oxford University Press, 2001.

Cargill, Thomas F., and Takayuki Sakamoto. *Japan Since 1980*. Cambridge: Cambridge University Press, 2008.

Carlile, Lonny E. 'The Japanese Labor Movement and Institutional Reform.' In Blomstrom, and La Croix, eds, *Institutional Change in Japan*, 177–201.

Carlile, Lonny E. 'Malleable Meaning, Shifting Practice, Lingering Rigidities: Postwar Japanese Industrial and Post-Industrial Policy in Historical Perspective.' Paper presented at the Conference, 'Revisiting Postwar Japan as History: A Twenty Year Check-up on the State of the Field,' 1–25. Sophia University, Tokyo, 31 May 2009.

Carlile, Lonny E., and Mark C. Tilton, eds. *Is Japan Really Changing its Ways? Regulatory Reform and the Japanese Economy*. Washington, DC: Brookings Institution Press, 1998.

Chan, Steve, Cal Clark, and Danny Lam. *Beyond the Developmental State: East Asia's Political Economies Reconsidered*. New York: St. Martin's Press, 1998.

Chang, Ha-Joon. 'Breaking the Mould: An Institutionalist Political Economy Alternative to the Neo-Liberal Theory of the Market and the State.' *Cambridge Journal of Economics* 26, no. 5 (2002): 539–59.

Chang, Ha-Joon. 'An Institutionalist Perspective on the Role of the State: Towards an Institutionalist Political Economy.' In Leonardo Burlamaqui, Ana Célia Castro, and Ha-Joon Chang, eds, *Institutions and the Role of the State*, 3–26.

Cheung, Anthony B. L., and Ian Scott. *Governance and Public Sector Reform in Asia: Paradigm Shifts or Business as Usual?* London: RoutledgeCurzon, 2003.

Chuma, Hiroyuki A. 'Employment Adjustments in Japanese Firms During the Current Crisis.' *Industrial Relations: A Journal of Economy and Society* 41, no. 04 (2002): 653–82.

Chuma, Hiroyuki A. 'Is Japan's Long-Term Employment System Changing?' In Isao Ohashi, and Toshiaki Tachibanaki, eds, *Internal Labour Markets, Incentives and Employment*, 225–68. New York: St. Martin's Press, 1998.

Citrin, Daniel, and Alexander Wolfson. 'Japan's BACK! After Its Lost Decade, Japan's Economy is Set On a Recovery Path.' *Finance and Development* 43, no. 2 (2006): 24–7.

Coates, David. *Models of Capitalism. Growth and Stagnation in the Modern Era*. Cambridge: Polity Press, 2000.

Coates, David. *Varieties of Capitalism, Varieties of Approaches*. New York: Palgrave Macmillan, 2005.

Cohen, Jerome B. *Japan's Economy in War and Reconstruction*. Minneapolis, MN: University of Minnesota Press, 1949.

Cole, Robert E. *Work, Mobility, and Participation: A Comparative Study of American and Japanese Industry*. Berkeley: University of California Press, 1979.

Comin, Diego A. 'An Exploration of the Japanese Slowdown During the 1990s.' In Hamada et al., *Japan's Bubble*, 375–98.

Cowling, Keith, and Philip R. Tomlinson. 'The Japanese Crisis – A Case of Strategic Failure?' *Economic Journal* 110, no. 464 (2000): 358–81.

Cowling, Keith, and Philip R. Tomlinson. 'Revisiting the Roots of Japan's Economic Stagnation: The Role of the Japanese Corporation.' *International Review of Applied Economics* 16, no. 4 (2002): 373–90.

Crafts, Nicholas. 'The East Asian Escape from Economic Backwardness: Retrospect and Prospect.' In Paul A. David, and Mark Thomas, eds, *The Economic Future in Historical Perspective*, 209–30. Oxford: Oxford University Press, 2006.

Crafts, Nicholas. 'East Asian Growth Before and After the Crisis.' *IMF Staff Papers* 46, no. 2 (1999): 139–66.

Crafts, Nicholas. 'Implications of Financial Crisis for East Asian Trend Growth.' *Oxford Review of Economic Policy* 15, no. 3 (1999): 110–31.

Dekle, Robert, and Ken Kletzer. 'Deposit Insurance, Regulatory Forbearance, and Economic Growth: Implications for the Japanese Banking Crisis.' In Michael M. Hutchison, and Frank Westermann, eds, *Japan's Great Stagnation: Financial and Monetary Policy Lessons for Advanced Economies*, 61–102. Cambridge, MA: MIT Press, 2006.

Dekle, Robert, and Ken Kletzer. 'The Japanese Banking Crisis and Economic Growth: Theoretical and Empirical Implications of Deposit Guarantees and Weak Financial Regulation.' *Journal of the Japanese and International Economies* 17, no. 3 (2003): 305–35.

Dell'Ariccia, Giovanni. 'Banks and Credit in Japan.' In Callen, and Ostry, eds, *Japan's Lost Decade*, 43–61.

Dewenter, Katryn L. 'The Risk-Sharing Role of Japanese Keiretsu Business Groups: Evidence from Restructuring in the 1990s.' *Japan and the World Economy* 15, no. 3 (2003): 261–74.

DeWit, Andrew, and Tobias Harris. 'Japan's Twenty Year Response to Economic Crisis.' *Asia-Pacific Journal: Japan Focus* 7, no. 3 (2009).

Dore, Ronald P. *Flexible Rigidities: Industrial Policy and Structural Adjustment in the Japanese Economy, 1970–1980.* Stanford: Stanford University Press, 1986.

Dore, Ronald P. *Taking Japan Seriously: A Confucian Perspective on Leading Economic Issues.* Stanford: Stanford University Press, 1987.

The Economist. 'Criss-Crossed Capitalism: Japanese Firms' Tradition of Cross-Shareholdings is Causing Problems.' *The Economist*, 6 November 2008. Available at http://www.economist.com/node/12564050

The Economist. 'Dead Firms Walking: Japan's Unproductive Service Industries are Holding Back Its Improving Economy from Achieving Even Better Performance.' *The Economist*, 23 September 2004. Available at http://www.economist.com/node/3219857.

Eichengreen, Barry. 'Capitalizing on Globalization.' *Asian Development Review* 19, no. 1 (2002): 14–67.

Eser, Zekeriya, Joe Peek, and Eric S. Rosengren. 'Secondary Bank Lending in Japan.' In Michael M. Hutchison, and Frank Westermann, eds, *Japan's Great Stagnation*, 129–56. Cambridge, MA: MIT Press, 2006.

Evans, Peter B. *Embedded Autonomy: States and Industrial Transformation.* Princeton, NJ: Princeton University Press, 1995.

Fishlow, Albert, Catherine Gwin, Stephan Haggard, Dani Rodrik, and Robert Wade, eds. *Miracle or Design? Lessons from the East Asian Experience.* Washington, DC: Overseas Development Council, 1994.

Fitzgerald, Robert, and Etsuo Abe. *The Development of Corporate Governance in Japan and Britain.* Burlington, VT: Ashgate Publishing, 2004.

Forsberg, Aaron. *America and the Japanese Miracle: The Cold War Context of Japan's Postwar Economic Revival, 1950–1960.* Chapel Hill: University of North Carolina Press, 2000.

Friedman, David B. *The Misunderstood Miracle: Industrial Development and Political Change in Japan.* Ithaca: Cornell University Press, 1988.

Friedman, Milton. 'No More Economic Stimulus Needed.' *The Wall Street Journal*, 10 October 2001.

Fruin, Mark W. *The Japanese Enterprise System: Competitive Strategies and Cooperative Structures.* New York: Oxford University Press, 1992.

Fuji, Mariko, and Kawai, Masahiro. 'Lessons from Japan's Banking Crisis, 1991–2005.' ADBI Working Paper, no. 222. Asian Development Bank Institute, Tokyo, 2010. Available at http://ssrn.com/abstract=1638784.

Fukao, Mitsuhiro. 'Financial Crisis and the Lost Decade.' *Asian Economic Policy Review* 2, no. 2 (2007): 273–97.

Fukao, Mitsuhiro. 'Japan's Lost Decade and its Financial System.' *The World Economy* 26, no. 3 (2003): 365–84.

Gao, Bai. *Japan's Economic Dilemma: The Institutional Origins of Prosperity and Stagnation.* Cambridge: Cambridge University Press, 2001.

Garside, W.R. 'A Very British Phenomenon? Industrial Policy and the Decline of the Japanese Coal Mining Industry Since the 1950s.' *Australian Economic History Review* 45, no. 2 (2005): 186–203.

Genda, Yuji, and Marcus E. Rebick. 'Japanese Labour in the 1990s: Stability and Stagnation.' *Oxford Review of Economic Policy* 16, no. 2 (2000): 85–102.

Gerlach, Michael L. *Alliance Capitalism: The Social Organization of Japanese Businesses.* Berkeley: University of California Press, 1992.

Gibney, Frank. *Unlocking the Bureaucrat's Kingdom: Deregulation and the Japanese Economy.* Washington, DC: Brookings Institution Press, 1998.

Gordon, Andrew. *The Evolution of Labor Relations in Japan: Heavy Industry, 1853–1955.* Cambridge, MA: Harvard University Press, 1962.

Gordon, Andrew. *The Wages of Affluence: Labor and Management in Postwar Japan.* Cambridge, MA: Harvard University Press, 1998.

Gottfried, Heidi. 'Pathways to Economic Security: Gender and Nonstandard Employment in Contemporary Japan.' *Social Indicator Research* 88, no. 1 (2008): 179–96.

Griffin, Naomi N., and Kazuhiko Odaki. 'Reallocation and Productivity Growth in Japan: Revisiting the Lost Decade of the 1990s.' *Journal of Productivity Analysis* 31, no. 2 (2009): 125–36.

Grimes, William W. *Unmaking the Japanese Miracle: Macroeconomic Politics, 1985–2000.* Ithaca: Cornell University Press, 2001.

Haley, John O. 'Governance by Negotiation: A Reappraisal of Bureaucratic Power in Japan.' *Journal of Japanese Studies* 13, no. 2 (1987): 343–57.

Haley, John O. 'The Paradox of Weak Power and Strong Authority in the Japanese State.' In Boyd and Ngo, eds, *Asian States*, 67–82.

Hamada, Koichi. 'Policy Making in Deflationary Japan.' *Japanese Economic Review* 55, no. 3 (2004): 221–39.

Hamada, Koichi, Anil K. Kayshap, and David E. Weinstein, eds. *Japan's Bubble, Deflation and Long-Term Stagnation.* Cambridge, MA: MIT Press, 2011.

Hamada, Koichi, and Asahi Noguchi. 'The Role of Preconceived Ideas in Macroeconomic Policy: Japan's Experiences in Two Deflationary Periods.' *International Economics and Economic Policy* 2, no. 2–3 (2005): 101–26.

Hamada, Koichi, Keijiro Otsuka, Gustav Ranis, and Ken Togo, eds. *Miraculous Growth and Stagnation in Post-War Japan*. London: Routledge, 2011.

Harrigan, James, and Kenneth N. Kuttner. 'Lost Decade in Translation: Did the United States Learn from Japan's Post-Bubble Mistakes?' In Takatoshi Ito, Hugh Patrick, and David E. Weinstein, eds, *Reviving Japan's Economy*, 79–106.

Hashimoto, Masanori, and Yoshio Higuchi. 'Issues Facing the Japanese Labor Market.' In Ito et al., *Reviving Japan's Economy*, 341–85.

Hashino, Tomoko, and Osamu Saito. 'Tradition and Interaction: Research Trends in Modern Japanese Industrial History.' *Australian Economic History Review* 44, no. 3 (2004): 241–58.

Hassard, John, Jonathan Morris, and Leo McCann. 'Hard Times for the Salaryman: Corporate Restructuring and Middle Managers' Working Lives.' In Peter C. D. Matanle, and Wim Lunsing, eds, *Perspectives on Work, Employment and Society in Japan*, 98–117. Basingstoke: Palgrave, 2006.

Hattori, Masazumi, Hyun Song Shin, and Wataru Takahashi. 'A Financial System Perspective on Japan's Experience in the Late 1980s.' Paper presented at the 16th International Conference hosted by the Institute for Monetary and Economic Studies, Bank of Japan, Tokyo, May 2009.

Hayami, Yujiro, and Masahiko Aoki, eds. *The Institutional Foundations of East Asian Economic Development: Proceedings of the IEA Conference Held in Tokyo, Japan*. Basingstoke: Palgrave Macmillan, 1998.

Hayami, Yujiro, and Yoshihisa Godo. 'The Role of Education in the Economic Catch-Up: Comparative Growth Experiences From Japan, Korea, Taiwan, and the United States.' In Hamada et al., *Miraculous Growth and Stagnation*.

Hayami, Yujiro. 'Towards an East Asian Model of Economic Development.' In Yujiro Hayami, and Masahiko Aoki, eds, *The Institutional Foundations of East Asian Economic Development: Proceedings of the IEA Conference Held in Tokyo, Japan*, 3–35.

Hayashi, Fumio, and Edward C. Prescott. 'The 1990s in Japan: A Lost Decade.' *Review of Economic Dynamics* 5, no. 1 (2002): 206–35.

Hidaka, Chikage, and Takeo Kikkawa. 'The Main Bank System and Corporate Governance in Post War Japan.' In Robert Fitzgerald, and Etsuo Abe, eds, *The Development of Corporate Governance in Japan and Britain*, 124–40. Burlington, VT: Ashgate Publishing, 2004.

Higuchi, Yoshio. 'Trends in Japanese Labour Markets'. In Sako and Sato, eds, *Japanese Labour and Management in Transition,* 27–52.

Hopkins, Anthony G. *Global History: Interactions Between the Universal and the Local*. Basingstoke: Palgrave Macmillan, 2006.

Hoshi, Takeo, Satoshi Koibuchi, and Ulrike Schaede. 'Corporate Restructuring in Japan During the Lost Decade.' In Hamada et al., *Japan's Bubble*, 343–74.

Hoshi, Takeo, and Hugh Patrick. *Crisis and Change in the Japanese Financial System*. Boston, MA: Kluwer Academic Publishers, 2000.

Hoshi, Takeo, and Anil K. Kashyap. 'Japan's Financial Crisis and Economic Stagnation.' *Journal of Economic Perspectives* 18, no. 1 (2004): 3–26.

Hoshi, Takeo, and Anil K. Kashyap. 'The Japanese Banking Crisis: Where Did it Come from and How Will it End?' In Ben S. Bernanke, and Julio J. Rotemberg, eds, *NBER Macroeconomics Annual 1999, Volume 14*, 129–221. Chicago: University of Chicago Press, 1999.

Hoshi, Takeo, and Anil K. Kashyap. 'Solutions to Japan's Banking Problems: What Might Work and What Will Definitely Fail.' In Ito et al., *Reviving Japan's Economy*, 147–95.

Houseman, Susan N., and Katharine G. Abraham. 'Female Workers as a Buffer in the Japanese Economy.' *American Economic Review* 83, no. 2 (1993): 45–51.

Huang, Xiaoming. *The Rise and Fall of the East Asian Growth System, 1951–2000: Institutional Competitiveness and Rapid Economic Growth*. London: RoutledgeCurzon, 2005.

Hughes, Christopher W. 'Japanese Policy and the East Asian Currency Crisis: Abject Defeat or Quiet Victory?' *Review of International Political Economy* 7, no. 2 (2000): 219–53.

Hunter, Janet, and Cornelia Storz. *Institutional and Technological Change in Japan's Economy: Past and Present*. New York: Routledge, 2006.

Hutchison, Michael M., Takatoshi Ito, and Frank Westermann. 'The Great Japanese Stagnation: Lessons for Industrial Countries.' In Hutchison, and Westermann, eds, *Japan's Great Stagnation*, 1–32.

Hutchison, Michael M., and Frank Westermann, eds. *Japan's Great Stagnation: Financial and Monetary Policy Lessons for Advanced Economies*. Cambridge, MA: MIT Press, 2006.

Ibata-Arens, Kathryn. *Innovation and Entrepreneurship in Japan: Politics, Organization, and High Technology*. New York: Cambridge University Press, 2005.

Ihori, Toshihiro, and Atsushi Nakamoto. 'Japan's Fiscal Policy and Fiscal Reconstruction.' *International Economics and Economic Policy* 2, no. 2–3 (2005): 153–72.

Ihori, Toshihiro, Toru Nakazato, and Masumi Kawade. 'Japan's Fiscal Policies in the 1990s.' *World Economy* 26, no. 3 (2003): 325–38.

Iida, Tetsuya, and Morris Jonathan. 'Farewell to the Salaryman? The Changing Roles and Work of Middle Managers in Japan.' *International Journal of Human Resource Management* 19, no. 6 (2008): 1072–87.

International Monetary Fund. Japan: 2007 Article IV Consultation-Staff Report; and Public Information Notice on the Executive Board Discussion: IMF Country Report No. 07/280. Washington, DC: International Monetary Fund, 2007.

International Monetary Fund. Japan: Economic and Policy Developments: IMF Country Report No. 01/221. Washington, DC: International Monetary Fund, 2001.

International Monetary Fund. Japan: Selected Issues: IMF Country Report No. 04/247. Washington, DC: International Monetary Fund, 2004.

International Monetary Fund. World Economic Outlook: Financial Turbulence and the World Economy, Chapter IV Japan's Economic Crisis and Policy Options. Washington, DC: International Monetary Fund, 1998.

Ishi, Hiromitsu. 'Macroeconomic Fundamentals of Postwar Economic Growth in Japan – A Great Success and Recent Frustration Lessons in Asian Economies.' *Journal of Asian Economics* 10, no. 2 (1999): 247–61.

Ishi, Hiromitsu. *Making Fiscal Policy in Japan: Economic Effects and Institutional Settings.* New York: Oxford University Press, 2000.

Ishii, Hiroko, and Erika Wada. 'Local Government Spending: Solving the Mystery of Japanese Fiscal Packages.' IIE Working Paper, no. 98–5. Washington, DC: Peterson Institute for International Economics, 1998. Available at http://www.piie.com/publications/wp/wp.cfm?ResearchID=146.

Ito, Takatoshi. 'Japan and the Asian Economies: A "Miracle" in Transition.' *Brookings Papers on Economic Activity*, no. 2 (1996): 205–72.

Ito, Takatoshi, and Andrew K. Rose. *Monetary Policy with Very Low Inflation in the Pacific Rim.* Chicago: University of Chicago Press, 2006.

Ito, Takatoshi. 'Retrospective on the Bubble Period and Its Relationship to Developments in the 1990s.' *World Economy* 26, no. 3 (2003): 283–300.

Ito, Takatoshi, and Frederic S. Mishkin. 'Monetary Policy in Japan: Problems and Solutions.' In Ito et al., *Reviving Japan's Economy*, 107–46.

Ito, Takatoshi, Hugh Patrick, and David E. Weinstein. *Reviving Japan's Economy.* Cambridge, MA: MIT Press, 2005.

Ito, Takatoshi, and Frederic S. Mishkin. 'Two Decades of Japanese Monetary Policy and the Deflation Problem.' In Takatoshi Ito, and Andrew K.

Rose, eds, *Monetary Policy with Very Low Inflation in the Pacific Rim*, 131–201. Chicago: University of Chicago Press, 2006.

Iu, Selahattin, and Nao Sudo. 'Will a Growth Miracle Reduce Debt in Japan?' Institute of Monetary and Economic Studies, Discussion Paper Series 2011-E-1, Bank of Japan, January 2011.

Iwai, Katsuhito. 'What Will Become of the Japanese Corporation?' In Hamada, et al., *Miraculous Growth and Stagnation in Post-War Japan*, 54–73.

Iwaisako, Tokuo. 'Corporate Investment and Restructuring.' In Ito et al., *Reviving Japan's Economy*, 275–310.

Jackson, Gregory, and Andreas Moerke. 'Continuity and Change in Corporate Governance: Comparing Germany and Japan.' *Corporate Governance: An International Review* 13, no. 3 (2005): 351–61.

Jackson, Gregory. 'Employment Adjustment and Distributional Conflict in Japanese Firms.' In Aoki et al., *Corporate Governance in Japan*, 282–309.

Jackson, Gregory, and Hideaki Miyajima. 'Introduction: Diversity and Change of Corporate Governance in Japan.' In Aoki et al., *Corporate Governance in Japan*, 1–47.

Jackson, Gregory. 'The Japanese Firm and Its Diversity.' *Economy and Society* 38, no. 4 (November 2009): 606–29.

Jessop, Bob. 'A Regulationist and State-Theoretical Analysis.' In Richard Boyd, and Tak-Wing Ngo, eds, *Asian States: Beyond the Developmental Perspective*, 19–42.

Jinushi, Toshiki, Yoshihiro Kuroki, and Ryuzo Miyao. 'Monetary Policy in Japan Since the Late 1980s: Delayed Policy Actions and Some Explanations.' In Ryoichi Mikitani, and Adam S. Posen, eds, *Japan's Financial Crisis and its Parallels to U.S. Experience*, 115–48.

Johnson, Chalmers A. 'The Developmental State: Odyssey of a Concept.' In Meredith Woo-Cumings, ed., *The Developmental State*, 32–60. Ithaca: Cornell University Press, 1999.

Johnson, Chalmers A. 'Economic Crisis in East Asia: The Clash of Capitalism.' *Cambridge Journal of Economics* 22, no. 6 (1998): 653–61.

Johnson, Chalmers A. 'How to Think About Economic Competition from Japan.' *Journal of Japanese Studies* 13, no. 2 (1987): 415–27.

Johnson, Chalmers A., ed. *The Industrial Policy Debate*. San Francisco, CA: ICS Press, 1984.

Johnson, Chalmers A. 'Japanese "Capitalism" Revisited.' *Thesis Eleven* 66, no. 1 (2001): 57–78.

Johnson, Chalmers A. *MITI and the Japanese Miracle: The Growth of Industrial Policy, 1925–1975*. Stanford: Stanford University Press, 1982.

Jones, Eric L. *The Record of Global Economic Development*. Cheltenham, UK and Northampton, MA: Edward Elgar, 2002.

Kalra, S. 'Fiscal Policy: An Evaluation of Its Effectiveness.' In Tim Callen, and Jonathan D. Ostry, eds, *Japan's Lost Decade: Policies for Economic Revival*, 164–76.

Kambayashi, Ryo, and Takao Kato. 'The Japanese Employment System After the Bubble Burst: New Evidence.' In Hamada et al., *Japan's Bubble*, 217–62.

Kamiya, Mitsuhiro, and Tokutaka Ito. 'Corporate Governance at the Coalface: Comparing Japan's Complex Case Law on Hostile Takeovers and Defensive Measures.' In Luke Nottage, Leon Wolff, and Kent Anderson, eds, *Corporate Governance in the 21st Century: Japan's Gradual Transformation*, 178–96.

Kanaya, Akihiro, and David Woo. *The Japanese Banking Crisis of the 1990s: Sources and Lessons*. Essays in International Economics No. 222. Princeton, NJ: Department of Economics, Princeton University, 2001.

Kang, Jun-Koo, and Rene M. Stulz. 'Do Banking Shocks Affect Borrowing Firm Performance? An Analysis of the Japanese Experience.' *Journal of Business* 73, no. 1 (2000): 1–23.

Kang, Kenneth. 'The Resolution and Collection Corporation and the Market for Distressed Debt in Japan.' In Callen, and Ostry, eds, *Japan's Lost Decade*, 65–79.

Kato, Junko, and Bo Rothstein. 'Government Partisanship and Managing the Economy: Japan and Sweden in Comparative Perspective.' *Governance: An International Journal of Policy, Administration, and Institutions* 19, no. 1 (2006): 75–97.

Kato, Takao. 'The End of Lifetime Employment in Japan? Evidence from National Surveys and Field Research.' *Journal of the Japanese and International Economies* 15, no. 04 (2001): 489–514.

Katz, Richard. *Japan: The System That Soured: The Rise and Fall of the Japanese Economic Miracle*. Armonk, NY: M. E. Sharpe, 1998.

Katz, Richard. *Japanese Phoenix: The Long Road to Economic Revival*. Armonk, NY: M. E. Sharpe, 2003.

Katz, Richard. 'A Nordic Mirror: Why Structural Reform Has Proceeded Faster in Scandinavia Than in Japan.' Center on Japanese Economy and Business Working Papers, No. 265, Columbia Business School, New York, 2008. Available at http://academiccommons.columbia.edu/catalog/ac:100544.

Katz, Richard. 'Tokyo's Intervention That Can't.' *The Wall Street Journal*, 1 November 2011.

Katzner, Donald W. 'Explaining the Japanese Economic Miracle.' *Japan and the World Economy* 13, no. 3 (2001): 303–19.

Kawai, Masahiro. 'Reform of the Japanese Banking System.' *International Economics and Economic Policy* 2, no. 4 (2005): 307–35.

Keizer, Arjan B. *Changes in Japanese Employment Practices: Beyond the Japanese Model.* New York: Routledge, 2010.

Keizer, Arjan B. 'Non-Regular Employment in Japan: Continued and Renewed Dualities.' *Work, Employment and Society* 22, no. 3 (2008): 407–25.

Kim, Jong-Il, and Lawrence J. Lau. 'The Sources of Economic Growth of East Asian Newly Industrialized Countries.' *Journal of the Japanese and International Economies* 8, no. 3 (1994): 235–71.

Kim, Sangho, and Young Hoon Lee. 'The Productivity Debate of East Asia Revisited: A Stochastic Frontier Approach.' *Applied Economics* 38, no. 14 (2006): 1697–1706.

Kimura, Tatsuya, and Martin Schulz. 'Industry in Japan: Structural Change, Productivity, and Chances for Growth.' *The Japanese Economy* 32, no. 1 (2004): 5–44.

Kitson, Michael. 'Measuring Capitalism: Output, Growth and Economic Policy.' In David Coates, ed., *Varieties of Capitalism, Varieties of Approaches*, 29–46.

Kiyota, Kozo, and Tetsuji Okazaki. 'Industrial Policy Cuts Two Ways: Evidence from Cotton Spinning Firms in Japan, 1956–1964.' *Journal of Law and Economics* 53, no. 3 (2010): 587–609.

Konoe, Sara. 'Financial Crisis, Politics and Financial Sector Restructuring: A Comparison Between Japan and the United States.' *Journal of Asian and African Studies* 44, no. 5 (2009): 497–515.

Koo, Richard C. *Balance Sheet Recession. Japan's Struggle With Unchartered Economics and Its Global Implications.* Singapore: John Wiley & Sons, 2003.

Koo, Richard C. 'A Different Kind of Crisis.' *The Economist*, Vol. 400, Issue 8747, 20 August 2011.

Koo, Richard C. *The Holy Grail of Macroeconomics: Lessons from Japan's Great Recession.* Singapore: John Wiley & Sons, 2008.

Krauss, Ellis S. 'Political Economy: Policymaking and Industrial Policy in Japan.' *PS: Political Science and Politics* 25, no. 1 (1992): 44–57.

Krawczyk, Mariusz. 'Changes and Crisis in the Japanese Banking Industry.' In Janet Hunter, and Cornelia Storz, eds, *Institutional and Technological Change in Japan's Economy: Past and Present*, 120–39. New York: Routledge, 2006.

Krugman, Paul. 'It's Baaack? Japan's Slump and the Return of the Liquidity Trap.' *Brookings Papers on Economic Activity*, no. 2 (1998): 137–205.

Krugman, Paul. 'The Myth of Asia's Miracle.' *Foreign Affairs* 73, no. 6 (1994): 62–78.

Krugman, Paul. *The Return of Depression Economics*. London: Allen Lane, 1999.

Kuttner, Kenneth N., and Adam S. Posen. 'Fiscal Policy Effectiveness in Japan.' *Journal of the Japanese and International Economies* 16, no. 4 (2002): 536–58.

Kuttner, Kenneth N., and Adam S. Posen. 'The Great Recession: Lessons for Macroeconomic Policy from Japan.' *Brookings Papers on Economic Activity* 2001, no. 2 (2001): 93–185.

Lane, Philip R. 'International Financial Integration and Japanese Economic Performance.' In Hamada et al., *Japan's Bubble*, 129–74.

Lazonick, William, and William Mass, eds. *Organizational Capability and Competitive Advantage: Debates, Dynamics and Policy*. Aldershot, UK and Brookfield, VT: Edward Elgar, 1995.

Lin, Chelsea C. 'The Transition of the Japanese Keiretsu in the Changing Economy.' *Journal of the Japanese and International Economies* 19, no. 1 (2005): 96–109.

Lincoln, Edward J. *Arthritic Japan: The Slow Pace of Economic Reform*. Washington, DC: Brookings Institution Press, 2001.

Lincoln, Edward J. 'The Heisei Economy: Puzzles, Problems, Prospects.' *Journal of Japanese Studies* 37, no. 2 (2011): 351–75.

Lincoln, James R., and Michael L. Gerlach. *Japan's Network Economy: Structure, Persistence, and Change*. Cambridge: Cambridge University Press, 2004.

Lockwood, William W. *The Economic Development of Japan: Growth and Structural Change*. Princeton, NJ: Princeton University Press, 1968.

Low, Linda. *Developmental States: Relevancy, Redundancy or Reconfiguration?* New York: Nova Science Publishers, 2004.

Maddison, Angus, *Explaining The Economic Performance of Nations: Essays in Time and Space*. Aldershot, UK and Brookfield, VT: Edward Elgar, 1995.

Madsen, Robert A. 'What Went Wrong. Aggregate Demand, Structural Reform, and the Politics of 1990s Japan.' Berkeley Roundtable on the International Economy (BRIE) Working Paper 162, University of California, Berkeley, September 2004.

Matanle, Peter C. D., and Wim Lunsing. *Perspectives on Work, Employment and Society in Japan.* Basingstoke: Palgrave, 2006.

Matsumoto, Koji. *The Rise of the Japanese Corporate System: The Inside View of a MITI Official.* Translated by Thomas I. Elliott. London: Kegan Paul International, 1983.

Meltzer, Allan H. 'Monetary Transmission at Low Inflation: Some Clues from Japan in the 1990s.' Special issue, *Monetary and Economic Studies* 19, no. 1 (2001): 13–34.

Metzler, Mark. 'The Cosmopolitanism of National Economics: Friedrich List in a Japanese Mirror.' In Anthony G. Hopkins, ed., *Global History*, 98–130. Basingstoke: Palgrave Macmillan, 2006.

Metzler, Mark. 'Japan: Toward a Financial History of Japan's Long Stagnation, 1990–2003.' *Journal of Asian Studies* 67, no. 2 (2008): 653–66.

Mikitani, Ryoichi, and Adam S. Posen. *Japan's Financial Crisis and Its Parallels to U.S. Experience.* Washington, DC: Institute for International Economics, 2000.

Mikuni, Akio, and R. Taggart Murphy. *Japan's Policy Trap: Dollars, Deflation, and the Crisis of Japanese Finance.* Washington DC: Brookings Institution Press, 2002.

Miwa, Yoshiro. *State Competence and Economic Growth in Japan.* London: RoutledgeCurzon, 2004.

Miwa, Yoshiro, and Mark J. Ramseyer. 'The Myth of the Main Bank: Japan and Comparative Corporate Governance,' *Law & Social Inquiry* 27, no. 2 (2002): 401–24.

Miwa, Yoshiro, and Mark J. Ramseyer. 'The Fable of the Keiretsu.' *Journal of Economics & Management Strategy* 11, no. 2 (2002): 169–224.

Miyajima, Hideaki, and Fumiaki Kuroki. 'The Unwinding of Cross-Shareholding in Japan: Causes, Effects, and Implications.' In Aoki et al., *Corporate Governance in Japan*, 79–124.

Miyazaki, Tomomi. 'The Effects of Fiscal Policy in the 1990s in Japan: A VAR Analysis with Event Studies.' *Japan and the World Economy* 22, no. 2 (2010): 80–87.

Moerke, Andreas. 'Japanese Inter-Firm Relations: On the Way Towards a Market-Oriented Structure?' In Hunter and Storz, eds, *Institutional and Technological Change*, 75–90.

Molteni, Corrado. 'Structural Reforms in Japan: The Attempt to Transform the Country's Economic System.' In Maria Weber, ed., *Reforming Economic Systems in Asia: A Comparative Analysis of China, Japan, South Korea, Malaysia, and Thailand*, 43–60. Cheltenham, UK and Northampton, MA: Edward Elgar, 2001.

Montgomery, Heather, and Satoshi Shimizutani. 'The Effectiveness of Bank Recapitalization Policies in Japan.' *Japan and the World Economy* 21, no. 1 (2009): 1–25.

Moon, Chung-In, and Rashemi Prasad. 'Beyond the Developmental State: Networks, Politics, and Institutions.' In Steve Chan, Cal Clark, and Danny Lam, eds, *Beyond the Developmental State: East Asia's Political Economies Reconsidered*, 9–24. New York: St. Martin's Press, 1998.

Mori, Naruki, Shigenori Shiratsuka, and Hiroo Taguchi. 'Policy Responses to the Post-Bubble Adjustments in Japan: A Tentative Review.' Special issue, *Monetary and Economic Studies* 19, no. 1 (2001): 53–102.

Moriguchi, Chiaki, and Hiroshi Ono. 'Japanese Lifetime Employment: A Century's Perspective.' In Blomstrom, and La Croix, eds, *Institutional Change in Japan*, 152–76.

Morishima, Michio. *Why Has Japan Succeeded? Western Technology and the Japanese Ethos*. Cambridge: Cambridge University Press, 1982.

Motonishi, Taizo, and Hiroshi, Yoshikawa. 'Causes of the Long Stagnation of Japan During the 1990s: Financial or Real?' *Journal of the Japanese and International Economies* 13, no. 3 (1999): 181–200.

Muellbauer, John, and Keiko Murata. 'Consumption, Land Prices and the Monetary Transmission Mechanism in Japan.' In Hamada et al., *Japan's Bubble*, 175–216.

Muhleisen, Martin. 'Too Much of a Good Thing? The Effectiveness of Fiscal Stimulus.' In Tamim A. Bayoumi and Charles Collyns, eds, *Post-Bubble Blues: How Japan Responded to Asset Price Collapse*, 107–42.

Mulgan, Aurelia George. *Japan's Agricultural Policy Regime*. New York: Routledge, 2006.

Muramatsu, Michio, and Ellis S. Krauss. 'Bureaucrats and Politicians in Policymaking: the Case of Japan.' *American Political Science Review* 78, no. 1 (1984): 126–46.

Murphy, R. Taggart. 'The Financial Crisis and the Tectonic Shifts in the US-Japan Relationship.' *Asia-Pacific Journal: Japan Focus* 32, no. 2 (October 2009).

Murphy, R. Taggart. 'A Loyal Retainer? Japan, Capitalism, and the Perpetuation of American Hegemony.' *The Asia-Pacific Journal: Japan Focus* 41, no. 3 (August 2010).

Nakamura, Takafusa. *The Postwar Japanese Economy: Its Development and Structure, 1937–1994.* Tokyo: University of Tokyo Press, 1995.

Nakaso, Hiroshi. 'The financial crisis in Japan during the 1990s: how the Bank of Japan responded and the lessons learnt.' BIS paper no. 6, Bank for International Settlements, Basel, Switzerland, 2001. Available at http://www.bis.org/publ/bppdf/bispap06.htm.

Nakatani, Iwao. 'The Role of Financial Corporate Grouping.' In Masahiko Aoki, ed., *Economic Analysis of the Japanese Firm*, 227–58. New York: North Holland, 1984.

Narai, Osamu. *Exploring the Japanese Economy: Historical Background, Current Topics and Japan's Role in the Global Integration.* Kashiwa, Chiba: Reitaku University Press, 2005.

Noble, Gregory W., ed. *Collective Action in East Asia: How Ruling Parties Shape Industrial Policy.* Ithaca: Cornell University Press, 1998.

Noguchi, Yukio. 'The 1940 System: Japan under the Wartime Economy.' *American Economic Review* 88, no. 2 (1998): 404–7.

Noguchi, Yukio. 'The "Bubble" and Economic Policies in the 1980s.' *Journal of Japanese Studies* 20, no. 2 (1994): 291–329.

Noland, Marcus, and Howard Pack. *Industrial Policy in an Era of Globalization: Lessons From Asia.* Washington, DC: Institute for International Economics, 2003.

North, Douglass C. *Institutions, Institutional Change and Economic Performance.* Cambridge: Cambridge University Press, 1990.

Nottage, Luke, Leon Wolff, and Kent Anderson, eds. *Corporate Governance in the 21st Century: Japan's Gradual Transformation.* Cheltenham, UK and Northampton, MA: Edward Elgar 2008.

Nottage, Luke, Leon Wolff and Kent Anderson, 'Introduction: Japan's Gradual Transformation in Corporate Governance.' In Nottage et. al., *Corporate Governance*, 1–20.

Obstfeld, Maurice. 'Time of Troubles: The Yen and Japan's Economy, 1985–2008.' In Hamada et al., *Japan's Bubble*, 51–104.

Odagiri, Hiroyuki. *Growth Through Competition, Competition Through Growth: Strategic Management and the Economy in Japan.* New York: Oxford University Press, 1992.

Ogata, Shijuro. 'Financial Markets in Japan.' In Suzanne Berger, and Ronald P. Dore, eds, *National Diversity and Global Capitalism*, 171–8. Ithaca: Cornell University Press, 1996.

Okamoto, Itaru. 'The Failure of the Japanese "Big Bang": Bureaucracy-Driven Reforms and Political Intervention', *The Japanese Economy*, 33, no. 1 (Spring 2005): 69–106.

Okazaki, Tetsuji. 'From Wartime Controls to Postwar Recovery.' In Frank Gibney, ed., *Unlocking the Bureaucrat's Kingdom: Deregulation and the Japanese Economy*, 19–30.

Okazaki, Tetsuji. 'The Government-Firm Relationship in Postwar Japan: The Success and Failure of Bureau Pluralism.' In Joseph E. Stiglitz, and Shahid Yusuf, eds, *Rethinking the East Asian Miracle*, 323–42. New York: Oxford University Press, 2001.

Okazaki, Tetsuji. 'The Supply Network and Aircraft Production in Wartime Japan', *The Economic History Review*, 64, no. 3 (August 2011): 973–94.

Okazaki, Tetsuji, and Masahiro Okuno-Fujiwara, eds. *The Japanese Economic System and Its Historical Origins*. Oxford: Oxford University Press, 1999.

Okazaki, Tetsuji, and Masahiro Okuno-Fujiwara. 'Japan's Present-Day Economic System and Its Historical Origins.' In Okazaki and Okuno-Fujiwara, eds, *The Japanese Economic System*, 1–37.

Okimoto, Daniel I. *Between MITI and the Market: Japanese Industrial Policy for High Technology*. Stanford: Stanford University Press, 1989.

Okimoto, Daniel. I., Takuo Sugano, and Franklin B. Weinstein. *Competitive Edge: The Semiconductor Industry in the U.S. and Japan*. Stanford: Stanford University Press 1984.

Okina, Kunio, Masaaki Shirakawa, and Shigenori Shiratsuka. 'The Asset Price Bubble and Monetary Policy: Japan's Experience in the Late 1980s and the Lessons.' Special issue, *Monetary and Economic Studies* 19, no. 1 (2001): 395–450.

Okina, Kunio, and Shigenori Shiratsuka. 'Asset Price Fluctuations, Structural Adjustments, and Sustained Economic Growth: Lessons from Japan's Experience Since the Late 1980s.' Special issue, *Monetary and Economic Studies* 22, no. 1 (2004): 143–67.

Okina, Kunio, and Shigenori Shiratsuka. 'Japan's Experience with Asset Price Bubbles: Is It a Case for Inflation Targeting?' In William C. Hunter, George G. Kaufman, and Michael Pomerleano, eds, *Asset Price Bubbles: The Implication for Monetary, Regulatory, and International Policies*, 81–100. Cambridge, MA: The MIT Press, 2003.

Okina, Kunio, and Shigenori Shiratsuka. 'Policy Commitment and Expectation Formation: Japan's Experience Under Zero Interest Rates.' *North American Journal of Economics and Finance*, no. 1 (2004): 75–100.

Ono, Hiroshi. 'Lifetime Employment in Japan: Concepts and Measurements.' *Journal of the Japanese and International Economies* 24, no. 1 (2010): 1–27.

Organisation for Economic Co-operation and Development. *Historical Statistics, 1960–1997.* OECD, 1999.

Ozawa, Terutomo. 'Institutionally Driven Growth and Stagnation – and Struggle for Reform.' In David Bailey, Dan Coffey, and Phil Tomlinson, eds, *Crisis or Recovery in Japan: State and Industrial Economy*, 106–33.

Palat, Ravi A. '"Eyes Wide Shut": Reconceptualizing the Asian Crisis.' *Review of International Political Economy* 10, no. 2 (2003): 169–95.

Peek, Joe. 'The Changing Role of Main Banks in Aiding Distressed Firms in Japan.' In Hamada et al., *Japan's Bubble*, 309–42.

Peek, Joe, and Eric S. Rosengren. 'Unnatural Selection: Perverse Incentives and the Misallocation of Credit in Japan.' *American Economic Review* 95, no. 4 (2005): 1144–66.

Pekkanen, Saadia M. *Picking Winners? From Technology Catch-Up to the Space Race in Japan.* Stanford, CA: Stanford University Press, 2003.

Pempel, T. J. 'The Bureaucratization of Policymaking in Postwar Japan.' *American Journal of Political Science* 18, no. 4 (1974): 647–64.

Pempel, T. J. 'The Developmental Regime in a Changing World Economy.' In Meredith Woo-Cumings, ed., *The Developmental State*, 137–81.

Pempel, T. J. *Regime Shift: Comparative Dynamics of the Japanese Political Economy.* Ithaca: Cornell University Press, 1998.

Pempel, T. J. 'The Unbundling of "Japan, Inc.": The Changing Dynamics of Japanese Policy Formation.' Special issue, *Journal of Japanese Studies* 13, no. 2 (1987): 271–306.

Polanyi, Karl. *The Great Transformation: The Political and Economic Origins of Our Time.* Boston: Beacon Press, 1957.

Porter, Michael E., Hirotaka Takeuchi, and Mariko Sakakibara. *Can Japan Compete?* Cambridge, MA: Basic Books and Perseus, 2000.

Posen, Adam S. 'Deflation and the Bank of Japan.' *The Japan Times*, 23 September 2002. Available at http://search.japantimes.co.jp/cgi-bin/nb20020923a1.html.

Posen, Adam S. 'It Takes More Than a Bubble to Become Japan.' Institute for International Economics Working Paper No. 03–9, Peterson Institute for International Economics, Washington, DC, 2003. Available at http://ssrn.com/abstract=472962.

Posen, Adam S. 'The Realities and Relevance of Japan's Great Recession: Neither Ran Nor Rashomon.' Institute for International Economics Working Paper No. 10–7, Peterson Institute for International Economics, Washington, DC, 2010. Available at http://ssrn.com/abstract=1623828.

Posen, Adam S. *Restoring Japan's Economic Growth*. Washington, DC: Institute for International Economics, 1998.

Price, John. *Japan Works: Power and Paradox in Postwar Industrial Relations*. Ithaca: Cornell University Press, 1997.

Puchniak, Dan W. 'Perverse Rescue in the Lost Decade: Main Banks in the Post-Bubble Era.' In Nottage et al., *Corporate Governance*, 81–107.

Pyle, Kenneth B. 'Profound Forces in the Making of Modern Japan.' *Journal of Japanese Studies* 32, no. 2 (2006): 393–418.

Rebick, Marcus E. *The Japanese Employment System: Adapting to a New Economic Environment*. Oxford: Oxford University Press, 2005.

Rebick, Marcus E. 'Japanese Labor Markets: Can We Expect Significant Change?' In Blomstrom et al., *Japan's New Economy*, 120–41.

Richardson, Bradley M. *Japanese Democracy: Power, Coordination, and Performance*. New Haven, CT: Yale University Press, 1997.

Rodrik, Dani. 'King Kong meets Godzilla: The World Bank and the East Asian Miracle.' In Fishlow, et al., *Miracle or Design?*, 13–53.

Rodrik, Dani. *One Economics, Many Recipes: Globalization, Institutions, and Economic Growth*. Princeton, NJ: Princeton University Press, 2007.

Rodrik, Dani. 'Understanding Economic Policy Reform.' *Journal of Economic Literature* 34, no. 1 (1996): 9–41.

Saito, Osamu. 'The Economic History of the Restoration Period, 1853–1885.' Institute of Economic Research, Global COE Hi-Stat Discussion Paper Series 163. Institute of Economic Research, Hitotsubashi University, Tokyo, 2011. Available at http://gcoe.ier.hit-u.ac.jp/research/discussion/2008/pdf/gd10–163.pdf.

Sako, Mari, and Hiroki Sato, eds. *Japanese Labour and Management in Transition: Diversity, Flexibility and Participation*. New York: Routledge, 1997.

Samuels, Richard J. *The Business of the Japanese State: Energy Markets in Comparative and Historical Perspective*. Ithaca: Cornell University Press, 1987.

Saxonhouse, Gary R., and Robert M. Stern. 'The Bubble and the Lost Decade.' *World Economy* 26, no. 3 (2003): 267–81.

Schaede, Ulrike. *Choose and Focus: Japanese Business Strategies for the 21st Century*. Ithaca: Cornell University Press, 2008.

Schaede, Ulrike. *Cooperative Capitalism: Self-Regulation, Trade Associations, and the Antimonopoly Law in Japan.* Oxford: Oxford University Press, 2000.

Schaede, Ulrike. 'Globalization and the Japanese Subcontractor System.' In David Bailey, Dan Coffey, and Phil Tomlinson, eds, *Crisis or Recovery in Japan: State and Industrial Economy*, 82–105.

Schaede, Ulrike. 'The "Old Boy" Network and Government-Business Relationships in Japan.' *Journal of Japanese Studies* 21, no. 2 (1995): 293–317.

Schaede, Ulrike, and William W. Grimes. 'Introduction: The Emergence of Permeable Insulation.' *The Japanese Economy* 28, no. 4 (July–August 2000): 3–17.

Schaede, Ulrike, and William W. Grimes, eds. *Japan's Managed Globalization: Adapting to the Twenty-First Century.* Armonk, NY: M. E. Sharpe, 2003.

Schaede, Ulrike and William W. Grimes. 'Permeable Insulation and Japan's Managed Globalization.' In Schaede and Grimes, eds, *Japan's Managed Globalization*, 243–54.

Schaller, Michael. *The American Occupation of Japan. The Origins of the Cold War in Asia.* New York: Oxford University Press, 1985.

Segers, Rien T., ed., *A New Japan For the Twenty-First Century: An Inside Overview of Current Fundamental Changes and Problems.* New York: Routledge, 2008.

Sekine, Toshitaka, Keiichiro Kobayashi, and Yumi Saita. 'Forbearance Lending: The Case of Japanese Firms.' *Monetary and Economic Studies* 21, no. 2 (2003): 69–92.

Sheard, Paul. 'The Main Bank System and Corporate Monitoring and Control in Japan.' *Journal of Economic Behavior & Organization* 11, no. 3 (1989): 399–422.

Sheard, Paul. 'Main Banks and the Governance of Financial Distress.' In Masahiko Aoki, and Hugh Patrick, eds, *The Japanese Main Bank System*, 188–230.

Shimada, Haruo. 'Japan's Industrial Culture and Labor-Management Relations.' In Shumpei Kumon, and Henry Rosovski, eds, *The Political Economy of Japan, Vol. 3: Cultural and Social Dynamics*, 267–91. Stanford: Stanford University Press, 1992.

Shimizu, Yoshinori. 'Convoy Regulation, Bank Management, and the Financial Crisis in Japan.' In Mikitani and Posen eds, *Japan's Financial Crisis and Its Parallels to U.S. Experience*, 57–100.

Shimizutani, Satoshi, and Izumi Yokoyama. 'Has Japan's Long-Term Employment Practice Survived? Developments Since the 1990s.' *Industrial and Labor Relations Review* 62, no. 3 (2009): 313–26.

Shinoda, Toru. 'Rengo and Policy Participation: Japanese-Style Neo-Corporatism?' In Mari Sako, and Hiroki Sato, eds, *Japanese Labour and Management in Transition*, 187–214.

Smith, David C. 'Loans to Japanese Borrowers.' *Journal of the Japanese and International Economies* 17, no. 3 (2003): 283–304.

Solis, Mireya. 'Adjustment Through Globalization: The Role of State FDI Finance.' *Japanese Economy* 28, no. 5 (2000): 27–49.

Stiglitz, Joseph E. 'From Miracle to Crisis to Recovery: Lessons from Four Decades of East Asian Experience.' In Joseph E. Stiglitz, and Shahid Yusuf, eds, *Rethinking the East Asian Miracle*, 509–26.

Stiglitz, Joseph E., and Shahid Yusuf, eds. *Rethinking the East Asian Miracle*. New York: Oxford University Press, 2001.

Stubbs, Richard. *Rethinking Asia's Economic Miracle: The Political Economy of War, Prosperity and Crisis*. New York: Palgrave Macmillan, 2005.

Suzuki, Hiromasa. 'Employment Relations in Japan: Recent Changes Under Global Competition and Recession.' *Journal of Industrial Relations* 52, no.3 (2010): 387–401.

Tabb, William K. *The Postwar Japanese System: Cultural Economy and Economic Transformation*. New York: Oxford University Press, 1995.

Taira, Koji. 'Characteristics of Japanese Labor Markets.' *Economic Development and Cultural Change* 10, no. 2 (1962): 150–68.

Tamura, Kentaro. 'Challenges to Japanese Compliance with the Basel Capital Accord: Domestic Politics and International Banking Standards.' *Japanese Economy* 33, no. 1 (2005): 23–49.

Tan, Li. *The Paradox of Catching Up: Rethinking State-Led Economic Development*. Basingstoke: Palgrave Macmillan, 2005.

Tandon, Rameshwar. *The Japanese Economy and the Way Forward*. New York: Palgrave Macmillan, 2005.

Teranishi, Juro. *Evolution of the Economic System in Japan*. Cheltenham, UK and Northampton, MA: Edward Elgar, 2005.

Tolliday, Steven. *The Economic Development of Modern Japan, 1945–1995: From Occupation to the Bubble Economy*. 2 vols. Cheltenham, UK and Northampton, MA: Edward Elgar, 2001.

Toshiki, Jinushi, Yoshihiro Kuroki and Ryuzo Miyao. 'Monetary Policy in Japan Since the Late 1980s: Delayed Policy Actions and Some Explanation,' in Mikitani and Posen, eds, *Japan's Financial Crisis*, 115–48.

Toya, Tetsuro. *The Political Economy of the Japanese Financial Big Bang: Institutional Change in Finance and Public Policymaking*, edited by Jennifer A. Amyx. New York: Oxford University Press, 2006.

Ueda, Kazuo. 'Causes of Japan's Banking Problems in the 1990s.' In Hoshi and Patrick, *Crisis and Change*, 59–81.

Underhill, Geoffrey R. D., and Xiaoke Zhang. 'The State-Market Condominium Approach.' In Boyd, and Ngo, eds, *Asian States*, 43–66.

Usui, Chikako, and Richard A. Colignon. 'Corporate Restructuring: Converging World Pattern or Societally Specific Embeddedness?' *Sociological Quarterly* 37, no. 4 (1996): 551–78.

Van Wolferin, Karel. *The Enigma of Japanese Power: People and Politics in a Stateless Nation*. New York: Alfred A. Knopf, 1989.

Vogel, Steven K. *Freer Markets, More Rules: Regulatory Reform in Advanced Industrial Countries*. Ithaca: Cornell University Press, 1996.

Vogel, Steven K. *Japan Remodeled: How Government and Industry Are Reforming Japanese Capitalism*. Ithaca: Cornell University Press, 2006.

Wade, Robert. 'Selective Industrial Policies in East Asia: Is the East Asian Miracle Right?' In Fishlow et al., *Miracle or Design?* 55–79.

Walter, Andrew. 'From Developmental to Regulatory State: Japan's New Financial Regulatory System.' *Pacific Review* 19, no. 4 (2006): 405–28.

Watanabe, Susumu. 'The Japan Model and the Future of Employment and Wage Systems.' *International Labour Review* 139, no. 3 (2000): 307–33.

Watanabe, Wako. 'Does a Large Loss of Bank Capital Cause Evergreening? Evidence from Japan.' *Journal of the Japanese and International Economies* 24, no. 1 (2010): 116–36.

Watanabe, Wako. 'Prudent Regulation and the "Credit Crunch": Evidence from Japan.' *Journal of Money, Credit and Banking* 39, no. 2–3 (2007): 639–65.

Weber, Maria, ed. *Reforming Economic Systems in Asia: A Comparative Analysis of China, Japan, South, Korea, Malaysia, and Thailand*. Cheltenham, UK and Northampton, MA: Edward Elgar, 2001.

Weinstein, David E. 'Historical, Structural, and Macroeconomic Perspectives on the Japanese Economic Crisis.' In Blomstrom et al., *Japan's New Economy*, 29–47.

Weinstein, David E., and Yishay Yafeh. 'On the Costs of a Bank-Centered Financial System: Evidence from the Changing Main Bank Relations in Japan.' *Journal of Finance* 53, no. 2 (1998): 635–72.

Weiss, Linda. *The Myth of the Powerless State: Governing the Economy in a Global Era*. Cambridge: Polity Press, 1998.

Werner, Richard A. 'The Cause of Japan's Recession and the Lessons for the World.' In Bailey et al., *Crisis or Recovery in Japan*, 31–60.

Werner, Richard A. *Princes of the Yen: Japan's Central Bankers and the Transformation of the Economy.* Armonk, NY: M. E. Sharpe, 2003.

Werner, Richard A. 'A Reconsideration of the Rationale for Bank-Centered Economic Systems and the Effectiveness of Directed Credit Policies in Light of Japanese Evidence.' *Japanese Economy* 30, no. 3 (2002): 3–45.

Whittaker, Hugh D., and Simon Deakin, eds. *Corporate Governance and Managerial Reform in Japan.* New York: Oxford University Press, 2009.

Witt, Michael A. *Changing Japanese Capitalism: Societal Coordination and Institutional Adjustment.* Cambridge: Cambridge University Press, 2006.

Wolf, Martin. 'Japanese Lessons for a World of Balance-Sheet Deflation.' *Financial Times*, 18 February 2009.

Wolf, Martin. 'Saving Japan, A Permanent Cure.' *Financial Times*, 7 April 1998.

Wolff, Leon. 'The Death of Lifetime Employment in Japan?' In Nottage et al., *Corporate Governance*, 53–80.

Woo, David. 'In Search of "Capital Crunch": Supply Factors Behind the Credit Slowdown in Japan.' *Journal of Money, Credit and Banking* 35, no. 6 (2003): 1019–38.

Woo-Cumings, Meredith, ed. *The Developmental State.* Ithaca: Cornell University Press, 1999.

Wright, Maurice. *Japan's Fiscal Crisis: The Ministry of Finance and the Politics of Public Spending, 1975–2000.* Oxford: Oxford University Press, 2002.

Yamori, Nobuyoshi, and Narunto Nishigaki. 'Japanese Banks: The Lost Decade and New Challenges.' In Rien T. Segers, ed., *A New Japan For the Twenty-First Century*, 35–54.

Yoshikawa, Hiroshi. *Japan's Lost Decade.* Tokyo: International House of Japan, 2001.

Yoshikawa, Hiroshi. 'Japan's Lost Decade: What Have We Learned and Where Are We Heading.' *Asian Economic Policy Review* 2, no. 2 (2007): 186–203.

Yoshikawa, Toru, and Jean McGuire. 'Change and Continuity in Japanese Corporate Governance.' *Asia Pacific Journal of Management* 25, no. 1 (2008): 5–24.

Yoshikawa, Toru, Lai Si Tsui-Auch, and Jean McGuire. 'Corporate Governance Reform as Institutional Innovation: The Case of Japan.' *Organization Science* 18, no. 6 (2007): 973–88.

Yoshino, Naoyuki, and Eisuke Sakakibara. 'The Current State of the Japanese Economy and Remedies.' *Asian Economic Papers* 1, no. 2 (2002): 110–26.

Zhou, Yanfei. 'The Trend Toward Nonregular Employment Among Young Workers, 1994–2003.' *Japanese Economy* 36, no. 4 (2009): 105–34.

Index

Abramovitz, Moses 51
administrative guidance 7, 9, 25, 40, 75,
  148–9
aggregate demand 62, 106, 109, 126–9,
  152–3, 168, 173
agricultural credit associations 104
agricultural sector 3, 17, 27, 33, 47, 55,
  150
aircraft industry 9
aluminium sector 27
amakudari 8, 76
Ansen Credit Cooperative 98
Asian financial crisis 1997 117, 121
asset prices 70–71, 78, 80, 83, 86, 98,
  101
automobile sector 5, 9, 14, 36, 40–41,
  62, 149, 161, 179, 184

balance sheet adjustments 108–9
balanced budgets 11
Bank of Japan 9–10, 20, 22, 63, 70,
  75–6, 78–9, 80, 86–7, 120, 124–5,
  130, 146, 170–72, 184
banking regulations 99, 103–4
banks 18–23, *see also* individual banks
  bank bailouts 171–2
  bank-centred finance 18, 67–8
  bank deposit guarantees 22, 75, 94,
    98, 105, 120, 133, 172
  bank-firm relationships 22–4
  bank mergers 19
  bank rescues 23–4
  main banks 9, 22, 30, 33, 74–5, 88,
    92, 100–101, 103, 139, 154, 176
  recapitalization of 96, 122–3, 133–4,
    142
  regulatory control of 74–5
  segmentation of 67
'bargained compromise' 54

Basic Law for Administrative Reform
  1999 136
Basle 1 capital asset requirements 94
'Big Bang' financial reforms 136–9,
  152
boards of directors 136, 140, 177
bond markets 18–19, 23, 67, 91
Bretton Woods 61
'bubble economy' 67–73
budget deficits 116, 127
bureaucracy 5–7, 10, 17–18, 25–6,
  28–9, 38, 44, 49, 52, 142–3,
  144–5, 147
'bureaupluralism' 17, 29, 36, 103
buyer-supplier relationships 5

Canon 140, 177
capacity utilization 90, 174
capital adequacy rules 99, 120, 122, 135
capital flows 65
capital markets 66, 73
catch-up growth 2, 41, 48–9, 54, 58
cement 35, 37
cheap money 70–71
chemicals 19, 21, 35
China 173–4
coalmining 12, 27–8
Cold War politics 178
Communism 10, 12
compensating balances 65
Comprehensive Survey of Living
  Conditions 1985–2000 182
'consensual technocracy' 54
construction sector 27, 90
'consultative capitalism' 8
consumption, domestic 41–2, 44, 53,
  68, 82, 106–8, 112, 128, 144, 165,
  178–9, 181
control associations 9

'convoy system' 20–21, 76, 99, 121
corporate governance 4, 9, 15, 24, 30,
     55, 75, 140, 154, 174, 176–7
Cosmo Credit Cooperative 98
cotton spinning 35
'creative destruction' 53, 87, 147
credit
   credit allocation 87–8
   credit crunch 88, 94, 122, 124, 129
   misallocation of 141, 143
'crony capitalism' 35
cross shareholding 5, 23–4, 30, 37, 46,
     75, 90, 136–8, 154, 184

Dai-Ichi Kango Bank 170
debt-to-equity ratios 169
deflation 9, 83–4, 114, 127–31, 143–4,
     153, 168, 171, 173, 181, 184, 186
debt
   corporate 108–12
   national (public) 127, 129, 179–81,
      185–6
Deposit Insurance Corporation of Japan
     98
deregulation 73, 148–50, 176, 183, 186
Development Bank of Japan 141
developmental state 2–3, 6, 8, 11, 16,
     20, 25, 30, 33, 35–8, 41, 43, 47, 57,
     145–7
distribution 17, 33
'Dodge plan' 19
'dual economy' 17–18, 36, 43, 77, 88

East Asian financial crisis 178
economic nationalism *see* mercantilism
Economic Planning Agency 10, 58
electronics 14, 26–8, 36, 149, 159, 161,
     169, 179, 184
employment system, Japanese
   characteristics of 12–17, 55, 154–5
   'lifetime employment' 9, 15, 37, 55,
      134, 146–7, 155–9
endaka recession 1985–6 62, 85
enterprise unions 12–14
European Union 173–4
'evergreening' 90–92, 94
excessive competition 12

exchange rate 10, 29, 61, 71, 109, 165,
     173
export-led development 11, 43, 60–61,
     64, 144, 178–9

factor utilization 152
Federation of Business Organizations
     (Keidanren) 134, 149
financial crisis management 96–8
financial integration 66
financial liberalization 65–7
Financial Reconstruction Commission
     (FRC) 135
Financial Reconstruction Law 135
financial regulation 74–6
financial services 28, 33, 41
Financial Supervisory Agency 135,
     140–41, 170, 172
Finland 84–5
firm creations 93
firm exists 93
Five Year Plan for Economic
     Independence 1955 3–4
Fiscal Investment and Loan Programme
     77, 115, 141
Fiscal Structural Reform Law 126
fiscal policy 62, 76–7, 105, 109, 126–7,
     143–4, 151, 173, 177, 180, 185–6
   fiscal consolidation 70, 173, 186
   fiscal multiplier 110, 115
   'real water' spending 115
'flexicurity' 147
forbearance lending 90–94
foreign exchange 5, 136
foreign ownership of shares 174
Fuji Bank 170
Fukui, Toshihiko 172

General Agreement on Tariffs and Trade
     [GATT] 47
'governed interdependence' 45
government-business interface 40, 45–6
growth, economic [in Japan] 30–31, 73,
     83, 86, 113, 117, 124, 127, 152,
     169, 173–4, 180
growth accounting 31, 48, 50, 52

Hashimoto, Ryutaro 105, 126, 133, 173

Hayami, Masaru 131
high-tech sectors 27, 40, 180
Hitachi 12, 36
Hokkaido Takushoku Bank 121
holding company 136
'hollowing out' 97
Honda 184
Hyogo Bank 98

Ibuki, Bunmei 183
income, distribution of 54, 181–2
Income Doubling Plan 47
indicative planning 26
industrial associations 12, 17, 29, 38,
    44, 55, 56
Industrial Bank of Japan 19, 170
industrial policy 4, 6, 9, 10, 17, 28, 35,
    44
  industrial concentration 11
  industrial 'losers' 35–6, 46
  industrial protection 35
  industrial restructuring 91–2, 95, 100
  industrial targeting 28
  industry-science linkages 150
  'picking winners' 36
  structural reform 93, 112–13,
    130–32, 146, 173
Industrial Revitalization Corporation of
  Japan [IRCJ] 140, 170
inflation 14, 35, 41, 72, 95, 153, 173
  inflation targeting 130–32, 146
  inflationary expectations 130–32
investment
  corporate 68, 82, 88, 96, 106, 108,
    110–11, 117
  foreign direct 10–11, 64, 97, 183, 186
information technology 151–2, 171,
  186
innovation 40, 180
integrated production systems 41
interest rates 11, 20, 21, 22, 23, 37, 63,
    67, 71, 76, 79, 80, 82–3, 86, 95,
    108, 128, 130, 153, 168, 173
  deregulation of 65–6
International Monetary Fund [IMF] 47,
  48
Internet 150, 152, 172–3

'iron triangle' 6–7
Iyo Bank 98

'J' model 140
Japan Business Federation 149
Japan Development Bank 9, 28, 115
Japan Federation of Employers'
    Association [Nikkeiren] 149
Japan Housing Loan Corporation 69
'Japan Inc.' 6, 67, 133
Japan Long-Term Credit Bank 19
Japan Trade Union Confederation
    (Rengo] 155, 181
'Japanese model' 176, 179–83
job retention rates 156–7
jusen companies 69, 104–5, 121

Keidanren, *see* Japan Business
    Federation and Federation of
    Business Organizations
keiretsu 5, 33, 37, 74, 99, 137–9, 174,
    176
'kigyoism' 15
Koizumi, Junichiro 172, 177
Korean war 11
Kizu Credit Corporation 98

labour
  disputes 12
  hours of work 152
  mobility 15, 37, 154
  productivity 89, 152, 186
  unions 12, 72
Labour Standards Law 2006 176
land prices 68–9, 70, 80–82
lending consortia 18
lending quotas 80
Liberal Democratic Party [LDP] 6, 17,
    26, 27, 38–40, 47, 76, 80, 103–4,
    108–9, 122, 134, 149–50, 173, 185
'lifetime employment' *see* employment
    system
liquidity trap 130
List, Frederick 46
Livedoor 183–4
loan syndicates 9
Long Term Credit Bank of Japan 123,
    133, 170

long-term credit banks 68
Louvre Accord 62

machine tool industry 26, 33, 36, 179
'main banks' *see* banks
market economy 8, 10, 54
market share 12, 21, 24, 35, 37, 46, 93
Mayekawa reports [Bank of Japan] 63
Meiji restoration 8, 54, 57, 59
mercantilism 11, 46–7, 53, 60, 149
merit payments 166
metals sector 35
mergers 183–4
Miike coalmining dispute 13
Ministry of Education 27
Ministry of Enterprise, Trade and
        Industry [METI] 145, 157, 163
Ministry of Health, Labour and Welfare
        182
Ministry of International Trade and
        Finance [MITI] 5, 7, 10, 20, 26,
        27, 29, 33, 36, 38, 40, 52, 58, 96–7,
        139
Ministry of Finance [MOF] 5, 7, 20–22,
        33, 38, 52, 58, 61, 63, 65, 74–6, 80,
        99–105, 116, 120, 134–6, 145
Ministry of Posts and
        Telecommunications 27, 38
Mitsubishi Tokyo Bank 170
Mitsui Bank 33
Mitsui Trust Bank 33
monetary policy 125–6, 172, 181, 184
moral hazard 21, 95
munitions industry 18

National Financial Control Association
        18
newly industrializing economies [NIEs]
        31–2
Nikkei stock index 71, 80–82
Nikkeiren *see* Japan Federation of
        Employers' Association
Nippon Broadcasting System 184
Nippon Credit Bank 123, 133, 170
Nippon Keidanren 155, 158
Nippon Steel 154
Nippon Telegraph and Telephone
        Corporation [NTT] 29, 38, 151–2

Nishimura, Yoshimasa 102
Nissan 12, 139, 154, 183, 184
'Nixon shock' 61
non performing loans [NPLs] 83, 86–7,
        92–4, 95, 98, 99–103, 120–24,
        132, 141, 153, 169–70, 174
Norway 84–5
non-regular employment 160–61, 167,
        182

Obuchi, Keizo 127
Occupation, American of Japan
        1945–52 10, 22
oil shocks 1970s 1, 14, 27, 35, 41, 61,
        72, 156, 159
Organisation for Economic
        Cooperation and Development
        [OECD] 30, 127, 150, 181–2

Panasonic 184
paper industry 37
performance-related pay 166
'permeable insulation' 149
petrochemicals 26, 37
pharmaceuticals 28, 183
Pioneer 26, 184
'Plaza accord' 62
Polanyi, Karl 49
post office privatization 173
process innovation 150
productivity 15, 16, 23, 35, 51, 89, 141,
        150, 186 (*see also* labour
        productivity]
'prompt corrective action' 135
property sector 68–9, 73–4, 77, 80
proportional representation 103
protectionism 29, 178 [*see also*
        mercantilism]
public works *see* fiscal policy

quality control 15
quantitative easing 171–2

recession cartels 35, 146
reciprocal consent 45
Reconstruction Finance Bank [RFB] 19
research and development 150

Resolution and Collection Corporation [RCC] 141
Resona bank 170
retail sector 17, 161, 183
retirement schemes 156, 163–4
Renault 139
Rengo *see* Japan Trade Union Confederation

savings, domestic 20, 22, 67, 73–4, 125, 129, 130, 141, 179, 180
seniority wages 9, 13, 55, 154, 166
shipbuilding 14
shareholders 15, 19, 22, 24
Shunto wage bargaining 14, 16, 159
small and medium-size businesses [SMEs] 3, 27, 33, 38, 47, 48, 68, 94, 122, 125, 126
social security 185–6
steel 12, 14, 27, 37, 40, 41, 56, 100, 149, 184
Sweden 84–5, 111

Takenaka, Heizo 172
taxation 111, 116–17, 153, 181
telecommunications 148, 151, 172–3
textiles 20, 27, 28, 35, 159
terms of trade 72
Toho Sogo Bank 98
Tokuyo City Bank 121
Tokyo Kyowa Credit Cooperative 98
Tokyo Kyoudou Bank 98
total factor productivity [TFP] 31–2, 89–90, 93, 146, 150, 152

Toshiba 12, 36, 184
Toyo Shinkin Bank 98
Toyota 12, 36, 139–40, 177, 184
trade associations 148
trade surpluses 60–62, 71
transaction costs 21, 37, 51, 58
'Triffin dilemma' 61

UFJ Bank 170
unemployment 9, 82, 117, 129, 152, 159–60, 165, 169, 173, 182
United States of America 4, 150, 151, 171, 173, 176, 178, 179 [*see also* Occupation]

venture capital 27, 40, 150–51, 180

wartime economy 1940–45 9, 10, 18–19, 56
Wartime Finance Bank 18–19
'Washington consensus' 48
'window guidance' 20, 76–7, 87
World Bank 48
wage policies 166–7

Yamaichi Securities 121
yen
    appreciation of 39, 43, 61, 62, 71, 72–3, 85–6, 113, 144, 179, 181
    depreciation of 61, 108, 113, 178, 179

zaibatsu 55, 56
zero interest rate policy 95, 132, 171–2
'zombie' firms 90, 127, 146